THE DARKNESS BELOW

THE DARKNESS BELOW

ROD MACDONALD

Whittles Publishing

Published by
Whittles Publishing Ltd.,
Dunbeath,
Caithness, KW6 6EG,
Scotland, UK

www.whittlespublishing.com

ISBN 978-184995-037-4

Printed by
4edge Limited, UK

Also by Rod Macdonald:

Dive Scapa Flow
Dive Scotland's Greatest Wrecks
Dive England's Greatest Wrecks
Into the Abyss: Diving to Adventure in the Liquid World

www.rod-macdonald.co.uk

To my wife Claire and my daughters
Nicola and Catriona

Rod Macdonald is the best selling author of four of the classic staples of UK diving: *Dive Scapa Flow*; *Dive Scotland's Greatest Wrecks*; *Dive England's Greatest Wrecks* and *Into the Abyss: Diving to Adventure in the Liquid World*. He specialises in wreck finding and research. Rod lives in Stonehaven in the northeast corner of Scotland with his wife Claire and two daughters Nicola and Catriona. He is a keen yachtsman and skier, and is a crewman on the Stonehaven Lifeboat.

www.rod-macdonald.co.uk

Cover Photograph: On a Tri-Services Expedition to the South China Sea, Rod hangs beside the Royal Navy ensign that had just been flown on the bridge of HMS *Repulse*. © Guy Wallis

CONTENTS

ACKNOWLEDGEMENTS

More than 30 years of diving has taken me to some of the greatest and some of the most remote dive locations in the world – and has brought me some of my closest friends. My diving career has been a journey from 1970s-style UK diving in a 7mm wetsuit with a Fenzy ABLJ and a single 10L aluminium tank, through deep air diving to open-circuit Trimix diving and latterly on to closed-circuit rebreather Trimix diving. My last book *Into the Abyss: Diving to Adventure in the Liquid World* charted the early part of that voyage. This book takes the story forward to the present time.

For helping me to achieve this, my thanks firstly are to my wife Claire who, when I ran out of steam or came up against a literary brick wall, would get me focussed and give me direction. She came up with some great ideas for the book – her best usually in our local, The Marine Inn down at Stonehaven harbour. Thanks also to my parents for reading my early draft manuscripts and helping with constructive feedback.

My long-time dive buddy Ewan Rowell was really the star of *Into the Abyss* – which wasn't so much autobiographical about me but more an account of Ewan's eclectic diving career. He features often again in this book and has kindly let me use some of his great underwater photos. We've had some tremendous fun over the years – topside and submerged – and I'm much obliged again, Ewan. His oil field work has recently taken him to Perth, Western Australia, so he has been out of the UK diving loop for a while and is thus sadly missing from the later chapters.

The Stonehaven Snorkellers Deep Cave Rescue Team (SSDCRT) (less than seriously named because we do not carry snorkels, do not go deep unless we really have to, seldom go into caves and have not rescued anyone) have had a glorious last few years with many virgin wrecks being located, dived and identified. Thanks to all the team – without whom none of this would have been possible. It is immensely reassuring on a deep scary dive – often in pitch-black 5-foot visibility hundreds of feet down – to know that such solid divers are around you. When we did have an incident this summer on the *Baku Standard* the team sprang into action and solved the problem at depth before making a perfect ascent to safety.

Up in Peterhead, the northern branch of the team – consisting of Jim Burke, Mike Rosie and Mike Wilcox, coxed by Roger Mathieson – diving off the *Buchan Elle* (say it quickly!) have successfully dived and identified most of the wrecks around the northeast and this has brought rewarding contact from survivors and relatives.

Down here in Stonehaven, thanks go to my regular dive buddies Paul Haynes, Richard Colliar, Tony Ray, Greg Booth and Gary Petrie – and of course to our own trusty boat handlers Dave Hadden and Simon Chalmers. We are out on the water together most weekends – more of all of them later.

A special thanks goes out to local fisherman and friend Ian Balgowan. Ian is a tough old sea dog now in his early 60s who my wife Claire first met when she was down at our harbour. I was out at sea and was overdue and she was getting a little anxious. She asked Ian, who was on his trawler *Harvester* berthed at the pier, if he could call me on his VHF, which he was happy to do. Our friendship has developed from there. Ian has fished the local wrecks since the early 1960s and indeed was wrecked himself in a fishing boat as it tried to get into Stonehaven harbour in an easterly storm. He knows the wrecks and the peculiarities of the seabed like the back of his hand, but had always wondered what the wrecks actually looked like. We have now been able to show him our wonderful underwater footage and I suspect that we may have changed his fisherman's view of the wrecks (as unwelcome snags and obstructions for his nets) to seeing them as we do – as things of beauty. Ian has been able to vicariously follow the journey with us as we unveiled wreck after wreck.

Thanks also to Guy Wallis, firstly for inviting me along as civilian expert on the Tri-Services Expedition to the South China Seas to dive and film the British warships HMS *Repulse* and HMS *Prince of Wales* (both sunk by Japanese aircraft during World War II 200 miles north of Singapore); and secondly for allowing me to use some of the images he shot. The cover image of me with the Ensign we had just flown on HMS *Repulse* is his.

Noel Blacklock – an ex Royal Navy Radio Officer – kindly gave me much first hand information on the sinking of his ship SS *Creemuir* during World War II and allowed me to set out *verbatim* his survivor account. Noel's wish is to preserve the story of what happened on the day of the sinking and to highlight the role of the Merchant Navy during the war – and I hope the last chapter of this book accomplishes that.

Thanks also to Gordon Wadsworth of *Jane R* fame for ensuring that our week's diving with him from Bergen in Norway turned out to be so good, and for letting me use his underwater images. I cannot recommend Gordon, the *Jane R*, his food and his home brew enough. Try diving Norway with him.

Gráinne Patton kindly allowed me to use some of her underwater photos of the classic North Channel wrecks, HMS *Audacious* and SS *Empire Heritage* – stunning images shot in available light 200 feet down.

Up in Orkney I have used the *Radiant Queen* as my regular dive boat to work from for many years. It is skippered by opera-singing Emily Turton – who does a mean line in home baking. I am sure that part of the allure (second of course to her skilful handling of the boat) is that when Ewan and I climb up the ladder after a dive and heavily plonk ourselves fully kitted down on a bench, as we pull off mask and hood we get a steaming pint mug of tea and a chunk of homemade cake thrust into our hands. Now that's what I call service. Us men are so fickle…

INTRODUCTION

THE WRECK OF THE WHITE STAR LINER *JUSTICIA*

25 miles off Northern Ireland

Seventy metres below the surface, 25 miles off the Northern Irish coast, my regular dive buddy Ewan Rowell and myself were speeding over the remains of the White Star liner RMS *Justicia* on our bright orange Aquazepp underwater scooters. Frantically, we were trying to complete a grand tour from stem to stern before it was time to start our long, slow ascent to the surface. We had already had three dives on this sunken leviathan's remains in the days before. This was the last dive of a ten-day dive trip.

The *Justicia* was sunk during World War I whilst in use as a troop ship and was remarkably similar in size and scale to her rather-better-known fellow White Star liner, RMS *Titanic*. Like *Titanic* she was also built by Harland & Wolff in Belfast and weighed in at a massive 32,234 gross tons. She was 740 feet long – the length of a modern aircraft carrier.

The White Star liner, Justicia

Ewan and I had spent the first minutes of our planned 20 minute bottom-time exploring the massive intact bow section, which sits on an even keel in an underwater desert of clean, white sand. Think of the classic Hollywood footage of the *Titanic*'s bows and you'll get the idea.

Making our way onto the fo'c'stle deck we found ourselves dwarfed by massive anchor chains running out along the deck and disappearing into hawse pipes at either side. Huge anchor capstans and winches were dotted around the deck here and there.

We turned our scooters and pointed them directly astern. Gunning the motors we moved off the fo'c'stle deck and dropped down to her forward cargo holds which now lay collapsed and flattened. At a steady 2 knots we sped aft hovering some 10 metres above the collapsed plating – staying a bit shallower would be good for minimising decompression stops later in the dive.

We sped over the foredeck. Next up was the massive bridge superstructure that lay fallen to the seabed on the port side of the wreck – its large square windows rimmed in brass, still in place.

From the bridge aft the ship had collapsed, pulverised by the might of the Atlantic, and her innards were laid bare before us. Ewan and I flew side-by-side over two massive boilers – each the size of a small house – then two more, and then two more – they just kept coming and coming.

After the boiler rooms had passed astern of us, her massive engines emerged from the gloom ahead. I couldn't help thinking of the *Titanic* movie scene where the engines are ordered astern as the iceberg is sighted – colossal engines; engineering on a grand Victorian scale. We pressed on and just as the final minute of our 20-minute bottom time clocked up we reached the stern. It was time to leave.

Ewan and I turned our scooters upwards and motored slowly up from the wreck at 70 metres towards our first scheduled decompression stop at 48 metres. The underwater visibility 25 miles out from the coast in clear Atlantic waters was a staggering 50 metres and as we halted for our first 'deep stop' at 48 metres we could look down and still see the wreck clearly beneath us. As the first tiny bubbles of compressed breathing gas started being released from my body, far below I could pick out teams of our divers exploring different sections of her remains. These tiny bubbles would have expanded eight times in size by the time they reached the surface. Better let them out slowly on a controlled, leisurely ascent.

Bubble streams of exhaled breathing gas from the open-circuit divers below billowed upwards, the bubbles expanding and flattening as they forced their way towards the surface. Larger bubbles – too large to hold together as a single bubble – broke up into three or four smaller bubbles. As they reached the surface far above, the massively expanded bubbles blooped and burst in the languid calm seas freeing the gas to the atmosphere, and easily audible to those on the dive boat.

We hung at our 48-metre decompression stop for a couple of minutes and I unclipped my yellow reel and attached decompression buoy (a 6-foot long red sausage marker buoy). Cracking open the valve on its small cylinder, the buoy rapidly filled with air. When it was straining to pull me to the surface I let it go, my reel paying out line at an increasingly fierce speed. The reel handle spun round ferociously as the buoy accelerated to the distant surface.

Within seconds the reel handle abruptly stopped turning – the buoy had reached the surface and our position was now marked for the dive boat above. It would shadow us as we carried out our inwater decompression, drifting freely with the current. All around us the other divers in our team were finishing their time down on the wreck and starting the same ascent process. On the surface loose groups of red deco buoys were popping up – each one with the individual diver's name written on it in bold black for the benefit of those topside.

Suspended, neutrally buoyant in oceanic mid water, I wound in the reel line and pulled it tight and vertical as we moved up to our next scheduled deco stop at 39 metres.

The ascent went flawlessly – and we stuck rigidly to our pre-calculated run time for the ascent, taking one minute to ascend every three-metre increment up to a depth of 30 metres. From there we started pausing increasingly longer at each three-metre step up towards the surface.

At 20 metres I spat out the regulator mouthpiece for my back-mounted helium-rich bottom gas and stuck the regulator for my oxygen-rich decompression gas into my mouth. This deco gas was 50% oxygen – as opposed to the 21% oxygen in the air normally breathed on the surface – and I would breathe it for the final part of the ascent. The high level of oxygen would shorten the length of time required to fully decompress and rid my body of the dangerous bubbles. This deco gas had its own range of dangers – it could only be breathed in the shallows from 20 metres up to the surface. If I breathed it on the bottom by mistake it would very quickly kill me.

The decompression stops ticked away slowly. Two more minutes at 18 metres, three minutes at 15 metres, five minutes at 12 metres, six minutes at nine metres and then 28 minutes at six metres. Some 62 minutes after leaving the wreck below it was time to break the surface. In all we had probably drifted in the current about a mile during the hour we had been rising up from the wreck.

My head broke the oily calm surface of the water and upon seeing me, the skipper of the 75-foot long dive boat, motored over. As the boat arrived beside me, I gunned my scooter and moved over to grab hold of the steel ladder that led 6 feet up the side of the boat from the water to the main deck.

In the water the weight of my cumbersome equipment – four large steel dive tanks, weights and other gear – had been suspended to the point that I barely knew it was there. But as I got my feet on the rungs of the ladder and started climbing up slowly, the full weight of my kit started to bear down upon me. In all, the total weight of all my kit would be about 80 lbs, and here I was climbing up a 6-foot-high ladder after an exerting technical dive.

I reached the gunwale of the dive boat, clambered inboard and sat down on a fixed bench. As I started stripping off my heavy kit, the boat was already motoring over to pick up the next group of divers who had broken the surface about 200 yards away. Soon we were slowing beside them and now free of my own equipment, I started helping them to their seats as well as ferrying their tanks and weights to their storage positions to clear the area around the top of the ladder for the next divers to board.

For perhaps half an hour after surfacing I helped shift kit and tanks around. Then once everyone was aboard I stripped off my black dry suit and went into the lounge to grab some lunch.

Very shortly after finishing lunch – and in all perhaps one hour after surfacing – I started to feel fatigued and slightly unwell. I imagined it was just mild post-dive fatigue, and made an excuse to the rest of the team that I was going below decks to my cabin for a wee snooze – not unusual after a hard dive and some food. This was the last dive of a gruelling ten-day trip and we had been diving to 70 metres nearly every day. In fact, the day before we had carried out two 70-metre dives: one on the *Justicia* again; and a second on the U boat *U- 155*. It was little wonder that I was feeling tired.

Below decks I swung myself onto my bunk, closed my eyes and tried to nod off. But sleep wouldn't come to me – in fact what came was not all what I expected. A sharp pain developed in my right elbow: 'That's from hauling myself and all my kit up that ladder', I rationalised. Maybe I strained something.

Next, a sharp pain developed quite quickly in my right knee, like a pinprick. It then seemed to spread out slowly over the whole of my knee. Shortly after that I developed a similar pinprick pain in my left knee, which also started to radiate outwards. Soon my head was feeling a little fuzzy and there were tears rolling down my cheeks from the pain in my knees.

Twenty-five miles out to sea I had decompression sickness – the dreaded bends.

CHAPTER ONE

FIRST BEGINNINGS

Scuba diving took over my life in 1981.

Up until then I had been a gangly youth growing up by the sea in the tough, bustling, northeast of Scotland fishing port of Fraserburgh. Like all kids of my age I was captivated by the Jacques Cousteau TV series of underwater adventures. They allowed a glimpse into an exotic underwater world far removed from the brutally tough lives of the local fishermen. There was more to the sea than fishing – there was a different world, hidden from sight but filled with strange creatures, danger and excitement. Shipwrecks lay in the depths holding mystery and intrigue. I never dreamt that one day I would become part of that world.

In the late 1970s I went to study law at Aberdeen University. It was only 42 miles away from where I had grown up – but in those days that seemed a long way. I got myself a motorbike and my interest in the sea took a backseat during those frenetic years as study and a wild student/biker lifestyle consumed my days and nights.

I graduated in law in 1979 although it's fair to say that whilst I knew how to party I hadn't the faintest clue about what being a lawyer was all about. That was grown-up stuff that I didn't really want to get too involved in.

Nevertheless I secured a law apprenticeship with a legal firm in the nearby fishing town of Peterhead. As student threads and my fringed black leather biker jacket grudgingly gave way to business suits and shirt and tie, I started looking around for a sport that would take me away from the stresses and worries of life in a legal office. I had snorkelled abroad on past holidays and had liked the experience, so I thought I would try out scuba diving and see if I liked it. I joined the local branch of the Scottish Sub Aqua Club and started going along to their weekly pool training sessions.

My interest in trying my hand at scuba diving had really been whetted during a summer working in America before my last year at University, when I was able to go on a few snorkelling trips in the Florida Keys. It's funny how the direction of your life is moulded by chance twists and turns. I hadn't gone to America to go to Florida – I had gone to work in Detroit – and it was a pure fluke that I ended up in Florida.

As part of the British Universities' North America student exchange programme (B.U.N.A.C.) I had gone for the summer to a job as an ice cream van driver in Detroit – the then murder capital of America. It would be a summer of adventure, excitement and danger.

About 25 of us from different UK universities had flown out together to New York and then made our way independently to Detroit, where we were met by a series of drivers hired by our employer. Eventually at about 1am, we were dropped off by the drivers somewhere in the industrial outskirts. It seemed like the middle of nowhere – just a collection of a few ramshackle buildings and a large yard full of cannibalised white ice cream vans. It was the ice cream depot and it looked dire.

It was the middle of the night and pitch black – and we were tired, dirty and hungry. But the place was silent – all the buildings were closed and locked. The drivers had been told just to drop us off and knew nothing more. So once we got out of the cars, they just turned and drove away into the darkness, leaving us standing lost in the Michigan night. We thought someone would come to get us but after an hour of waiting forlornly for someone to turn up and tell us where we could bunk the penny dropped: no one was coming.

In frustration, one of the guys smashed a window of the house. We all climbed in through it and settled down where we could on armchairs or the floor.

Early the next morning our employer arrived – a big, tough loud American who was less than impressed at the damage we had caused and the chaos in the house with our kit lying everywhere. Not the best of job starts but what did he expect? This attitude was to characterise our work there – he was just using the exchange programme to get cheap labour for the summer. Conditions were appalling.

Detroit is a large sprawling city with massive suburbs. We were each assigned an ice cream van and given a map of a small section of the city outlined in red. That was the area you were allotted to sell ice cream in – it was your turf. All the ice cream companies had divided Detroit up between them and jealously guarded their own areas – they didn't suffer any other van coming onto their turf to sell.

That's fine in principle, but I had only passed my driving test a few months before and my driving and road craft was in its very infancy. It's fair to say that for the first week or two I didn't find my designated area once. I had no idea where I was, knew nothing of ice cream turf wars and just naively drove around in my van with the music blaring, stopping to sell in areas that looked promising.

Inevitably I unwittingly strayed onto other ice cream company turf – and this didn't go down particularly well. On one occasion I got seriously chased and buzzed by another van. The driver was half out his door window bellowing at me that he had a gun, as I tried to leg it flat out in my wee van. And then he turned to pursue me. It was extremely scary but with hindsight it must have looked comical to see two white ice cream vans chasing after each other through the Detroit suburbs – a scared, thin Scottish driver in one and a furious local driver screaming murder in the other.

On another evening, far from where I should have been and seriously lost as ever, my van broke down in a very dangerous suburb where I soon realised I was the only white face around. As darkness descended the mood turned ugly when the locals realised there was a thin white

Scotsman crapping it in a broken-down van in their neighbourhood. I had thankfully broken down not far from a pay phone and had called in to the base to report where I was, but it was a couple of hours before help appeared. By that time I was locked in my van with a large gang of youths milling around outside, throwing stones at it. I was extremely relieved to see help arrive.

The mechanic who came wasn't able to fix my van there and then, so rather than leave it (it would be torched overnight), he got me to jump back into the van and let off the handbrake. He then manoeuvred his pickup behind my van and gave it a bump to get it rolling. Once we were moving he would come up periodically behind me and push my van with his bumper so I went faster and faster. We made it onto the nearest freeway and got up to a creditable 40mph or so in this fashion, as we pushed and bumped our way about 12 miles all the way back to the base.

Needless to say, breaking a window to get in the night before your first day on the job wasn't the best of starts with our new boss. He was in the process of building a bunkroom for his cheap summer labour, but it was far from finished. The 25 of us had to sleep night after night where we could on scabby armchairs, sofas or the floor. There was only one toilet – it never got cleaned and was disgusting.

As days turned into weeks of working there, conditions didn't improve and one by one our band of students started leaving to secure other jobs. After about six weeks of working we had about 15 or so of us left – and we decided that enough was enough. We were all going to leave en masse and sort out our dreadful boss.

We decided on a plot for all of us to walk out on a set day a week ahead – the day before the weekly stock take of the vans' contents. We were all skint, so this would allow time for those who wanted to take some cash unnoticed from the day's takings for several days in the lead up to the stock check. Most took out $10 a day from the takings – not a lot but at least it would give a little extra above the meagre spending money we had left. One guy had got involved with some local black youths and arranged that they would stage a hold up of his van and take the whole day's takings – several hundred dollars in cash. They duly obliged complete with a gun, which was brandished to great effect. The driver reported the robbery to the local police but by Detroit standards it was small beer and of course he couldn't ID any of the robbers. Nothing came of it and the youths got their cut.

When Americans want to vacation in another part of America and have their car available for them there, they can pay a 'drive away' agency a fee to have their car driven to their holiday destination. The agencies proclaimed the quality of their drivers and the care taken with the cars – but they were always short of drivers and would take anyone. We thought they might even take us.

The day before the great walk out, my buddy and I went to AAAcon as soon as we finished work – it was the biggest 'drive away' agency downtown. We were immediately offered a drive away car to Florida – perfect. We were given a week to drive it down from Detroit to Florida – basically the whole length of America from north to south. It was a seriously long way. We collected the car.

The day of the walk out arrived. I was nervous about the whole thing and thought we should just leave without notice and get going. We would be well on our way and the boss would never find us. It was the easy option and was what most of the other guys were doing.

The boss was a big guy with a fierce temper – I wouldn't like a rumble with him. But my mate (bless him) wanted to do the decent thing and go confront the boss and tell him to his face why we were all doing what we were. It took a lot of guts.

I remember vividly sitting in the car outside the yard – engine running – as my mate went in, walked up to the boss and calmly told him why we were leaving. The boss went berserk when he realised that his whole work-force had disappeared overnight. We had just closed his business down and cut off his income until he could hire another set of drivers. The shouting match reached a crescendo and the boss picked up an alternator and threw it across the yard. My mate turned and marched – rather quickly – back to the car leaving the boss standing alone in his yard, surrounded by silent ice cream vans. What goes around comes around.

My mate jumped into the car, closed the door and we were off – loose and free in America with just a couple of hundred dollars between us and our pre-booked, prepaid, non refundable, non changeable, cheapest of the cheap flights set for the end of September – three months away.

We had been given a week to drive to Florida, but we had no work lined up there and nowhere to stay sorted out and we were seriously short of cash as well. Unless we got a job quickly we would be in big trouble. There were no cash points in walls then and as a poor student, I had no savings anyway. We talked about the options and decided we couldn't afford to hire a car down there to get us to potential employers – but we had the drive away car for the week. So we thought that if we drove non-stop the length of America from Detroit to Fort Lauderdale in Florida in say 24 hours, then it would mean that we would have the remaining five days allocated for the drive, to use the car down there and hopefully secure employment. The car could also provide six nights free lodging. We settled down into three-hour shifts: one driving whilst the other slept; and in this fashion we made it down in a straight 22-hour drive.

Once we started looking for work however we knew we had a problem. We didn't have the right work permits and no one would hire us. We even drove to Disneyland and asked to see the HR boss to see if he would offer a couple of Scots lads in a bind work for a month or two. We got a lot of sympathy – but no job. Each night we drove out into the countryside and slept in the car at a rest area to save cash. Things weren't going well.

Our money dwindled away until we were down to our last $20 – and it was still three months until our flight home. The tickets we had could not be brought forward. We went to the British Embassy to see if they could help us out with a loan or flights back home – we got sympathy but no assistance.

The last full day's use of the car arrived and it was dawning on us that we were completely screwed. We were fed up driving around begging for jobs all over the place. Bugger this, we thought as we drove over to SeaWorld and spent our last $20 on a day out there. That was it: three months to go and no money at all. We then had to give the car back to the owner who had arrived from Detroit. Now we had no car and nowhere to stay.

We scraped together $3 for a pitch for our small two-man tent at a campsite on Alligator Alley, the freeway that runs through the Everglade swamps from the east coast to the west coast. That night we walked in darkness along Alligator Alley to a local bar – we had no money and couldn't buy a drink but we sat at the bar asked for water and started talking to a bar maid. She told us that a BBQ restaurant a few blocks along Alligator Alley was short of staff and was hiring.

In the steamy hot darkness of a Florida night we walked a couple of miles further along Alligator Alley to the Country BBQ Cabin and asked to see the boss. They had just lost some staff and were extremely stretched – we seemed to be something of a gift from on high for him and were hired immediately. There were no questions or worries about work visas. We would start the following morning.

As we started working and earning cash we were able to move out of our bug-and-ant-infested campsite and hire an apartment. The next thing we did was to buy a wreck of an ancient Mustang coupé for $200. After having to walk all over the place in Florida's 100C heat (we were working five miles out from the town centre) we suddenly had wheels again.

As we neared our flight date back home we decided to take four weeks off and go on a road trip around Florida. We drove south from Fort Lauderdale through Miami and on down to the chain of islands off the southern tip of Florida – called the Keys. The road linking the various islands of the Keys runs over bridges built on the coral beds that link all the islands – for almost a hundred miles all the way down to Key West. One bridge is 7 miles long.

Once we got down to the Keys we went on a few snorkelling day trips out to the offshore coral reefs. Sharks and barracudas and all sorts of exotic sea creatures swam past me. I loved the feeling of looking down from the boat at the surface of the sea – seemingly a floor – and then breaking that surface and entering a new world where the surface of the sea became the ceiling of another world. It was my experience probing the Florida undersea world that opened a door and turned my interest in the sea from a passing inquisitiveness to something more serious. The future course of my life had just unknowingly been changed.

A year or so later and now a young lawyer in Peterhead, I went along to my first evening pool training session with the Scottish Sub Aqua Association. I was given a brief shot of an aqualung and immediately fell in love with the experience. I started going regularly.

After six months of learning the basics of diving at the weekly pool sessions and after a move nearer Aberdeen to Ellon, I was fully equipped in the diving tools of the day: 7mm wetsuit; bright orange Fenzy Adjustable Buoyancy Life Jacket (ABLJ); and a 72 cubic feet aluminium dive tank with single breathing regulator. For £1.50 I bought a second hand capillary depth gauge with a large circular face like a watch. A thin tube, open at one end, ran around the outside of the face. As you dived the increasing water pressure forced water into the tube, compressing the air inside more and more, the deeper you got. A scale on the face along the outside of the tube (which you read from where the air bubble was compressed to) revealed your depth. Simples – as the meerkat says. A mate gave me a dive watch that he had won as a school prize years before. I was ready for the sea.

My first sea dive took place that summer: a shore dive from a shingle beach into some 15 metres of clear water at Aberdour on Scotland's northeast coast. I was surprised and awed by the beautiful underwater seascape that met me – towering sheer rock faces covered with kelp, sponges and sea urchins. Crabs, conger eels and lobsters crammed every nook and cranny. A myriad of fish life drifted past my face plate, from the mundane fish like cod and ling to the intimidating ones like the blue grey wolf fish some 4–5 feet long with the fiercest bulbous head and menacing jaws you will find.

The somewhat inoffensive sounding monkfish can sometimes be a problem underwater. With a name like that you'd think it would be a gentle fish that wouldn't hurt a fly, perhaps brewing its own ale from honey. But not so. It's a flat, mean looking fish that resembles an oversized naan bread from your local curry shop. Both eyes are on top at the wide end and it has a large curved half-circle of a mouth with a menacing strip of sharp teeth like a zip round its front edge. This semi-circular mouth can open in an instant, from being flat into a perfect circle to bite at its foe. Once it bites it doesn't let go.

On one of my earliest dives we came across a monkfish sitting flat on the seabed, minding its own business. I was all for giving it a body swerve but my fearless and more experienced buddy diver Richard Cook decided to investigate. He took out his thin, pencil torch and gave the docile monkfish a prod on the mouth. It didn't budge. Not to be deterred, my buddy diver gave it a second, harder, prod on the snout. This was too much for the fish. In a blinding flash it opened up its mouth into a perfect circle and tried to swallow the whole torch in one go, getting its circular mouth around it and getting a few inches of it into its mouth. Once it had bitten it wouldn't let go no matter how hard my buddy waved and thrashed the torch around. Eventually it decided that modern hard plastics weren't good for its dental care regime. It let go and settled back down on the seabed, eyeing us cautiously with cold eyes. It seemed to be saying: 'You wanna try that again, laddie?' We gave it a wide berth this time.

Monkfish are quite a worry for trawler men gutting a catch of fish. Sometimes they'll stick a hand blindly into a haul of landed fish to get a fish out for gutting. If there's a live monkfish in the catch it can do a lot of damage to fingers and hands.

From shore diving I progressed to my first panic-stricken boat dive out of Portsoy harbour in a grey battered and patched Zodiac inflatable. Along with about five other divers (all bearded as was the fashion at the time [one I'm pleased to say I never embraced]), we motored out for a few miles from the harbour before randomly slinging the anchor over the side into unknown depths.

Dive boats then were almost completely devoid of any electronics at all – an echo sounder was as rare as snow in summer. There was a delicate (and very inaccurate) art to working out your approximate depth. As the rope and anchor went over the side, you would stretch the rope across your chest from outstretched hand to outstretched hand. One such length was about a metre, so counting the number of lengths gave you a rough idea of the depth of water you were going into. Not that on my first boat dive I had any concept of what diving to any sort of depth was like.

The cox of the dive boat reckoned we were in about 20 metres of water, but we seemed an awfully long way from shore and I couldn't believe it could be that shallow that far out. Additionally, all my diving experience had been from the shore when I could swim back to safety. I was a little concerned about being so far offshore with little chance of being able to swim ashore if things went pear shaped.

After the usual pre-dive buddy checks of each other's kit, I rolled backwards off the Zodiac and swam up to the anchor line at the bow. Looking down all I could see was the anchor line disappearing down into an inky blackness. It looked an awfully long way down – and that wasn't even to the bottom. On all my dives to date I'd been able to see the seabed throughout the whole of the dive. This was something different.

My dive buddy was vastly more experienced than me – and this was my first dive from a boat and my first dive to this sort of significant depth. There was a lot of hesitation and worry charging around inside my head as I swam to the anchor line.

After an exchange of 'OK' hand signals we started to swim down the anchor line into the depths. My buddy – a gentle, bearded and very capable diver called Colin Rivers – went down faster than my hesitant attempt. Soon there was a considerable gap between us. It also became clear that I hadn't seated my mask properly on my face - as water was trickling into my mask and pooling on the faceplate as I looked down. The rubber seal around the mask should sit flush on your skin, but a section of the seal was sitting overlapping the hood of my wetsuit stopping a perfect, watertight seal.

The world beneath me blurred and became indistinct as my buddy diver disappeared from sight below me. Then, as the volume of water in my mask started to get significant, everything below and around me disappeared. If you've ever swum underwater in a pool without a mask or goggles you'll know how difficult it is to make anything out with your eyes open. Well, I had that effect, but in the very dark all-embracing water around me, my blurred vision couldn't pick out any variation in my surroundings. I had no vision and was in an unknown depth of deep water, a couple of miles offshore. It was disconcerting and unnerving. I was already starting to lose it.

I tried to persevere going downwards and tried a mask clearing drill that I had been taught as part of my recent training. To clear a flooded mask you hold the top part of the mask against your forehead and pull the bottom part slightly away from your face. Blowing through your nose, the air rushes into the mask and is trapped at your forehead seal. Blowing more air through your nose displaces the rest of the water, which is driven down and out from your mask. However, this drill only works when you're in the heads up position, so that the air gets trapped in the closed part of your mask at your higher forehead seal.

In my panic of inexperience, I stupidly carried out this drill with my head downwards as I was finning *down* the anchor rope. By pulling the upmost part of my mask (between mouth and nose) away from my face, this allowed a route for the last remaining vestiges of air in my mask to disappear up through the open seal. My mask became completely flooded.

Nowadays, I'm completely at ease taking my mask off underwater and putting it back on again – but back then, it was all too much for me. I bottled it. I halted my descent and started climbing back up the rope hand over hand not knowing, with my waterlogged mask and vision, what depth I was in or where I was.

When with some relief my head finally broke the surface, I pulled my mask off my face and normal vision returned to me. The boat cox was concerned at first but saw there was nothing wrong with me. Shortly afterwards my dive buddy (who had gone all the way down to the bottom at 25 metres and waited for me to appear) returned to the surface and came over to me. Rather sheepishly I explained what had happened. In reality it was a very simple situation to sort out – but with my inexperience compounded by my fear I had screwed it all up. I was all for giving up on the planned dive there and then – but very patiently he persuaded me to give it another go. He would stay right beside me.

My male sense of pride being prodded I agreed to try descending again. I sometimes wonder how my life would have turned out if I had just given up there and then. Would I have continued diving? If not I'd have missed out on a lifetime of travel, adventure and exploration. In that one moment, the direction of my life was fixed.

We swam back to the line and restarted the descent. My dive buddy stayed right beside me, shepherding me like an errant pupil. At times he would hold the back harness strap of my ABLJ, lest I lose my bottle again and bolt for the surface.

We pressed on downwards into the darkness – and I found it hugely intimidating not being able to see the seabed. But eventually we came through a visibility horizon. One minute the seabed was out of sight; the next minute the whole scene beneath me swam into focus as though a curtain or veil had been drawn back. I found myself floating with my buddy about 10 metres above a wonderful seascape of flat rocks and boulders, peppered with fish, crabs and lobsters all going about their business unaware of the noisy and cumbersome visitors that were descending towards them from a distant surface they knew nothing of.

We let ourselves free fall down to the seabed and as I neared the seabed I righted myself into a standing position. Then… touchdown – we were on the bottom.

I took a deep breath on my breathing regulator, pulled it out of my mouth and stuck the oral inflator tube of my ABLJ into my mouth. I breathed out hard into the ABLJ, puffing it up slightly. I was still too heavy so I repeated the trick a couple of times more until I achieved what divers call 'neutral buoyancy'. This is the Holy Grail of diving: it is the perfect state of equilibrium to be in. You are neither too heavy nor too light.

If you are neutrally buoyant, when you breathe in, that simple breath into your lungs makes you slightly positively buoyant. You rise up almost imperceptibly. When you breathe out the small loss of buoyant air from your lungs is enough to make you sink slightly.

Once perfectly neutrally buoyant, we had a 20-minute dive exploring the nooks and crannies of this wonderful undersea world and seeing my first six-foot long conger eels out in the open.

Our bottom time was up all too soon and we returned to the anchor rope nearby – we hadn't strayed far – and made a slow ascent hand over hand back to the safety of the dive boat. My novice diver's inexperience had almost ruined the day – and stopped my diving career there and then. But my dive buddy's stoic perseverance had saved the dive and I suspect, my diving career. A door into the fascinating underwater world had just opened for me. I had embarked on a journey – a journey that I am still making more than 30 years later.

CHAPTER TWO

EVOLUTION IS A SLOW PROCESS

As the 1980s progressed, so did my diving – and the technology we were using also changed radically. Diving mutated from being a poor man's sport where all your kit was cobbled together on a shoestring budget, to a very expensive and technical sport. Today, diving is glamorous big business – you have a bewildering choice of a multitude of manufacturers' products in a kaleidoscope of colours. The generation of divers before me had only fairly recently stopped making their own DIY wetsuits from self-cut black sharkskin neoprene held together by yellow tape.

Wet suits gave way to dry suits – but not without a fight. The prevailing mentality was that real divers dived in wet suits despite the fact that they compressed at moderate depths and seemingly completely lost all their insulating properties at about 25 metres. The 7mm of neoprene was compressed by water pressure until, at about 40 metres down it felt as though the neoprene was only wafer thin. In truth there was nothing worse than pulling on a wet, wet suit in a rain-swept car park before a second dive. The wetsuit took on the adhesive qualities of glue and became nearly impossible to pull up your legs.

But, wet suit diving was the way real men dived – and there were lots of little tricks to make life bearable. A flask of hot water poured down the inside of a cold, wet, wet suit warmed it up enough to make it getting it on realistic. I still have memories of doing just this, standing in a wet car park at Kyle of Lochalsh and getting ready for a second dive on the *Port Napier* as hailstones, driven by a biting November wind, travelled horizontally across the car park.

Once in the water, if your wet suit didn't fit you too well, cold seawater continually flooded into the space between your skin and the wet suit, flushing out the water your body heat had warmed up. Putting on a T-shirt, or two (or three) under your long johns and jacket filled the space between wet suit and skin. This gave extra warmth and stopped the flushing effect, but you did go through a heck of a lot of T-shirts.

Wet suits were good at keeping you warm underwater in moderate depths – but were completely useless at keeping you warm topside. Once out of the water after a dive, all the warm water in your suit rushed downwards, pooling in your wetsuit boots. These ballooned out comically and the water soon cooled down.

The wind chill of being in an open boat – particularly in a cold, windswept remote part of Scotland in a wet, wetsuit was severe. The wind seemed to slice right through the wet suit as though it wasn't there. We learned to put an old waterproof (usually bright orange) or cagoule over our wetsuit as we travelled to and from dive sites to cut out the chill. Who said diving is a glamorous sport?

The 'real divers' who dived in wet suits rebelled against the wide-spread introduction of dry suits to sport diving. Dry suit divers were seen as soft – and dry suits themselves were seen as dangerous. They introduced all sorts of new ways to get hurt underwater – such as the much-feared, ballistic feet-first ascent from depth. Unlike wet suits – which fitted snugly over your body (in theory at least) – dry suits were a loose-fitting dry bag sealed onto your body at the neck and cuffs. As you dived, the increasing water pressure compressed the air trapped inside your dry suit, causing it to crease and start nipping at your skin. To relieve the squeeze an air hose ran from your scuba tank to a port in the suit. Press the port's inflator and air was fed into your suit, essentially blowing the drysuit off your skin. On one occasion in my early days I forgot to connect up my direct air feed hose on a 35-metre dive with a 8mm neoprene dry suit. It was very uncomfortable during the dive – and when I peeled off my kit after the dive my body had large black and blue streaks across it where the creases had squeezed.

However, if you remembered to connect up the new-fangled direct suit inflation feed and mistakenly bled too much air at depth from your tank into the suit to relieve the 'squeeze'; the air would migrate to the highest point in your suit. On occasion, as a diver pressed the suit inflator button it could (if not maintained properly) stick in the 'inflate' position, bleeding an endless amount of air into your suit until you managed to disconnect the air hose from the inflator. If you were finning head downwards, the air rushed up to your feet – so if you got too buoyant you would start to go up feet first. As you started (sometimes unknowingly) to go up, the surrounding water pressure got less, so the air already inside your suit would start to expand and fill the airtight legs of your suit even more. The air volume got greater and greater the shallower you got and a diver could get into an accelerating ascent, soon reaching the point of no return.

There are a number of ways to get rid of excess air if you were the right way up, through air dump valves on your chest or arm. Lifting one arm up would allow air to escape past your wrist seal and sometimes the air pressure inside your suit could overcome the tension of the neck seal, lifting it off the skin and allowing a large bubble to bloop out. But if you were in the head down/ feet up position there was no escape for the trapped air as there were no air dumps on the legs. Some divers bragged how if they had started a feet-first buoyant ascent they would puncture their drysuit legs with their knife to vent the excess air – but in reality, the suits were so tough that that would be easier said than done. You also only have the first 5–10 seconds of a buoyant ascent to get things under control – after that the ascent becomes completely uncontrollable. Once your legs are full and above you, it becomes physically impossible to get them down. Your feet-first ascent accelerates remorselessly as you rocket upwards.

Stories abounded of divers, out of control, blowing up from depth and exploding out of the water as they reached the surface. Such a rapid ascent could easily kill you from a number of causes – even from a moderate depth. It was as a result of these fears whipping round the dive world, that I recall one headline in a national dive magazine of the time urging the sport's governing UK body, the British Sub Aqua Club (BSAC), to 'Throw the dry baggers out'. But like the contemporary war between VHS and Betamax video formats, dry suits won the day over wetsuits. Today hardly anyone dives in a wet suit in the UK.

Dive boats evolved too. In the early days they were usually small grey, beat-up, patched inflatables (with inflatable keels) – such as the hugely reliable Zodiac – often with small tiller driven outboard engines ranging from 25–55 hp (never more). Nowadays we dive from 5–8 metre long bright orange or yellow, spacious rigid-hulled inflatables (RIB's) with bigger engines of up to 140 hp, sometimes twinned up for safety and power – unthinkable in the 1980s.

ABLJ's to the fore as divers, some in wet suits, pack a small Zodiac 'squidgy' for a trip out to dive HMS Port Napier. A young Rod is seated right.

A Zodiac inflatable with six divers crammed into it and a 25 hp engine would wallow and struggle to ride up and over its bow wave onto the plane. To achieve this hallowed state, the cox had to nurse the boat and marshal his divers into a synchronised ballet.

Initially, the cox would wave all his divers forward to the front of the 'squidgy' (as we lovingly called our dive boats). This added weight to the front of the inflatable, which would be up at an angle of 45 degrees as it forlornly tried to ride over the mountain of water it was pushing along. The added weight would help drop the bow down.

As the inflatable eventually crested its bow wave, the bow became too heavy with all the divers up there – so they'd promptly be directed towards the stern of the boat as it was trimmed to run smoothly. As it got onto the plane, the boat's speed would shoot up in an instant from a displacement speed of say 9 knots to 15 or even as much as 20 knots on a good day. The cox could then throttle back to the perfect speed – one that kept the boat just up on the plane (and no more) whilst at the same time minimised the fuel guzzled by the labouring 25 hp engine.

Sometimes the boat would just be too heavily laden and wouldn't be able to get up on the plane at all. It would just plough along slowly at about 8 knots, the engine labouring at full throttle. Nowadays, boats and hulls are so good – and engines so big and powerful – that getting up on the plane is never an issue. But it was in the 1980s.

On one occasion at Kyle of Lochalsh, off Skye on the west coast of Scotland, I had loaded up my small 5-metre long Aberglen Gordon inflatable dive boat with about eight divers for the short journey of about a mile across to dive the remains of one of Scotland's most famous wrecks, the mine layer HMS *Port Napier*. The boat was so heavily laden that the side tubes only had about 8 inches of freeboard sticking up proud above the water. We just couldn't make more than 7–8 knots flat out with my 35 hp engine. There was not even the slimmest of chances that we would get up on the plane.

We laboured, painfully slowly across the sea loch Loch Alsh, towards Skye. Thankfully it was pretty calm, as even in the short seas, waves would wash completely over the bow, flooding the boat before passing out at the stern through the elephant trunk self drainer. I remember thinking that at least the boat would be lighter on the way back because all the air tanks would be empty.

We would also memorise 'no stop' dive times for different maximum depths – that is the length of time you could stay at a certain depth and still be able to swim straight to the surface without any 'dangerous' decompression stops. We would use a cheap digital watch to note our dive time underwater and would always use the 'no stop' time for the maximum depth we reached during the dive. If you went to 35 metres at one point of a dive, your no stop time for the dive was 15 minutes. It didn't matter if you had only dipped down there for five minutes at the beginning of the dive and then risen up and spent the rest of the dive at 10 metres. We knew that using a square profile for 15 minutes on the bottom at 35 metres (when we had spent most of the dive at 10 metres taking on far less nitrogen) was way over the top – but we had no way of calculating the decompression benefit we were gaining from the shallower depth. Using the deepest depth reached on the dive built in a huge safety factor.

Thankfully, in the late 1980s and early 1990s we saw the widespread introduction of dive computers to the sport. These sense and monitor your depth and time underwater, continuously calculating (using specially developed decompression software programmes) how long you can stay down before having to carry out a decompression stop. Instead of a square profile based on the deepest depth reached, dive computers take into account all the various levels you might be at during the one single dive. Multi-level decompression diving was a huge step forward.

Decompression diving itself was frowned upon and considered to be fraught with danger. Much better not to get into that danger area and do a 'no stop' dive where you could ascend straight to the surface. This straight ascent without stopping is in turn now hugely frowned upon, even on the simplest shallow dive. On a dive where you don't need to carry out any formal decompression stops, you still carry out a safety decompression stop at the end for a few minutes at 6 metres to let any rogue bubbles in your system escape.

When we first started looking at straying into the length of dive that would require decompression stops we thought it hugely unfamiliar and dangerous if we racked up decompression stops of a few minutes. Every dive I do nowadays is a decompression dive and more often than not I am carrying out inwater decompression stops from 30 minutes to often well in excess of over an hour – something completely alien to us in the 1980s.

I gave up wet suit diving in 1984 and got myself a second-hand Poseidon 8mm red neoprene dry suit, which I acquired in a dodgy straight exchange for a wide-angle Nikonos underwater camera viewfinder that I had found lying on the seabed on a dive, dropped aeons before by an unlucky diver.

With a few years wet suit diving under my belt, the cumbersome, restrictive and hugely buoyant dry suit was an eye opener and it took some time getting used to. I didn't get any training on it at all – it was just a case of trying it out and seeing what happened. There weren't any dry suit introduction course badges to be won then.

I had no idea what weight to carry to counteract this new hugely increased buoyancy and I still remember my first dry suit dive vividly. It was an experiment with something new and unfamiliar, a battle to physically haul myself down the shot-line against the buoyancy of the suit – of course I had failed to get all the air out of it properly.

Once I got down a few metres and the water pressure compressed the suit and air inside, I overcame the buoyancy of the alien suit and got down to the wreck – but I spent the whole of the dive worrying about how I was going to surface at a reasonable speed and avoid an ascent like a Polaris missile, spiralling out of control and getting faster and faster as the air in my suit expanded in volume many times. You have never seen anyone as happy as I was when I managed to navigate back to the shot-line to ascend. I think I can't be the only diver who has ascended from depth clinging grimly onto the shot-line to stay down whilst my feet swung up above me to point to the surface. I think I even lifted the wreck we were tied to up by a few feet, and I'm sure you could see my face flushed red with embarrassment from the shore when I surfaced.

As diving suits progressed, so did the undergarments that went beneath your dry suit. The original woolly bear undersuit seemed great at the time – but why were they always blue? In reality they were fine for thick neoprene suits, but poor when thin membrane dry suits (which don't have their own insulation like neoprene suits) appeared on the scene again. We have now progressed to fantastically warm under-suits using fabric technology developed to keep polar explorers and Everest climbers warm – a magical material that cleverly wicks sweat away from your skin and even if your dry suit floods is still 80% efficient at keeping you warm.

The scuba tanks we used also progressed from low-pressure tanks that held 210 bar of air (210 times atmospheric pressure) to 232 bar tanks and then to 300 bar tanks. These higher-pressure tanks allowed you to carry a lot more air in the same tank. More air = longer underwater. Better dive suits and undergarments and more air = longer, more comfortable dives at greater depths.

We doubled up our single air tanks into manifolded twin-sets so we could carry *even* more air underwater, go *even* deeper and stay longer. We had entered the world of decompression diving – deep air diving – a form of diving that would be king for a decade. And yet, all of us who made the transition during the 1980s from a low-tech diving scene to a much more technical scene had no idea how the introduction of mixed gas diving in the 1990s would radically change our diving with another quantum leap forward. But more of that later.

The new technology made diving in places like Scapa Flow even more rewarding. Scapa Flow is known around the world as the last resting place of the remaining dreadnoughts from the German World War I High Seas Fleet and is without doubt one of the world's top dive sites. Most divers will make the pilgrimage there to dive these sunken relics of a bygone era at least once in their career. Some come back year after year, learning more about these warships with every visit. Some divers visit once – and simply never leave. I have been going back there once or twice a year for nearly 30 years and it is a pleasure to see and spend time with the local folk I know as well as meeting divers who I see returning year after year – sometimes several times in the same year.

Divers talk in awe of the German wrecks at Scapa Flow – and every diver has a favourite. To be a true wreck diver you have to understand the wreck you are diving on, to appreciate what you are looking at. To understand Scapa Flow, you need to understand something of the history that makes it such a special place for divers.

At the very end of World War I, the German Imperial Navy's High Seas Fleet of some 74 warships was taken into internment at Scapa Flow as a condition of the Armistice that had halted the fighting in November 1918.

The interned dreadnought Fleet was made up of five battle cruisers, 11 battleships, eight light cruisers and 50 destroyers and it languished at anchor under guard for seven long, cold months from November through the fierce northern winter of 1918/1919.

Built up over the preceding 20 years in a naval arms race with Britain, the High Seas Fleet had been created at huge cost to the German nation to challenge the traditional naval supremacy of Britain. However, the High Seas Fleet had not been surrendered to the Allies, nor had it been crushed in any sea battle. For as German land forces faced outright defeat during 1918 and their leaders pressed for surrender terms with the Allies, the Armistice had been negotiated to halt the fighting whilst the two sides thrashed out a final deal for peace. The High Seas Fleet (which had not fought against the Royal Navy in any significant fleet action since the Battle of Jutland in 1916) had survived the War relatively intact and still would pose a significant threat should the Armistice break down and the fighting recommence.

Therefore, as a condition of the Armistice, the High Seas Fleet would be taken into internment and be heavily guarded at Scapa Flow, until the Treaty of Versailles was finalised and determined its fate.

Once the Armistice was called, arrangements were made by the Allies to receive the High Seas Fleet into internment. The entire British Grand Fleet rendezvoused at an agreed location in the North Sea with the High Seas Fleet to escort it to Scapa Flow, where it was thought the German Fleet could be kept safely under guard. No such combined sea force had ever been

The German World War I High Seas Fleet at anchor in Scapa Flow prior to the scuttling in 1919.

gathered before – a staggering 90,000 men were afloat, on a grand total of 370 warships. The British Fleet took no risk of any German treachery. Their guns were loaded and crews were at action stations, alertly looking out for any signs of trouble.

The British Grand Fleet split into two long lines of battleships, 6 miles apart and stretching out of sight over the horizon into the distance. The German High Seas Fleet then sailed in single column into the passage thus created – flanked on both sides by the lines of British warships which escorted it on the long voyage up to internment at Scapa Flow. Once the combined Fleets reached Scapa Flow, the German ships were lined up in neat compact rows in their predesignated anchorages, with up to three or four of the smaller vessels moored to a single buoy.

The German warships – although under Allied guard – were interned (not surrendered) and thus legally remained German property. The bulk of the 20,000 German sailors who had brought the Fleet to Scapa Flow were repatriated, leaving only a skeleton crew (of up to 200 on the larger ships) on each vessel. No British guards were permitted aboard the German ships, which were also prohibited from flying the German Imperial Navy ensign with its black cross and eagle.

The German sailors who remained behind in Scapa Flow had to endure a savage, long Orcadian winter as their cold, damp ships swung at their moorings. They were not allowed ashore and all their provisions other than water and coal had to be sent to them from Germany. The peace negotiations dragged on as Germany and the Allies made demand and counter-demand. The snows and cold of the 1918 winter gave way to the spring of 1919 – and then in turn to early summer. And still the German ships swung at their moorings.

Then, after seven months of this hell, Rear Admiral Ludwig von Reuter (in charge of the German High Seas Fleet) learned from a four-day-old newspaper given to him by the British that the Armistice was due to end on 21 June 1919. He read that the peace negotiations were in trouble and the reports indicated that it was unlikely that an agreement would be reached. He concluded that if the peace negotiations broke down then the fighting would start again. Manned by a skeleton crew and with its guns disarmed, his Fleet could not defend itself if the British tried to seize it when the Armistice ended. That had to be avoided at all costs.

At 9.00 a.m. on the 21 June – the very day the newspaper reports had indicated to Reuter that the Armistice would end – to the surprise of the Germans, the British battleships of the Grand Fleet sailed out of the Flow with their supporting cruisers and destroyers leaving only two serviceable destroyers on guard duty. The Armistice had been extended by two days and they were under instructions to be back in the Flow by then to deal with any trouble that might arise should the Armistice not be further extended. Did Reuter know about the extension? The jury is still out on that one.

At 10.00 a.m. von Reuter appeared in full dress uniform on the quarterdeck of his flagship, the cruiser *Emden*. Reuter proudly bore the insignia of his highest decorations around his neck and his Iron Cross and other medals were pinned to the breast of his frock coat. He studied his ships through a telescope and was advised by one of his staff that the British Fleet had left on exercise earlier that morning. He could hardly believe his luck. Reuter issued an order that the international code flags 'DG' be raised on *Emden*. This alerted officers on the other ships that they should be alert and watch for other orders.

At 10.30 a.m. Rear Admiral von Reuter addressed an attendant signaller and shortly afterwards a string of command flags appeared over his ship, even although this was well outside

The German battleship Bayern *goes down by the stern during the scuttling of the entire Fleet at Scapa Flow on 21 June 1919.*

the permitted times for issuing signals. The order read 'PARAGRAPH 11. BESTÄTIGEN': 'Paragraph 11. Confirm'. The prearranged coded order to the commanders of the other ships in the Fleet to scuttle had just been given.

The details of the plan to scuttle the Fleet had been finalised four days earlier on 17 June with a view to avoiding the Allies seizing the powerful warships (unbeknown to Reuter, the Allies had formulated just such a plan months before, as part of their contingency planning).

The signal to scuttle was passed from ship to ship by semaphore and Morse code on signal lamps and travelled slowly around the Fleet. The southernmost ships of the long lines of destroyers were not visible from the *Emden*. They had to wait for a full hour until the order reached them.

The prearranged formal responses came back, slowly to begin with. The first signal reached *Emden* at about 11.30 a.m., just as the original signal reached the last of the destroyers: 'Paragraph 11 is confirmed'.

In a patriotic gesture of defiance, many of the German ships ran up the prohibited Imperial Navy ensign at their sterns. The white flags with their bold black cross and eagle had not been seen at Scapa Flow before. Others ran up the red flag, the letter 'Z' which in international code signalled: 'Advance on the enemy.'

Noon. An artist who had hitched a ride on one of the patrolling Royal Navy trawlers to sketch the assembled might of the interned German Fleet, noticed that small boats were being lowered down the side of some of the German ships, against British standing orders. Sixteen minutes later the first of the German ships to sink, the *Friedrich der Grosse*, turned turtle and went to the bottom.

The other ships in the Fleet also began to list as the water rushing into their hulls altered their buoyancy. For the last four days, Reuter's trusted sailors had been opening all the internal doors and hatches and fixing or welding them in the open position, to allow water to flood through the hull more easily. Seacocks were set on a hair, turning and lubricated very thoroughly. Large hammers had been placed beside any valves that would allow water to flood in if knocked off. Sea valves were opened and disconnected from the upper deck to prevent the British closing them if they boarded a ship before it went down. Sea water pipes were smashed and condensers opened. Bulkhead rivets were prised out.

As soon as the valves and seacocks were open, their keys and handles were thrown overboard. They could never be closed again. Once the vessels had started to sink, they could not be saved other than by taking them in tow and beaching them.

Some of the great vessels rolled slowly on to their sides while others went down by the bow or stern first, forcing the other end of the vessel to rise high out of the water. Others sank on an even keel. Some had been moored in shallow water and came to rest on the seabed with their upper superstructures and masts jutting proud of the surface.

Blasts of steam, oil and air roared out of the ship's vents and white clouds of vapour billowed up from the sides of the ships as they sank. Great anchor chains snapped with the strain and crashed into the sea or whip-lashed against the decks and sides of the ship. Ships groaned and protested as they were subjected to stresses and strains for which they had never been designed.

As each vessel passed from sight a whirlpool was created. Debris swirled around in it, slowly being sucked inwards and eventually, remorselessly, being pulled under into the murky depths.

Gradually, oil escaping from the submerged ships spread upwards and outwards to cover the surface of the Flow with a dark film. Scattered across the wide expanse of the Flow were boats, hammocks, lifebelts, chests, matchwood and debris. Hundreds of German sailors abandoned ship into lifeboats.

The British guard force, which had left the Flow that morning on exercise for the first time in the seven long months of internment were advised that the scuttling had started and turned to charge back to the Flow at full speed. The first ship however would only be able to get back around 2.00 p.m. By 4.00 p.m. when the last British ship returned, only three German battleships, three light cruisers and a few destroyers were still afloat out of the total interned force of 74 warships. It was – and still is – the single greatest act of maritime suicide the world has ever seen.

British tug alongside the scuttled German destroyer G102 shortly after the scuttling. A British rating is pulling down the German flags and ensign.

At first the Admiralty resolved to leave the scuttled ships to rust away in the dark depths of Scapa Flow. There was so much scrap metal about after the War that prices were low. By the 1920s however, the price of scrap metal had picked up and the attentions of entrepreneurial salvers started to turn to the seemingly inexhaustible supply of finest German scrap metal at the bottom of the Flow.

Over the course of the coming decades the majority of the warships were salvaged, and today only eight of the original Fleet remain complete on the seabed waiting to be explored. They are: the 26,000-ton battleships, *König*; *Markgraf* and *Kronprinz Wilhelm*; the 5,500-ton light cruisers *Dresden*; *Brummer*; *Cöln* and *Karlsruhe*; and the 900-ton destroyer *V 83*.

But Scapa Flow is not just all about the remaining German warships lying in its depths. Over the years many other vessels have also come to grief in Scapa Flow. Steamers and tugs have struck mines. Attacking U-boats have been depth charged and trawlers have succumbed to the fierce northern gales.

The scale of human loss in Scapa Flow is huge – some tragedies took hundreds of young lives together in a single instant. These war graves of course are not for divers – but again it is important to understand what lies at the bottom of the Flow.

On 9 July 1917 the 19,560-ton British battleship HMS *Vanguard* was destroyed in a cataclysmic magazine explosion with the loss of more than 700 men.

On 14 October 1939 a U-boat managed to slip past the British defences in the dead of night and torpedo the 29,000-ton British battleship HMS *Royal Oak* at anchor in Scapa Bay. *Royal Oak* turned turtle and sank within five minutes into 30 metres of water with most of her crew trapped inside her. The torpedo explosions destroyed the power circuits and the whole of the ship below decks was pitched into darkness. Desperately the crew stumbled around in the darkness groping for a way out as the ship heeled over. Flash fires of burning cordite swept around the corridors. In all, 833 officers and men died in that one attack and they are remembered each year in a ceremony where Royal Navy divers fly an ensign down on the wreck.

Today, this concentrated profusion of wrecks in one relatively small area of sea some 12 miles wide draws thousands of divers annually to Scapa Flow from all over the UK, Europe and the United States. Diving has become big business in Orkney and from April to October, there are usually 10–15 charter hard boats taking parties of up to 12 divers per boat out to dive the wrecks each day.

In the early 1980s we used to dive Scapa Flow in 7mm wet suits. Scapa Flow then was regarded as deep, dangerous, on the edge diving. The wrecks all lay in 35 to 45 metres of water and even though the tops of the wrecks rose up to 15 to 20 metres from the surface, it was pretty much at the edge of what you could do then. Your wet suit was compressed to a wafer thin garment at those sorts of depths and it was exceedingly cold in the water. It was not uncommon to surface from a dive shaking and shivering and I remember trying to take a hot cup of coffee from a thermos after a dive on the light cruiser *Cöln* – because I was shaking so much I couldn't hold the cup to my mouth to drink any of it and it was spilled all over my front.

Dry suits stripped all that away. Almost overnight with their introduction, we became warm and comfortable at depth. Diving deep and long on the German wrecks became less on the edge. The colossal battleship *Markgraf* lies upside down in the deepest water of all

The German World War I High Seas Fleet battleship Kronprinz Wilhelm *at Scapa Flow.*
In the background, her sister dreadnaughts Markgraf *and* König.

the remaining German wrecks: 45 metres. Suddenly we could venture to the very bottom in comfort and explore under her upturned deck. By using decompression stops, we could stay there longer. Diving was indeed changing.

Nowadays, thanks to wrist-mounted decompression computers there is no difficulty in having two dives in the one day on the deeper German wrecks, separated by just a few hours of a surface decompression interval. But in the 1980s if you were going to do a second deep dive on the German wrecks you would usually leave a six-hour surface interval before you went in the water again. But it was more common after the deep morning dive on one of the German wrecks to have a shallower second dive on one of the 'block ships' that guard the eastern and western approaches into the Flow.

The eastern side of Orkney is a collection of small islands: Lamb Holm, Glims Holm, Burray and South Ronaldsay. During the First World War, old ships were sunk as 'block ships' in the small tidal channels separating these islands to protect the British Grand Fleet that was using Scapa Flow as its North Sea and Atlantic base. The Admiralty thought they had constructed a wall of steel with their block ships through which no enemy shipping could pass. These block ships, allied with the other shore and sea defences such as underwater detector loops (which could pick up the sound of a U-boat operating in the Flow and allowed shore based operators to detonate mines remotely) earned Scapa Flow the nickname 'Impregnable Scapa Flow'.

By the time the Second World War erupted over Europe the First World War defences at Scapa Flow had decayed or been removed. The Flow was no longer impregnable and that old

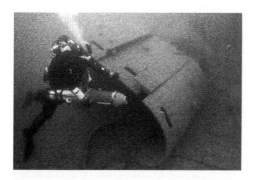

Rod beside the foremast spotting top on the German World War I battleship Kronprinz Wilhelm *at Scapa Flow.* © *Ewan Rowell*

nametag was to be proved tragically inaccurate by the U-boat attack on HMS *Royal Oak* in September 1939, just six weeks after the start of World War II during the so-called 'phoney war'.

U-47, under the daring and skilful command of Günther Prien, managed to thread its way between the block ships sunk in Kirk Sound – the channel between the main section of Orkney and the small island of Lamb Holm. These block ships had not been set nose to tail but had been set parallel and overlapping - leaving a zigzag path possible between them. Once through them and into the Flow, Prien was able to close on *Royal Oak* and fire a number of torpedoes into the unsuspecting battleship. As mentioned above, *Royal Oak* turned turtle and sank with in five minutes with the loss of 833 officers and men.

Similarly the smaller channel into the Flow to the west, Burra Sound, also was blocked by eight sunken hulks: the *Ronda*; *Budrie*; *Urmstone Grange*; *Rotherfield*; *Tabarka*; *Doyle*; *Gobernador Bories*; and the most striking block ship of all, the tanker *Inverlane*.

The *Inverlane* was built in 1938 at Vegesack in West Germany, an 8,900-ton tanker registered in Dublin. She was damaged by a mine off South Shields in 1939 and broke in two. The stern section sunk there but the bow to midships section was made watertight and then towed to Scapa Flow for use as a block ship. She was sunk broadside on across Burra Sound in 1944.

The bow section was one of the most dramatic sights in Scapa Flow from the war until its collapse in 1996. The massive tanker bows, fo'c'stle, forward main deck, oil tank hatches and midships bridge superstructure – some 100 feet in all – projected clear of the water, even at high tide. About another 75 feet of her aft of that, was permanently submerged.

The common practice was for the dive boat to approach in the lee of the wreck and tie onto it. Divers would then board her and pass all their kit over onto the main deck of the wreck. You could then go for a walk around the wreck peering down into the massive empty oil tanks, which still had fixed rotted steel ladders leading down into them.

Burra Sound was justly famous for the clarity of its gin clear water. Twenty to 30 metre underwater visibility was the norm and on the wreck itself you could peer way down into the empty water filled oil tanks. Despite being a hugely tidal channel, where the full might of the Atlantic ebbs and flows daily (at about 7 knots around the bows itself), once divers entered the water inside the wreck they were completely protected from the current raging outside.

Entry into the water was made from the small pump room just in front of the bridge by a step entry, dropping a few feet down through the top of a stair well into the water-filled stairway below. Although the water always looked clear but dark from above, once in the water the true beauty of the wreck was revealed. Shafts of sunlight penetrated down through openings in the hull and the open oil tanks, filling the wreck with light. The huge open oil tanks, their sides corroded away to reveal the latticework of her hull, became vast underwater cathedrals. Doors at the bottom of each tank led from one tank to the next and it was possible to navigate through the wreck right up to the bow itself. Companionway stairs led from one deck to the next beside the tanks.

Moving astern from the bridge, once you exited the last complete tank, you came to a mass of coiled towing cables and then – from the darkened interior – your eyes were dazzled by the brilliant blue of open water where the hull had been completely sheared off after striking the mine. Moving to the very edge of the wreck, the kelp just outside was laid flat by the fierce current and it was very intimidating to have that mass of water moving past you so ferociously and so close.

For the bolder diver however, this was one of the highlights of ending a dive on the *Inverlane* on a flood tide. Divers could venture out from the confines of the wreck into the moving open water. As soon as they did the current would pick them up in an instant and whisk them off towards the centre of Scapa Flow. They could carry out a drift dive at speed sometimes passing over the remains of one or more of the other block ships in the Sound.

The fast flowing tide was famous for producing a vortex or eddy just outside the wreck at the side facing in towards the Flow, the starboard side.

On one memorable dive, I was diving with a certain dive buddy called Ewan Rowell. For most divers in Scotland, Ewan needs no introduction - he is something of a legend. He started off as a civil engineer and specialised in bridges, being involved in the construction of the Kessock Bridge over the Moray Firth at Inverness and latterly with the construction of the Thames Barrier. After that he became a commercial oil field diver. He is now in a very responsible managerial position controlling subsea work off Western Australia – all very grown up stuff.

Ewan is fair haired, 6'1" and built like an ox – he is a black belt at karate, an ex motorcycle rider and sax player and never has a bad word to say about anyone. You get the drift. But it's his zany, edgy humour that endears him to anyone who meets him. In fact meeting him for the first time is always something of a shock to a newbie – it certainly was to me. But once you get him, you find he is an intensely intelligent, thoughtful guy. Latterly he has been a bit of a crash test dummy for the development of the Inspiration Rebreather and has filled rebreather forums with his witty banter. Try googling 'Ewan's stories' and enjoy.

By this time Ewan had become my regular dive buddy and on this dive on the *Inverlane* we had been moving aft through the wreck, following another group of divers. These were big, heavy men, but as they exited the confines of the wreck they were picked up like toys by the current and carried off at speed. One minute they were there – next minute they were whisked away down the Sound. When we, with some hesitation and a large dose of apprehension, ventured out into the current, we were caught up in the circular whirlpool. Our skipper had told us if we got caught in that, we were to fin to the right as hard as we could and we would break free of it. But no matter how hard I finned right I couldn't break free.

Quickly Ewan and I got separated – and then lost in the frothing water. I went round in a circle in this vortex, three or four times – vainly kicking right as hard as I could. To make matters worse, as I had left the wreck I had inflated my delayed deco buoy – a large 6-foot red sausage marker buoy on a hand held reel which marks a diver's position for the topside boat cover. I thought if we were going on a drift dive down the Sound at that speed the skipper should know where we were. It seemed like a good idea at the time – but in fact it was a seriously bad move. The buoy was whisked round and round above me like in a washing machine as I manfully struggled to hold onto the reel and line.

After being whisked around for three or four circumnavigations of the vortex, for some inexplicable reason I managed to break out of its grasp. As soon as I was out of the vortex I expected that I would be whisked off down the Sound at several knots. But that didn't happen – for although I was free of the vortex, my deco bag on its line to my reel wasn't. It was still in the vortex going round and round. I wonder what the skipper topside thought I was doing. The vortex was holding my deco bag – which in turn was holding me in a delicate equilibrium and stopping me going with the flow – literally.

I wedged my feet into some rocks on the seabed and pulling the reel and line with all my might managed to get the bag out of the vortex. I started to reel the bag in, but now free from the restraining pull of the vortex, I started to drift with the current down the Sound. Even although I was moving at a few knots over the seabed below it felt as if I was in completely still water. I was floating, suspended in a fixed body of water that was charging into Scapa Flow at a good rate of knots.

I had worked so hard trying to get out of the vortex that my regulator had almost given up the ghost and had started feeding me chunks of water along with the usual air. On top of that, I was panting, out of breath and probably suffering from a carbon dioxide build-up. I couldn't seem to get my breath back and my regulator wouldn't let me fill my lungs properly because of the water entering my mouth. I knew I had to get control of my breathing and recover.

I saw a large boulder a few metres ahead of and beneath me which offered a bit of shelter from the raging current so I kicked down as I approached it, and dipped in behind it into still, settled water. I sat down on the seabed, my back against the boulder and tried to slow my breathing in order to fill my lungs properly and get rid of the carbon dioxide. I wondered where Ewan was – but there was no hope of me finding him in these currents.

As I sat on the bottom, breathing long and slow, my composure just starting to recover, a large black shadow came over me. Before I knew it Ewan appeared beside me in a similar state, kicking hard to dip down and slow for a seat beside me and a bit of a rest too. How he found me I will never know – but I was grateful to have some company. It was strange to be sitting side by side in such relative tranquillity whilst only a few feet above our heads, the horizontal kelp frothed and waved about in the current.

After a few minutes rest and an exchange of 'OK' signals, Ewan and I stood up and kicked off into the current and carried out our drift dive. We flew like skydivers over the bottom some 5–10 metres above it. The underwater visibility was glorious and we could pick out every feature on the seabed. Very soon the wreck of another block ship – the 1,761 ton, single screw steamship *Doyle* – flew past beneath us, its brown rusted steel work starkly contrasted against the white sand surrounding it.

Once we surfaced and were picked up by our watchful skipper we learned that some of our group had ended up on one of the other wrecks: the 2,332-ton iron Chilean steamship *Gobernador Bories*.

Tankers like the *Inverlane* are extremely strongly constructed compared to ordinary steam ships. The *Inverlane* however sat broadside on to the massively strong current that charges up and down Burra Sound with the eternal ebbing and flooding of the tide. It couldn't last forever and sadly in the winter of 1996 the *Inverlane* collapsed in a storm. She didn't go completely without a fight as part of her foʼcʼstle remained sticking out of the water for a few years. It too however collapsed and sadly nothing of the *Inverlane* remains proud of the water today. The classic view from the mainland ferry of her tanker's bows and bridge sticking up from the water has been lost forever.

Shipwrecks decay and change naturally over time – eventually they all meet such a fate.

CHAPTER THREE

THE BECKONING DEPTHS

As the 1990s dawned I was right in the midst of my deep air diving days. The depth I was diving to was gradually increasing as I sought out new shipwrecks to explore – an interest that had been first whetted at Scapa Flow.

By now, I was diving shipwrecks almost exclusively and had managed to dive all the justly famous wrecks around the west coast of Scotland – famed amongst divers for its crystal clear underwater visibility. With one or two exceptions however, it soon became clear that all the wrecks I was diving, which lay in the mid air-diving range of up to about 40 metres, had been almost completely picked clean of anything of interest by the generation of divers before me.

It dawned on me that interesting though the wrecks were, I had never seen a porthole with opening glass in situ. I had never seen a ship's telegraph or compass binnacle still standing in a bridge. These artefacts would bring a vessel to life – but they were all gone, stripped away by the lump hammer divers of yesteryear.

The depth I was diving to in search of new unpillaged shipwrecks increased steadily from 30 to 40 metres, then to 50 metres and then on to 60 metres. The lure of virgin, undived shipwrecks was taking me into a depth where diving on compressed air became very hazardous. The increasing depth meant that the very air I was breathing to keep me alive was feeding me ever increasing amounts of its main constituent, nitrogen. Although largely inert on the surface, at high levels nitrogen has a narcotic effect – the nasty diving problem called 'nitrogen narcosis'.

This is a creeping (and at first largely unnoticeable) debilitating effect – which starts for me (when I'm diving on air) at a depth of about 30–35 metres. You need to know a little about the mechanics of diving to understand how it becomes a problem.

As a diver descends, the increasing weight of water surrounding him tries to compress internal air spaces such as his lungs. These are essentially bags of air – so a parallel would be taking say a crisp bag filled with air to any depth. It would very quickly be compressed to a fraction of its size by the surrounding water pressure. To avoid this eventually fatal effect on a diver's lungs, an aqualung (or breathing regulator) delivers increasing amounts of compressed air with each breath as he descends. The aqualung delicately and rather cleverly keeps the air pressure in the diver's lungs exactly equal to the increasing water pressure around him. So the lungs stay the same size as topside and no catastrophic collapse happens.

The aqualung is a clever piece of engineering but does however bring its own complications. Of the air we breathe on the surface 79% is nitrogen. It is by far the largest component of air, with oxygen and other trace elements making up the remaining 21%. This large amount of nitrogen has no discernable effect on us as we walk around on land – it is largely inert and just passes in and out of our bodies harmlessly. You're breathing it right now. However as you dive, your aqualung delivers higher volumes of compressed air to counter the water squeeze. Consequently you are breathing increasingly higher levels of nitrogen – and these high nitrogen levels bring on nitrogen narcosis. Cousteau called it 'the Rapture of the Depths'.

Once a diver has descended to a depth of 10 metres, the weight of the surrounding water in which he is immersed is conveniently exactly equal to the weight of the whole atmosphere pressing down upon us whilst standing on the surface. On the surface the weight of the atmosphere ('atmospheric pressure') is called one 'atmosphere' or one 'bar'. So adding the 1 atmosphere weight of the atmosphere itself to the 1 atmosphere weight of water at 10 metres produces a pressure ('water pressure') of 2 bar (or 2 atmospheres). The water pressure is exactly double the air pressure we experience on the surface. The doubled weight of water and atmosphere above the diver will compress the volume of any air spaces such as lungs to half its normal size if an aqualung is not used.

To combat this 'squeeze' (as the old hardhat divers called it), at a depth of 10 metres a diver's aqualung feeds him air at twice atmospheric pressure, i.e. at 2 bar. The delicate equilibrium between the pressure of air in the lungs and the surrounding water pressure is maintained.

At a depth of 40 metres the water pressure is five times atmospheric pressure: that's 5 bar made up of the 1 bar (atmosphere) on the surface plus 1 bar (atmosphere) for each of the four 10 metres. Any air spaces (like your lungs) would be compressed to a fifth of the volume they would be on the surface – not good. So the aqualung again cleverly feeds a diver air that is compressed to five times atmospheric pressure (5 bar). Again the air pressure in the diver's lungs is kept exactly the same as the surrounding water pressure and the diver's lungs remain exactly the same size as on the surface.

Boyle's Law – the law of inverse proportions – governs this effect. When scientists were trying to work out what happened to air underwater, some brave hardy men would sit in an upturned barrel cut in half, which was lowered into the water. As the barrel was taken down to predetermined depths the air inside was compressed and the water level rose. Marks would be made on the inside of the barrel at different depths. The depths and compression marks were studied and the Law became clear.

If each breath the diver takes holds five times as much air as normal (compressed into the same volume) he is absorbing five times as much of the individual constituents. So in every breath he breathes in five times as much nitrogen and five times as much oxygen. The deeper you dive, the more nitrogen (and oxygen) you take on and the greater is the nitrogen narcosis you will suffer.

For me, breathing air at 50 metres is roughly the same as drinking four pints of beer. The narcosis strips away your ability to understand and rationalise situations – and robs you of the ability to deal with things when they go wrong. The 'narcs' (as they are affectionately known) affect everyone in different ways. Some people get euphoric, some get paranoid. Some people get tunnel vision, others lose control and panic when the simplest thing goes wrong – something that could easily be dealt with normally by the same person on the surface. My quest to find and dive undived virgin wrecks meant that for most dives I was well under the influence of the narcs.

The one notable exception to this realisation that all the diveable wrecks around our coasts were picked clean came when I was researching my second book *Dive Scotland's Greatest Wrecks*, which was first published in 1993. A small, compact shipwreck called SS *Wallachia*, sunk in the closing years of the 19th century in the River Clyde, was to prove to be one of Scotland's little gems.

In fact, two of Scotland's greatest wrecks lie in the dark, murky depths of the River Clyde. As a complete contrast to the delicate 19th century steamship *Wallachia*, not far away, lies the huge modern wreck of the *MV Akka* – a 442-foot long Swedish steel motor vessel that ran aground on the Gantock Rocks off Dunoon in 1956 and sank nearby. She is the largest diveable wreck in the Clyde – a modern ore carrier, vast in scale.

But it was the small 19th century wreck *Wallachia* that fascinated me. After leaving Glasgow in 1895 she was rammed and sunk in fog by another steamship shortly after starting a voyage to the West Indies, before she had even got out of the River Clyde. She is a delicate ship from another era – the great age of steam – and is absolutely crammed full of artefacts.

Coming from the east coast of Scotland, I was completely unfamiliar with the River Clyde (on the west coast) and its associated shipwrecks. But I had resolved to write about these two vessels and it turned out that my dive buddy Ewan Rowell knew Peter Moir, the co-author of the bible on Clyde diving, *Clyde Shipwrecks*. Ewan got in touch with Peter and told him I wanted to dive these wrecks. The die was cast and within a few weeks, Ewan and I were strolling down the RNLI slip at Largs to meet Peter and his co-author Ian Crawford, who were going to take us out and give us the guided tour of both these wrecks. After shaking hands we were soon loading our kit into their well-equipped rigid-hulled inflatable boat (RIB) for the short journey out across the river to the last resting place of the *Wallachia*.

The SS *Wallachia* is 259 feet long – a contrast in scale to the 442 feet long *Akka*, which is almost double her size. When she sank in 1895 after being rammed, the cold dark waters of the Clyde closed over her, hiding her final resting place. She was soon forgotten about – just one more wreck to add to the long list of vessels that had foundered in the Clyde.

The last official trace of her was in 1905 – after that she disappeared from the Admiralty charts. Soon, all human memory of her had passed – she was perhaps known only as a snag for nets by a few local fishermen. For nearly 100 years she lay unsalvaged in the Clyde's murky depths, still carrying in her six cargo holds a treasure trove of artefacts: a time capsule that spans the centuries.

The *Wallachia* was built by Oswald Mordaunt & Sons in Southampton and launched in 1883. She was an iron single-screw steamship with a gross weight of 1,724 tons. In 1893 she was sold to William Burrell & Son of Glasgow and soon started plying Burrell's well-worn colonial passage from Glasgow out to the West Indies.

After two year's service on this passage, in September 1895 the *Wallachia* found herself berthed at the Queen's Dock in Glasgow, being filled to the gunwales with a mixed cargo of coal, gin, whisky, beer, books, building material, stationery, glassware, earthen ware, general goods and a deck cargo of stannous chloride in two-gallon jars – all destined to ease the rigours of colonial life in the West Indies.

By 10am on Sunday, 29 September 1895, lading was completed and she had a head of steam. Captain Walton ordered her mooring lines be cast off and she slipped out of the Queen's Dock. Her crew of 21 busily settled down to their well-established shipboard routine. Her one solitary passenger probably watched the crew attend to their duties, perhaps gazing longingly at Glasgow as it faded into the distance astern at the end of her wake and wondering when or if he would ever see Scotland again. It was to be sooner than he could ever have expected.

Sea conditions were poor: a heavy fog (common in autumn) hung in the air, making navigation dangerous and a test of seamanship.

Two hours into the journey, at noon, the *Wallachia* was heading south along the wide expanse of the river and was just off the Tail of the Bank, near Greenock. Here the fog was so thick that she had to halt her journey and wait for an improvement in the sea conditions.

By early afternoon, the fog had lifted slightly and Captain Walton – eager to get going – signalled engines ahead on the ship's telegraph. The *Wallachia* got underway again, slowly passing down the river and heading for the open water of the Firth of Clyde.

As the *Wallachia* passed the Cloch Lighthouse on her port beam, the fog thickened again. Captain Walton took the *Wallachia* across the wide expanse of the river towards the northerly Argyll shore. He then followed the shoreline southwards towards the Cowal Peninsula, keeping the land in sight in the poor conditions.

Just before 4pm, the *Wallachia* entered a thicker bank of fog and in the difficult conditions and poor visibility she grounded on a shoal off Innellan Pier, near the south most point of the Cowal Peninsula. Thankfully, the tide was rising and she quickly refloated and was able to continue with her journey southwards down the wide river.

That was the last piece of luck the *Wallachia* would have, for at about 4.10 p.m. disaster struck. A large steamship suddenly materialised out of the fog, bearing down hard on the *Wallachia*'s starboard bow. The poor visibility meant that the steamer was only seen at the last moment and Captain Walton had no time to take avoiding action. He was only able to order all hands clear of the fo'c'stle deck before the two vessels collided.

The oncoming bows of the 1,406 ton Norwegian steamship *Flos* rammed into the starboard side of the *Wallachia*, 10 feet back from the stem, slicing open the iron hull as though it were cardboard. A huge gash in the hull of the *Wallachia* appeared instantly and tons of cold, dark water started flooding into her hull. The two vessels were locked together in a mortal embrace as the initial shock gave way to a realisation of the calamity now facing the crews of both ships.

The captain of the *Flos* – alive to the situation – kept his engines ahead, helping to keep the two vessels locked together. This slowed the flood of water into her hull by plugging the gap. The order to abandon the *Wallachia* was given and the crew readied her four lifeboats for lowering from their davits to the water below.

The first lifeboat capsized as it was lowered but the crew of 22 and the sole passenger managed to safely lower and board the three remaining lifeboats and row clear of the two stricken ships. Toward Lighthouse was still visible to the northwest and the crew were able to row towards the shore and safety. Mercifully, no lives were lost.

The captain of the *Flos* decided to attempt to take the *Wallachia* in tow to shallower water where she could be grounded and the ship and her valuable cargo be saved. He put the *Flos'* engines astern, but as she backed away she unplugged the gap in the *Wallachia's* hull and the flow rate of water flooding into her hull dramatically increased. *Wallachia* immediately began to settle by the bow and the attempt to take her in tow was abandoned.

At about 4.35 p.m. – some 25 minutes after being rammed – the *Wallachia* went down by the bow, slipping under the dark waters of the Clyde. As she went under, the cold water made contact with her boilers causing an explosion. As she passed from sight, the waters of the Clyde around her frothed and boiled as air was forced from her hull by the pressure of the inrushing water.

The *Wallachia* plunged down through the depths, impacting into the seabed and coming to rest on an even keel in about 34 metres of water. Her tall masts rose to just one metre short of the surface – an obvious and very serious danger to navigation in the river. As a result, just 12 days later, on 11 October 1895, the salvage vessel *Torch* (owned by the Clyde Lighthouse Trustees) appeared at the scene of the sinking and anchored above the wreck.

A hardhat diver in standard dress was sent down to inspect the wreck and reported that she was sitting upright in 20 fathoms of water. Her two large tubular steel masts were then blasted off with explosives.

Once the danger to navigation had been removed, the *Wallachia* was left to lie in peace in her watery grave. The memory of the once proud ship faded with the passing of the years, and the passing of those who remembered her. *Wallachia* had passed into oblivion, just another short statistic haunting the pages of dusty, old record books. For more than 80 years, *Wallachia* lay forgotten on the seabed slowly rusting and decaying.

In December 1976 HMS *Sheraton*, carrying out a sonar seabed survey, located an unknown wreck. Three divers were sent down to investigate but they were unable to identify the mystery wreck, although they did note that the iron propeller was still on the wreck.

In March 1977 Navy divers went down on her again, this time noting that she was holed on her starboard side just aft of the bow and that this damage was probably the cause of her sinking.

In October 1977 the *Wallachia* was re-discovered for sport diving by members of the Girvan branch of the Scottish Sub Aqua Club, who had been tipped off about a large underwater obstruction by local fishermen who had also given them the Decca coordinates. On the same weekend they got the coordinates they were able to get onsite to check it out. After a few passes a large object was found on the seabed. It was every diver's dream – a virgin shipwreck.

Their initial exploratory dives confirmed that the obstruction was a large steel or iron hulled steamship but her identity couldn't be established easily through the lucky find of a bell or maker's plate. Research through the following winter also failed to establish her identity. The National Maritime Museum, HM Customs & Excise, Admiralty Hydrographic Department, Public Records Office, Glasgow Herald newspaper records, Nautical College and any other possible sources of a clue to her identity were all checked, but none allowed them to identify the mystery vessel.

The *Wallachia* held onto the secret of her identity until the following summer when, in August 1978, a breakthrough came which would finally allow identification of the wreck. On

The wreck of SS Wallachia, *lost in the Clyde in 1895 on a voyage to the West Indies.*

one dive, the ship builder's plate was located. As customary, it didn't have the vessel's name on it, but it did have the builder's name and the yard number:

OSWALD MORDAUNT & Co.
SHIPBUILDERS & ENGINEERS
SOUTHAMPTON
SHIP NO. 202
1883

Enquiries through Southampton Chamber of Commerce and Southampton Public Library allowed the divers to locate the shipyard's records and by the middle of 1979, the vessel's identity had been established as the SS *Wallachia*.

The Hydrographic Department of the MoD, acting on information from the club then asked HMS *Sheraton*, which was surveying the Clyde, to investigate the wreck and check the findings of the SSAC Girvan Branch. Using sonar, echo soundings and inspections by teams of divers, HMS *Sheraton* was able to confirm the Branch's information. The wreck, which had vanished from the Admiralty Charts in 1905, once again became marked on the charts after a gap of nearly 80 years. One of the Clyde's best-kept secrets had finally been revealed.

The wreck of the once proud *Wallachia* is now justly acclaimed as one of the most important of the many Clyde shipwrecks. When the first divers found her she had lain untouched and fully laden since she sank 80 years before. No one had salvaged her – and everything was exactly as it was at the moment of her passing. She was frozen in time at the moment of her doom – a time capsule from the 19th century.

Her cargo holds were found to be filled to the underside of her main deck and her deck cargo still stood stowed in place. The ship's bell was soon recovered and in the bridge deckhouse, the telegraph and compass binnacle were found still standing in position alongside the helm, which bore a brass centre plate embossed with her name:

WALLACHIA
1883
LIVERPOOL

The *Wallachia* – because of her story and her contents – screamed out to be included in my book, but to be fair, she is not every diver's idea of the perfect wreck. The darkness and poor visibility does put off those divers of a faint disposition and those not used to the peculiarities of Clyde diving. But if you treat it as a night dive and see past the limitations of the poor visibility you will be treated to one of Scotland's great wreck dives.

Once we had loaded up Peter's well-equipped 5.5 metre Tornado RIB we were soon heading away from the Largs slip bearing north for the short journey of a few miles out to the *Wallachia's* last resting place.

This was going to be my first taste of diving in the River Clyde. I didn't know what to expect but had heard and read a lot of reports, which suggested that the visibility would be poor: from a few metres at best to absolute zero. There were a lot of people living further up the river in Glasgow and its sprawling suburbs, so there would be a lot of pollution in the water. Additionally, there is a lot of natural run off of sediment from the surrounding lands. And here I was intent on trying to survey a 259-foot long steamship in one dive in that visibility – it was a daunting task.

Once we arrived on site, Peter very quickly made a pass over the wreck and its distinctive outline showed up on the bottom trace of his echo sounder – we were in business. He motored up river slightly and then dropped a shot-line with grapple over the side. We drifted back down river over the wreck waiting for the grapple to snag. Our downstream drift soon came to a halt as the grapple bit on something solid. Pete tugged hard a few times on the shot-line but the grapple stayed secure.

I rolled over backwards into the water, keeping a hold of the grab lines of the RIB to make sure the gentle current didn't drift me away downstream. I kicked my fins and moved up the side of the RIB and got a gloved hand around the downline. Peter was already there and after an exchange of 'OK' hand signals we got our heads down and started finning down the shot-line.

At first the visibility was a light brown/green 2–3 metres – something akin to diving in a whisky bottle. The particles in suspension being carried down from the upper reaches of the river clouded the water. As we headed downwards these particles quickly blotted out the ambient light penetrating from the surface. By about 10 metres down it was very dark and gloomy and I had to switch on my powerful dive torch to see anything.

By 20 metres down it was quite simply pitch black and the only thing you could see was what crossed the beam of your torch within a radius of 3–4 metres. My eyes were still adjusted to surface visibility and my night vision, which takes about 20 minutes to kick in, wasn't yet helping me.

Peter and I kept heading down through the darkness and surprisingly, once we neared the wreck – even though it was still pitch black – the water seemed to get clearer. .

Suddenly we arrived at the wreck – I almost banged into it before I saw it. The grapple was actually hooked to a 5-inch cylindrical davit from its mast system, which was lying across a foredeck hold. I could see one side of the wreck nearby – it looked like the starboard side. Peter led me down into the hold, which was about 25 feet across. It was largely silt filled but here and there a few encrusted old bottles were sticking out of the silt.

Moving forward we rose out of the hold and passed a cargo winch and then the stub of one of the two masts. I felt a long way down underwater and it was hard to think that this mast had reached up almost to the distant surface. More than 100 years ago, a hard hat diver in standard dress, from the salvage company had stood exactly where I was, fixing explosives to the mast before blowing it to remove the shipping obstruction.

Moving further forward we passed another silt-filled hold before we arrived at the raised foc'stle deckhouse with portholes either side, the brass and glass fitments themselves long gone. Moving over the starboard side Peter pointed out the large gash in the ship's side where the bows of the *Flos* had cut into her.

We turned here at the bow and moved aft quickly passing back over the two foredeck holds we had just examined and the davit with its grapple snagged on it. Now that I had been underwater for about ten minutes my night vision was starting to kick in and whereas on the descent my surroundings had seemed an impenetrable darkness, as I looked ahead of me now, I could make out the faint outline of the square frontage of the bridge silhouetted against the lighter green of the shallower water above me.

We entered the bridge itself looking forward through its portholes before passing by the captain's cabin aft of it and arriving at a large circular black hole some eight feet across where the long gone funnel had once stood. Peter swam up slightly and got himself into a standing position and then started to sink slowly feet first down into the funnel opening – interesting. I followed him.

The funnel led down to a small, tight engine room on two deck levels which had a pitched roof with ceiling skylights above and just enough space either side of the engine for a diver to swim along. Following ancient catwalks we passed by the engine and exited from the engine room through the roof skylights.

At the aft-most bulkhead of the engine room superstructure there is a drop down to the main deck where three more holds are set in the wooden planked deck.

Finning over the edge of the first of two open holds I immediately saw that there was only a drop of a few feet down into its silt filled void. The tops of a mound of hundreds of large dark, beer bottles and smaller stout bottles stuck up from the silt. I dropped down to investigate and realised that the hold (which is 35 feet wide and perhaps 30 feet deep) was filled right up to the underside of the main deck with this peculiar cargo. There must be thousands of bottles in here and I was just seeing the top of the mound – the tip of the iceberg. The second hold was exactly the same.

Further aft, a small deck hatch allowed access down into the covered Hold No. 5, down a fixed ladder. This hold was also well silt filled but Peter was to tell me later that he had heard of divers working in this hold wriggling their hands and arms up down into the silt up to their armpits and coming out with 100-year-old bottles of whisky still sealed and airtight. Some of these were rumoured to have sold at auction for as much as £500.

The *Wallachia* had proved to be something of a rare gem in Scottish air diving. A wreck in a reasonable depth of water (35 metres), which you could still visit and see artefacts and relics *in situ*. Although all of the brass ship's fitments – the bell, helm plate and portholes – had disappeared by the time I dived it, the sheer volume of its cargo of beer and spirits means that this wreck's cargo will be there for divers to see for years to come.

One of the divers brought up a bottle to the surface. With the change in pressure, the cork popped out clearly stamped 'McEwan's, Edinburgh'. Destined for export to the West Indies this was the original McEwan's Export, a beer still much favoured in Scotland to this day. The 100-year-old McEwan's Export smelled exactly the same as today's version sold in tins and pubs. None of us dared to try a sip of it though.

CHAPTER FOUR

DEEPER AND DEEPER

In my early diving years I had baulked at any dive deeper than 40 metres, but I now realised that to find virgin undived wrecks I had to range further offshore and dive a lot deeper.

In about 1990 I started looking at the Admiralty Charts specifically for my own coast on the northeast of Scotland. It is an area of the world where traditionally there haven't been too many divers about and to the best of my knowledge there had been no dive teams actively looking at deep-water shipwrecks.

The local charts seemed to show two hot spots of clusters of wrecks about five miles offshore. One cluster was directly out to sea from Stonehaven where I lived (a small fishing town about 12 miles south of Aberdeen). The other cluster lay about 10 miles further south and directly offshore from the coastal town of Inverbervie and the small fishing village of Gourdon, a further mile south.

The wrecks off Stonehaven looked to be in particularly deep water of well over 50 metres, the then maximum recommended depth for air diving. But a couple of the wrecks further south off Inverbervie and Gourdon looked to be on the shallower side of the 50-metre depth contour. Although they were many miles offshore, if we found a wreck sitting in 50 metres or less we thought that its shallowest parts like the bridge superstructure would rise up some 10 metres to a manageable depth and might give good diving. One wreck symbol on the charts in particular grabbed my immediate interest. It was marked some 2½ miles offshore and looked to be the shallowest of all the wrecks in that area.

I ordered from the Hydrographic Department of the Ministry of Defence a print-out of all the wreck information they had for the 50 miles of coastline from Montrose in the south, all the way up to Fraserburgh on the very northeast tip of Scotland.

When the print-out arrived from the Hydrographic Department a couple of weeks later it stated that the wreck symbol off Inverbervie that I was looking at on the Admiralty Chart was the World War I tanker *Baku Standard*. The wreck symbol (Wk) on the Chart had the figures '19.8' in a dotted circle beside and a line under it. This meant that it had been wire swept to identify the danger to shipping from its masts and top hamper sticking up below the water line, and found to be clear to 19.8 metres. There were *at least* 19.8 metres of clear water above the wreck, but that didn't mean that was where the top of the wreck was – it could be a lot deeper. We felt however that if a naval vessel had spent a lot of time wire sweeping the wreck, the position would be fairly accurate. Ewan and I determined to go out and find it.

Using an Admiralty Chart we took triangulation bearings to prominent land features from the charted wreck position. This was just before the advent of cheap and readily accessible Global Positioning Systems (GPS) and we were going to have to do it the old fashioned way. We knew that a lot of the charted positions were fairly inaccurate – a result of errors in the dead reckoning estimated positions reported at the actual time of the sinking. Additionally, once a vessel was abandoned it was common for it to drift some way away from its last reported position before sinking. It was therefore highly unlikely that the wreck position was 100% accurate but at least our compass bearings should get us in the right approximate position.

Early on a Saturday morning, togged up in red and yellow sailing gear, we launched my RIB *Stonehaven Diver* at Stonehaven harbour and set off on our quest to find the *Baku Standard*. It was a blustery, overcast morning – the clouds were a leaden grey, the sea dark and foreboding.

Once we had the RIB in the water we loaded into it four large pink Dhan buoys, each with 60 metres of thin, cheap blue nylon rope on it with a couple of 6 lb dive weights tied to the end. We planned to get out to the position and then drop one Dhan buoy to mark the general position – we would then make up a search box for about ¼ of a mile either side. Once we had set up our search area we would try to methodically mow the lawn with our echo sounder hoping to run over the wreck, which would show up on the echo sounder.

After a bouncy 12-mile ride down the coast we arrived in the approximate position. Whilst I sat at the steering console, Ewan stood behind me, his sighting compass held up to his eye shouting corrections to my course over the din of the engine and the wind. Once we thought we were in the right position we dropped a buoy and I started doing a crisscross search pattern outwards towards the south, my eyes glued to the echo sounder. There was nothing but a flat bottom trace.

Once we were about ¼ mile away from the first position we dropped another buoy and then headed off doing a crisscross search more to seaward or east of the first position. We repeated this methodical search pattern all morning. By lunchtime we had found nothing at all and we switched off the engine and let ourselves wallow silently beam on to the waves as we opened a flask of coffee and scoffed some sandwiches. We guessed that if it had been wire swept or surveyed by a surface vessel in the past that the position must be fairly accurate and the wreck would lie within a one-mile square box of the charted position. We decided to extend our search area.

Leaving the first Dhan buoy still in position to mark the charted position we started doing a haphazard search round and about the buoy extending it ever outwards – but still no result. Time was wearing on and in truth I had in my own mind given up ever finding the wreck, when at the outer limit of one of our sweeps the seabed bottom trace suddenly shot up from 49 metres to 39 metres. We had just passed over a large object on the seabed, which rose up 10 metres. Finally there was a wreck below us.

From a weary resignation to failure, Ewan and I leapt into action. We threw one of the Dhan buoys over the side. The weights rocketed down, the line went taught and the tell tale current stream past the buoy told us it wasn't moving. We had snagged into the wreck. We motored back and forth around the buoy watching the echo sounder and were able to see that the wreck was lying in an east–west direction, pointing towards the shore. We worked our way out to the extremity of the wreck in one direction and dropped another buoy. We then worked back along the wreck in the opposite direction until the wreck disappeared from our sounder and dropped another buoy. We now had both ends of the wreck buoyed and could work out its heading exactly – it was pointing towards the small fishing village of Johnshaven several miles south of Inverbervie. We could also have a go at roughly measuring the distance between the two buoys, which gave a length for the wreck of almost 400 feet. She was a big ship indeed.

We motored up beside the buoy and Ewan took compass bearings on land points. We also took land transits as best we could, lining up fixed objects on the shore with more distant recognisable landmarks – but we were some three miles offshore and it was difficult in the overcast visibility to make out buildings against the shadowy coastline.

We did however get one cracker of a transit. The large square sandstone spire of Inverbervie Church was silhouetted against the sky – it is the highest and most prominent of all the buildings in Inverbervie. By chance the spire nestled neatly in a small gap between two white square objects, which we presumed were houses on the shore. That transit would lead us to the wreck every time. Just line the spire up between the two houses and motor out until the depth got to about 49 metres and you were bound to run over the wreck. Or so we thought.

After pulling in our Dhan buoys and rope we decided to motor towards the shore to double-check exactly what the two white buildings were. We drove in towards shore keeping the spire wedged in the gap. As we neared the shore and our eyes started to be able to distinguish the buildings ashore, to our horror we saw that the two white square objects of our transit were not buildings at all, but large white lorries parked in a lorry park down at the shore. Worse still, as the lorries swung into focus, one of them slowly moved off. Our beautiful transit was driving off as we looked at it and there was no readily recognisable building behind it that we could use. Our golden transit was lost. Never the less we resolved to return the following week several hours before slack water, relocate the wreck and dive it.

The following Saturday we were motoring back down the coast. Ewan was going to boat-handle whilst I dived the wreck with Dave Hadden, a deep air dive buddy of mine. Dave had been air diving for longer than I had and had in the early days introduced to our group many of the techniques that would later go on to become staples of technical diving – like manifolded twin sets and deco reels. Dave was a tall, immensely strong diver (from a lifetime's body building) who had shown he had a level-head in difficult situations.

This was well before the advent of mixed gases such as 'Trimix' and 'Nitrox', so we would be breathing just standard compressed air on the bottom and as well as for all our decompression stops – and all from a twin set of two 12-litre tanks. At a depth of 49 metres we were right at the recommended depth limit for air diving of 50 metres. I knew that I would be severely affected by nitrogen narcosis.

Dave and I had kitted up facing each other on either side tube of the RIB. Once we were ready we simultaneously rolled backwards over the side splashing into the water. Righting ourselves we gave an 'OK' signal to Ewan and finned up to the bow of the boat, which was tied to the shot-line snagged on the wreck below. We started our descent.

It is a feature of east coast Scotland diving that the water is heavy with silt in the spring months. The run off from rivers disgorges sediment into the sea and clouds visibility. So as soon as we started our descent our surroundings grew darker as the silt in suspension in the increasing depth of water above us started to filter out the sunlight that was trying to penetrate down. By about 25 metres down it was almost completely dark and I turned on my powerful UK800 dive torch – its strong beam sliced through the darkness.

After a momentary pause and an exchange of 'OK' hand signals with Dave, I turned and pressed on downwards, headfirst into the darkness, keeping one hand lightly holding onto the downline. If I let go of it I'd very quickly be drifted away from the downline and would end up landing on a flat silty seabed away from the wreck.

Our boat's echo sounder had shown that the depth to the top of the wreck was about 40 metres and we had tried to drop the shot-line and weight right on top of the highest point. The seabed was showing a depth of 49/50 metres – right at the recommended extreme limit for air diving. I had been to that depth many times before and knew that if we hit 50 metres on the seabed we'd be heavily affected by the nitrogen narcosis and in pitch darkness on a new undived wreck, possibly with fishing nets snagged on it, we would be entering a very dangerous environment.

As I descended I continually checked my wrist-mounted depth gauge. Thirty metres came and went, then 35 metres. Shining my torch straight down there was no hoped-for sign of the wreck below – just the white downline disappearing relentlessly into the darkness, fluorescing in the glare of my torch.

Forty metres. I should be on top of the wreck by now with solid metal beneath me – at worst I was right beside the wreck. I knew it was tantalisingly close. I swept my torch beam around in the hope of glimpsing something manmade, but there was still no sign of the wreck. Had the downline been pulled off the wreck and was it now some way away from it? Was the whole dive going to be a complete failure?

I pressed on downwards to 45 metres. I realised now that the downline was off the wreck or perhaps in a collapsed section of it and that it was likely that I was going to have to go all the way down to the bottom at 50 metres. I felt waves of narcosis sweeping over me. In the all-consuming darkness I felt my heart rate accelerate and a gnawing fear and apprehension started to sweep over me.

Suddenly 3–4 metres below me, the sandy seabed materialised out of the gloom and I landed beside our anchor and chain, which was sitting on clean furrowed sand with a solitary starfish beside it. Dave's torch appeared out of the darkness above me and he landed on the seabed beside me. Two solitary specks of humanity standing in pitch darkness, 50 metres below the surface of the sea, 3 miles offshore looking for a large shipwreck which we knew was towering over us – but which was tantalisingly out of sight.

Narcosis washed over me like a fuzzy, warm velvet blanket. I looked down at my fins and the seabed and noticed the tell-tale scour left by our anchor dragging and bouncing through the silt. It must have failed to snag properly on the wreck and been pulled off by the current as we descended. If we followed the scour then it should lead us straight to the wreck.

We started to fin a few feet above the seabed following the track and I noticed from my depth gauge that our depth was decreasing slightly. The flat seabed soon started to change and suddenly, a wall of rotted brown steel covered in dead men's fingers and soft corals appeared out of the darkness ahead of us rising up perhaps for two metres. With a whoop of euphoria I kicked my fins and propelled myself up onto the top of the wall of steel and swept my torch around. It was immediately evident that this wasn't the tanker *Baku Standard*, but was the main deck of a freighter sitting on an even keel. I could dimly make out cargo winches and the stump of a large mast set in between the rims of two cargo holds. I finned over to one hold and pointed my torch into it, but to my dismay found that it was filled with silt to just a few metres short of the top. I checked my depth gauge – we were at 47 metres.

In the darkness, the feel of something manmade seemed to give me a sense of security, but the cloak of darkness also made it impossible to tell which way was aft – and which way was forward. Randomly I decided to head off to my right and started kicking my way along the main deck passing alongside the rim of one of the silt-filled holds.

The hold ended and I shone my torch across a short expanse of flat main deck. When we had arrived on the bottom, our surroundings had appeared completely black but my night vision was now starting to kick in. As I looked upwards I could make out a feeble lighter green to the water above – but there was also a large black rectangular silhouette blocking out the green in front of me. It looked something like the black monolith from *2001: a Space Odyssey* on its side. I realised with a start that I was looking at a large rectangular section of superstructure.

I moved over the deck to the base of the superstructure and found that it was almost completely covered with a carpet of sea life: sponges, anemones and dead man's fingers. A line of large portholes dotted its frontage at main deck level and thick old-fashioned electric cables hung down from above from ancient navigation lamps.

Two ominously black, open doorways faced towards me, their doors long ago fallen from rotted hinges. I checked my contents gauge – I had used less than one third of the air in my two back-mounted tanks. I moved to the left hand doorway, shone my torch inside and then moved through it.

I entered a large open space, which looked like it had once been a lounge. Silt several feet deep layered the bottom of the room, piled up even higher at the sides. As well as the portholes along the front of the room that I had seen from outside, portholes lined both sides as well and feeble shafts of weak green light penetrated the gloom through them. As I ventured further in, the brilliant glare of white ceramic sinks and toilets reflected in my torch beam. Once I had seen enough I exited through the same doorway back into open water outside.

Dave and I started to kick our way upwards in front of the wall of superstructure. As the second deck level approached I was staggered to see that instead of round portholes as on the deck below, large square glass windows rimmed with greened brass were set in its frontage. Some were missing, fallen from their mounts and smashed on the deck below.

We moved up a further deck level and I looked at my depth gauge. We had risen up to a mercifully shallower depth of 40 metres and I could feel the wash of narcosis that had been clouding my mind easing slightly. I was relieved to be in shallower water. Another row of square glass windows allowed glimpses into the interior of what could only be the bridge.

Dave and I finned round the starboard side of the bridge superstructure and dropped over a railing into the starboard bridge wing. As I looked across the flat top of this superstructure I saw collapsed sides of a smaller deckhouse with portholes studded in them and realised that there must have been a smaller deck house on top of the deck level where we were now standing.

The area we had arrived in was littered with rectangular bricks about a foot long by 6 inches across. I took up my knife and scraped away the crud on one of them and found a black bituminous material beneath. These had probably been layered over the roof of the bridge superstructure – a cheap form of armouring the bridge against machine gun fire from enemy planes. This was a wartime wreck.

Turning to my right, an aft facing doorway seemed to lead into the back of the bridge, the door itself long since rotted and fallen from its hinges. The remnants of an old fishing net snagged on the wreck aeons ago were draped across the doorway. Cutting away the worst of it with my knife I squeezed through the door and entered the bridge.

The bridge was heavily silt filled but to my left, on the centre line of the vessel, the compass binnacle was lying fallen over. I moved to the front of the bridge and peered out through one of the glass windows. With my night vision in full swing by now I could just make out the outline of one of the foredeck holds far below and a mast, which lay over another hold beyond.

Turning, as I backed out through the same bridge door the tell tale green gleam of verdigreed brass, partly obscured by the bituminous bricks, caught my attention. Moving a couple of bricks aside revealed a large telegraph, the white circular faceplate gone, lying on its side, well embedded into the crud below. I replaced the bricks over it and added a few more for good measure.

Dave and I moved aft over the top of the bridge deck until the superstructure dropped off, deck level by deck level down into the darkness below. We were already at our allotted time on the bottom and faced some 30 minutes of decompression stops on the ascent before we could reach the surface safely. We couldn't venture back down into the depths at this late stage of the dive – exploring aft of the bridge superstructure would have to wait for another day.

We took out our delayed deco reels and filled the deco buoys with air from one of our regulators. The bags went rushing up to the distant surface, our reels chattering wildly as they paid out line. The reels suddenly stopped spinning as our bags broke the surface. We wound in the slack and finned slowly upwards to our first deco stop.

Although we had started the dive at slack water (when there is no current), the tide had by now turned. So as we rose up from the wreck, the current drifted us over the top of the superstructure towards the port side, where I thought I caught a glimpse of the port bridge wing with a navigation lantern hanging limply on old thick electric cables.

Thirty minutes later our heads broke the surface. Ewan guided *Stonehaven Diver* deftly in between us and helped haul in our heavy kit, eagerly firing questions at us about what we had seen. For sure, this wasn't a World War I tanker: this was a merchant vessel with at least two holds and a large tubular mast collapsed down. But from this one dive I couldn't tell if this was a small freighter with just two holds and a bridge superstructure situated right at the very stern like a tanker – or whether we had just seen the bridge superstructure of a far larger vessel which might have more holds and superstructure aft of the bridge. We were pretty sure she was a war wreck from the bituminous bricks that lined her bridge roof. We resolved to dive her again as soon as we could.

The following week saw *Stonehaven Diver* flashing down the coast again towards our mystery wreck. After shotting her Dave and I once again made the descent into pitch darkness towards the wreck. We had now moved into the period of stronger tides called 'spring tides' where slack water only lasts for about 20 minutes on our coast (as opposed to the two hours of the weaker 'neap tides' of the month). As a consequence there was still a bit of current running as we moved down the line.

I reached the bottom of the line at about 48 metres and found myself in a confused jumble of collapsed ship's side. This was a new area for us – and I reckoned that the shot had landed in a hold where the ship's side had fallen in. Immediately I knew this wasn't either of the two intact holds we had seen the preceding week, so we now had this wreck confirmed as a far larger vessel than a simple two-hold freighter with her superstructure at the stern.

As I stood in the debris waiting for Dave to arrive beside me, my back was towards the current. Unseen by me a large lion's mane jellyfish – its translucent stinging tentacles some 6 feet long – was drifting towards me with the current. I felt a dull, barely perceptible, impact on the back of my head and then, driven on by the current, a mass of translucent stinging feelers carried round the front of my face and snared themselves over my mask and regulator. I started feeling the stings as they contacted the exposed area around my lips.

As I reeled from the pain of multiple stings I became aware that Dave was beside me prising the jellyfish off the back of my head and pushing it away to drift on in the current. Most of the stinging feelers seemed to come off my face and the immediate pain subsided a bit. I weighed up whether we should just abort the dive there and then and head for the surface – but after the initial stings, the pain wasn't that bad so I decided to tough it out and go on with the dive.

We kicked our legs and headed off. Very soon the hull regained its shape – we had indeed been inside a collapsed hold and as we finned out of it, we were met with an intact section of ship's hull with a single storey deck house atop it – most definitely not the 4–5 storey deckhouse we had explored the week before.

Moving to what I presumed was the starboard side of the deckhouse we entered a covered walkway along the side and finned along it. Portholes, some with the glass still in place studded the rotted deckhouse wall.

After perhaps 50 feet, the deckhouse came to an end and we moved in behind it. Here the deck sloped off abruptly downwards and we could see the rim of another aft hold. It seemed as though the hull had collapsed here as well.

In the aft facing section of this superstructure were set two doorways – their doors rotted off and fallen onto the deck. A large tubular mast, some 4 feet in diameter, had fallen down to rest on top of the superstructure. Its weight was clearly starting to collapse the deckhouse, as the walls were now bent and twisted out of line.

Dave and I gingerly swam in through the starboard side doorway and immediately came upon a large cooking range sitting athwartships with what looked like an oven nearby – we were in the galley.

We moved up the starboard side of the galley, passing a white sink, gleaming in our torches and were able to penetrate forward for perhaps 25 feet. As I swept my torch around, its beam picked out the outline of three square shapes in the deep silt covering the floor. Each was about 2 feet square with the edges protruding about 3–4 inches above the silt.

Resting on my knees on the silt, I wriggled my gloved hand deep into the silt inside one of them and started to feel large smooth objects. Grasping hold of one of the objects I pulled it out from its cloak of silt. It was a large white gleaming suturine, which had an unusual logo on it – a circular blue belt and buckle with a large 'W' inside it. Putting the suturine down I wriggled my hand deep into the silt again and pulled on what felt like a plate. It came out in a cloud of silt, gleaming white in the beam of my torch and it had the same blue shipping line logo glazed on it.

Replacing the crockery I turned and moved slowly out of the galley. We were now about 20 minutes into the dive and I was starting to feel decidedly unwell – presumably from the effects of the stings. I was starting to feel light-headed and slightly nauseous and a feeling of foreboding and apprehension was sweeping over me – the dread fear of a painful death far below the surface. I didn't know quite what was happening to me – but I did know we were already well into decompression stops and heading straight up to the surface was not an option.

As we came out of the galley, the current – which had continued to increase throughout our dive – took hold of us and started to drift us towards the port side of the wreck. The large collapsed tubular mast seemed to move towards us and Dave effortlessly swam over it and started to ascend. I wasn't able to go over it in time and had to duck and pass under it in the gap between it and the deck.

As I came out of the other side I saw Dave's fins above me as he rose up. Feeling this unwell I didn't want to lose sight of him – if I lost him and then passed out from the stings I was gone forever.

I kicked my legs and rose up towards him grabbing hold of one of his fins to slow him up. When I got level with him I gave him the hand signal that I was feeling unwell and hoped he would look after me as we ascended.

As my depth decreased I started to feel progressively more unwell. Whether the change in depth altered the way the stings were affecting me or whether this was how the reaction to the stings generally took place, I don't know. But by the time we rose up to our final 6-metre decompression stop I felt that I was in serious danger of blacking out. I was fighting to stay conscious and in control – and was so concerned about passing out that I clipped my deco reel (attached to my surface buoy) to my harness. At least if I blacked out I wouldn't sink back down into the darkness and be lost forever.

The deco stop seemed like an eternity as I grimly fought to stay conscious, but eventually we were clear to rise up to the surface. There Ewan stripped my kit off me and I tumbled into the boat. By the time we got ashore I had swollen marks of the stingers across my lower face and they stung like hell. We still managed however to go to our local harbour pub for a decompression pint of beer. I got some vinegar off a table and smeared it over the stinger marks but that didn't do much good. One of the guys offered another solution of peeing on the stings – which I kindly declined.

I toughed out the pain and gradually after a few hours it eased and then disappeared. In the jellyfish season on our coasts we get an explosion of many types of jellyfish, which flourish as they consume the preceding plankton bloom's harvest. Sometimes as you descend or ascend in a current they are so thick that it's like playing *Space Invaders* as you dodge them, twisting and turning to avoid contacting them or their translucent fan of stinging tentacles. Often translucent stingers cover the shot-line and worse still the stingers, which are sometimes hard to see, can get snared on the mouthpiece of your deco regulators. As you switch regulators, if you don't check and just stick it in your mouth, you can be stung on the soft mucous tissues inside your mouth. I've had that a couple of times and it isn't funny – you learn to check carefully and pick them off before you swap.

A week or two later I heard a report that a diver in the Moray Firth had also been stung by a lion's mane jellyfish and had surfaced unconscious. Talking to a doctor about what had happened he confirmed that unconsciousness on the surface could result from a severe set of stings.

In the succeeding weeks we continued to dive our mystery wreck and over the course of four or five dives managed to explore most of it. We sketched what we had seen on each dive and built up a full picture of the entire wreck.

The ship we reckoned was about 350 feet long with two foredeck holds, a bridge superstructure originally five to six levels high and a midships hold with the starboard side of the hull collapsed. Aft of that was a central superstructure one deck high and lined with cabins down either side, each with its own individual sink, and a galley at the aft most section. Aft of that were two further holds with the deck having collapsed downwards.

Although the main section of the hull from its two foredeck holds right back to its two aft holds was sitting on an even keel, the fo'c'stle had split off the hull and rolled over onto its port side causing the foremost hold to collapse. The wreck sat broadside onto the prevailing north/south current and on the southern side of the wreck, which faced towards the large tidal estuary at Montrose, there was a silt bank piled right up to main deck level.

The very stern itself, like the fo'c'stle had cracked and rolled off onto its port side. The prop was still *in situ* half buried in the silt.

The wreck seemed to be heading bows to shore and we knew the wreck was lined up with Johnshaven. We guessed that as the wreck sat broadside on to the powerful north/south currents that wash up and down this coastline, the current hitting the broad expanse of the side of the wreck would be channelled along the hull and would in time start to excavate and undermine the bow and stern. Eventually after long enough, the bow and stern would be suspended clear of the seabed above a scour. Then, as the wreck rotted and lost its structural integrity, the bow and stern would break off and fall down. Here both the bow and stern sections had then rolled onto their port side.

On one dive with Ewan we were exploring the flat expanse of the single story deckhouse superstructure towards the stern. I could see that the large tubular main mast had fallen down and was resting on top of the superstructure that housed the galley. A forest of mushroom forced draft ventilators had had their tops, seemingly cut off at the same level by a large knife. The large funnel had fallen towards the bow and the foremast also had been brought down and fallen towards the bow. The conclusion was inescapable and completely tied in with the wreck symbol on the chart – the wreck had been wire swept from stern to bow, chopping off the tops of all the ventilators. The main mast had fallen to rest on top of the uppermost starboard side of the collapsed fo'c'stle.

As we continued to explore the top of the superstructure we came across a large pitched roof, characteristic of an engine room. The pitched roof ran for 20–25 feet along the centre line of the vessel. The large rectangular opening fanlights were easily big enough for a man to get through and would originally have held glass. I peered inside and swept my torch around. It was pitch black but I could make out the tops of what appeared to be cylinders of a very large engine. The engine room itself was a cavernous space, which I thought could easily accommodate both of us.

I kicked up until I was directly above one of these openings and then, breathing out hard, let myself sink slowly down and through it. Once I had got myself fully in through the roof of the engine room I moved aside as Ewan followed. An enormous engine sitting fore and aft on the centreline of the vessel faced us. There seemed to be seven large cylinders each dropping down for perhaps 30–40 feet into the darkness below. At the side of each cylinder were set small oil-filled inspection gauges, which still had black oil in them. About 15 feet from the top of the engine – about halfway down – a catwalk grid wound around the whole seven cylinders. I dropped down and landed on the catwalk and peered further down, my eyes seeking the bottom of the engine – but this was well out of sight below. Checking my depth gauge, I had just dropped from 40 metres outside to 45 metres here. It was likely that the bottom of the engine room was well below the surrounding seabed, which I knew was at a depth of 50 metres – the maximum recommended depth for air diving. Enticing though it was, I couldn't venture down to the bottom.

On another dive we shotted the wreck in the two collapsed holds towards the stern of the wreck. Moving aft from the shot we came to the large broken-off stern section lying on its port side with a large opening where it had sheared off. I shone my torch around inside the hull. It seemed that all the internal walls and decks had completely rotted away as there was just one large common space. At the far side, a green opening in the hull looked back at me and seemed big enough to allow us to exit the wreck. With a sweep of my torch around to make sure there were no tangles or heavy objects likely to fall on me if disturbed, we finned into the hull and moved around it as we made our way over to the exit point, which was on the uppermost starboard side. With a feeling of relief I was able to squeeze through the exit point into free water and then move round the very stern itself back onto the main deck, which rested at an angle of about 60 degrees. Feeling our way forward we came across the auxiliary helm with its circular spokes some six feet across, still bolted *in situ* directly above the rudder. This would have been used if the main helm in the distant bridge had been disabled.

After some 20–30 dives on the wreck we felt that we had a good idea of the lay out and orientation of the wreck – but its identity still eluded us. Locals in the fishing villages directly ashore talked about a World War II wreck they called the *Roseberry*, from which barrels of rancid lard had washed ashore until the 1980s. When I looked at the Hydrographic Department print out however, there was no wreck named *Roseberry* listed as being lost in the 50 miles or so it covered from Fraserburgh in the north to Montrose in the south. There was however, a wreck called the *Queensbury*, which had been lost in a convoy attacked by German aircraft in World War II along with another Norwegian vessel, the motor ship *Taurus*, which was charted as sunk a few miles away.

I wrote the National Maritime Museum in Greenwich and the World Ship Society to order photographs of all of the ships listed as lost in this area. The World Ship Society came back with a photograph of the *Queensbury* but didn't have a photo of the MS *Taurus*. They suggested that as it was a Norwegian ship, I should contact the Norwegian Maritime Museum in Oslo – the quaintly named Norsk Sjøfartsmuseum.

I fired off a letter to the museum more in hope than expectation – and as I wasn't expecting much of a result I put my enquiry to the back of my mind. So I was completely stunned a few weeks later when I received a very polite reply from the museum stating that they were very familiar with MS *Taurus*, which it transpired had its own place in history as the first Norwegian ship to have a double acting diesel engine fitted. She had even been featured in Ship of the Year 1935. Furthermore they had some 200–300 photographs of her from her keel strip being laid in 1935 until her final launch and the start of her working life. They sent me copies of a few of these photos and lo and behold, there in front of me was a perfect match for the wreck we had surveyed and sketched.

The Norwegian Maritime Museum also went on to say that A/S Akers Mek Verk in Oslo had built *Taurus* for the Wilhelmsen Shipping Line, whose emblem or logo was the circular blue belt and buckle with a large 'W' inside it. This was the same logo I had seen on the crockery in the galley. The identity of our mystery wreck was confirmed.

To add icing to the cake the museum also held the log of the *Taurus* and sent me copies of the entries concerned with its last convoy duty and subsequent sinking. It was fascinating to read a first hand account of how this beautiful ship had ended up on the bottom off our coast.

The *Taurus* was a graceful fast vessel of 4,767 tons, measuring 408 feet in length with a beam of 55 feet. In 1939, four years after her launch, World War II had erupted over Europe. After the German occupation of Norway on 9 April 1940, *Taurus* was one of the many Norwegian vessels stranded in Swedish waters. As a result she – along with 43 of the other stranded Wilhelmsen Line vessels (situated outside Norwegian waters) – came under the control of the Norwegian Government in exile in London, and thus under the British Ministry of War Transport.

George Binney – a British citizen working in Sweden – drew up 'Operation Rubble', in which he would use five of these stranded ships to take vital cargoes of special steel through the Skagerrak minefields, past German patrol boats, submarines and aircraft, and on to Orkney. On 19 January 1941 *Taurus* and the other four chosen ships left the small Swedish port of Brofjord at 30-minute intervals.

The passage from Sweden to Orkney took the small flotilla 36 hours. En route *Taurus* burnt out an exhaust valve and was stopped dead in the water for two hours whilst it was repaired. German aircraft fired on all five vessels, but none were badly damaged and they succeeded in carrying 25,000 tons of precious steel to Britain. The five ship's captains were awarded OBEs by Britain and were decorated by the King of Norway. George Binney was knighted for his daring, dangerous and brilliantly executed operation.

In May 1941, just five months after the dash from Sweden, *Taurus* was in Freetown in West Africa, completing lading with a cargo of 2,000 tons of cocoa and 2,000 tons of groundnuts amongst other general cargo. Her route was to take her up the west coast of Africa and on up to Scotland where she would form up in the Oban Roads for a convoy which would pass around the north of Scotland and then down the east coast to her eventual destination at Hull. The English Channel was simply too dangerous to risk passing through.

The voyage from Africa went uneventfully and as the hours of 5 June 1941 passed slowly, she was making good progress in a large convoy heading south down the east coast of Scotland

MS Taurus *(1935). Norwegian Maritime Museum, Oslo.*

several miles offshore. Once the convoy had got in range of the German planes operating from their Norwegian airfields, continuous air attacks had started up against it. The convoy would have to fight its way down the whole east coast of the UK.

By nightfall, as the convoy passed Aberdeen and then Stonehaven, it stretched as far as the eye could see to the north and as far again to the south. Locals still talk of helplessly watching the attacks going in, from vantage points on cliffs and headlands. The night sky was lit up with the flashes of large explosions far offshore – followed some time after by the rumble of the distant explosions.

At 0044 hrs on 6 June, as *Taurus* passed south of Todhead lighthouse near Catterline, her crew suddenly heard the drone of an aircraft approaching in the darkness and three bombs were dropped from low altitude by the attacker. Although all three bombs missed, like so many near misses, the force of the explosions transmitted through the water and several of her hull plates were ruptured. She started to flood with water and her engines had to be stopped.

Slowly she took on a list to port and started to settle by the stern. A cable was passed to her and she was taken in tow by the escort trawler HMS *Tarantella*, bound for the port of Montrose some 15 miles away. The attacks on the rest of the convoy continued unabated.

About two hours later another aircraft attacked her and three more bombs were dropped. Like the last bombing run, these three bombs also narrowly missed the ship but exploded close enough to cause further damage. The rate of water flooding into her hull increased and she started to settle more quickly. There would be no time to tow her all the way to Montrose now.

The tow was diverted and a desperate dash developed to drag her water-filled hulk into shallow water and beach her near the small fishing village of Johnshaven. But the tow was destined to fail – and she sank some two and a half miles short of safety in 50 metres of water, her bows still pointed forlornly towards Johnshaven and the safety of the shore. She became a total loss.

In 1969, 200 tons of lard washed ashore at Johnshaven after a big storm, and right up until the 1980s, from time to time after a storm, large barrel shaped pieces of lard – the wooden barrel itself rotted away – would be washed up on the shore. Scraping off the rancid fat, some canny locals would heat up the good fat and use it for cooking, despite its long immersion in the sea. The locals did say you had to be careful how you heated the fat as from time to time you got a German machine gun bullet in it.

Having identified the beautiful wreck of the *Taurus* we were now buoyed with success. We had found, dived and identified a virgin shipwreck and the story of the wreck – largely forgotten since World War II – had been brought back to life. So when George Mair – another of my dive buddies of the time – called to say that he had located another big wreck five miles offshore in the same vicinity (which was recorded in the Hydrographic Department records as a probable U-boat), we jumped at the chance of diving it. The depth to the seabed was 60 metres and the shallowest parts of the wreck only reached up to 50–52 metres. This was

Right: The wreck of the MS Taurus, *North Sea.*

Below: The 1893 tanker Baku Standard *torpedoed during World War I off Inverbervie.*

diving at the very extreme edge of air diving and although I knew nitrogen narcosis would be a significant problem for me, I didn't really appreciate how disabled I would be by its insidious effects at that depth.

When we eventually took the plunge into the darkness above this wreck, the shot-line led us straight down to 50 metres where we arrived on the flat main deck of a World War I tanker complete with a large stern mounted defensive gun, which still had its firing panel *in situ*. Although the bridge superstructure amidships had collapsed, the pump room was still standing complete with portholes with glass in them. Large pipes ran fore and aft between the open, empty oil tank hatches. A curious tall and thin Victorian funnel near the stern, complete with brass and glass viewing ports, had come crashing down and fallen into one of the aft tanks.

On subsequent dives where the main deck had rotted away, we were able to duck down between the structural ribs of the ship into the tween deck and swim along under the main deck for 50–100 feet with an open oil tank to one side – allowing a safe exit – before popping up through the main deck at the very stern. Once we had surveyed and sketched this wreck we soon had it identified as the unmistakeable tanker *Baku Standard*, built in 1893 and torpedoed off Gourdon in 1917.

This wreck was right at the very limit of deep air diving and I found the effects of nitrogen narcosis quite severe beyond 50 metres. I seemed to be fine up to 40 metres but then felt progressively worse the deeper I got. At 50 metres, in complete darkness, I seemed to be just hanging on – just getting by with the dive and not really noticing as much as I should be. At night after a deep air dive I would suffer quite heavily from unearned fatigue – after a big meal, I just wanted to get to bed and rest. The physical exertion of the dive itself didn't seem to merit the tiredness I would feel.

There were no more virgin wrecks charted around here at less than 50 metres depth and our dive team, keen to explore more undived wrecks, had reached a physical barrier – one, which we did try to break through with potentially serious consequences.

CHAPTER FIVE

BAIL OUT ON THE SS *CUSHENDALL*

D riven on by the lure of finding and diving more virgin wrecks we started to regularly dive deeper than the recommended maximum BSAC depth limit for diving on compressed air of 50 metres – about 165 feet in old money.

Before long I had done a deep air dive to a newly found wreck in more than 55 metres off Girvan – a pitch black dive on a silty, virgin wreck far offshore. But I had felt comfortable and in control, able to spend the dive not just trying to stay alive but trying to take in what I was seeing and work out in the poor visibility what sort of ship it was and how it had met its end.

And then George Mair (who had found the *Baku Standard*) located another undived wreck some five miles off Stonehaven in 58 metres. It was the northmost of the triangle of three wrecks charted as lying 4–5 miles out of Stonehaven but we didn't know what precise vessel it was. Without any hesitation we decided to have a go at diving it. It couldn't be much worse than the Girvan 55 metre wreck – could it?

SS Cushendall, *one of the wrecks in Stonehaven Bay. World Ship Society.*

47

On a beautiful summer's evening with a languid rolling oily swell, we launched two RIBs at Stonehaven harbour and motored out to the position where George had run over the wreck previously. Sure enough the LCD of the echo sounder showed a flat seabed at 58 metres with the wreck trace itself rising up off the seabed for some 4–5 metres at its shallowest parts. I had hoped in the run up to the dive that we might find a large section of superstructure sticking up, to decrease the depth we would be diving at. But it was clear from the echo sounder that no matter where we landed on the wreck we were still going to be well over the 50 metre limit.

Strangely, in the run up to the dive I had experienced no pangs of hesitation about what we were planning. I had been to just a few metres short of that depth before. How could just another few metres make much of a difference?

But when we arrived on the site above the wreck and dropped our anchor into it, I just sat there at the steering console staring at my echo sounder as it scrolled out a flat bottom trace at 58 metres. The reality of the depth I was soon going to dive dawned on me, and a feeling of dread and apprehension swept over me. For the first time in my diving career I thought about chickening out of a dive. It was just *too* deep, but I didn't let on about my fears to my dive buddies.

George Mair and his dive partner Eric Ronsberg were to be the first divers to descend – a courtesy amongst wreck divers, as it was George who had managed to locate the wreck. Dave Hadden and I would go in the second wave.

Twenty to 25 minutes after they had disappeared beneath the surface on their descent, two red decompression marker buoys blooped to the surface. George and Eric had started their ascent.

At this stage of our diving we were used to carrying out inwater decompression stops at the end of a dive of about 25 minutes at most. But it was a massive 45 minutes later before their heads broke the surface. We motored our boats over to them and hauled in their equipment.

George told me as he de-kitted that the anchor was lying on the sand beside the wreck, but that the wreck was out of sight. They had followed the scour it had made in the sandy seabed as it had dragged along, and managed to find the wreck. He gave me the direction to head once I got to the bottom.

Slack water had come and gone and we were now entering a late evening dusk as Dave and I got dressed into our heavy gear, rolled backwards off the boat and splashed into the water. We started our descent and soon a familiar darkness enveloped us. We pressed on downwards, switching on our powerful dive torches as we went down.

Thirty-five metres came and went. The wreck was still a long way down beneath us. Forty metres came and went and the gnawing apprehension that I had felt on the surface came back to me as the first warm waves of narcosis swept through me. My mind focussed on trying to see the wreck as we went down – to get to the shallowest part of it and minimise the nitrogen narcosis building up in my body.

Forty-five metres down. Below and around us, nothing but darkness. We pressed on down. Fifty metres down. I knew the wreck would be only a few metres beneath me and off to one side. It might only be 15 feet away – but in which direction? The current would have reversed after slack water, so would that which had been the right direction when George had dived be the right direction now? I swept my torch round about me hoping to catch a reassuring glimpse of some rusted brown metal, but there was nothing but the all-consuming inky cocoon in which I was enveloped.

Fifty-five metres down. I should be right on top of the wreck now – or at worst just a few metres – 10 feet at best – off the seabed. Surely I must be near something solid now – but as I strained my eyes below me following the beam of my torch, I couldn't see the seabed. Why was the strong beam of my torch not lighting up the seabed beneath? For even though it was pitch black, my torch beam seemed to penetrate the darkness for about 6 feet. Was I dropping into a hole or scour in the seabed taking the depth even deeper than 58 metres? What was going on? It was all starting to be extremely confusing.

I was starting to lose control.

My breathing rate started to rise, as the recurring strong feelings of dread and apprehension clouded my thoughts. This was deeper than I had ever dived before on air – and it looked as if I was going to have to go deeper. Things just weren't working out as I'd planned.

Fifty-eight metres down. Suddenly I came through a visibility horizon and there was the sandy seabed about 3 feet beneath me. I landed on the seabed and swept my torch around hoping for a glimpse of wreckage. Dave arrived beside me, seemingly unperturbed.

About 5 feet away from our anchor I spotted the large rotted iron plate that George had told me to follow as this would lead me to the wreck. I was conscious that whereas the first divers had gone in at slack water, the tide had now turned and there was a perceptible current trying to sweep us away from that rotted piece of plating and away from the wreck.

Giving Dave an 'OK' hand signal, I kicked my legs and headed off in search of the wreck, swimming against the current and having to work a tad too hard. I was feeling distinctly narcosed and so, to try and minimise my depth as we finned along against the current (and thus reduce my narcosis level), I decided to try rising up a few metres but still keep the seabed in sight.

I rose up gently – and the seabed suddenly disappeared into the blackness again.

And then it happened.

For some inexplicable reason a huge wave of fear overcame me – a colossal rush of dread and apprehension. My vision noticeably changed: my lateral vision disappearing as tunnel vision took over. If you've never experienced tunnel vision, rest assured its name is a perfect description of the effect. The only thing I could see was a circular tunnel of vision directly ahead of me – I couldn't see anything outwith this corridor of vision. It was very strange – just a bright circle with nothingness around it. I recall seeing my torch beam flaring out ahead of me, cutting through the tunnel's enveloping cocoon of inky blackness as I moved it about.

With the seabed having disappeared out of sight, in an instant I became sure that I had lost control of my buoyancy and was starting a ballistic buoyant ascent. It took just one stupid simple thought to make me come undone. As soon as that unfounded thought wedged in my mind an uncontrollable series of physical reactions took over – my breathing rate increased further and my tunnel vision closed in even more. I remember for some obscure reason feeling that my forehead was grey and covered with pinpricks of sweat breaking out. I was starting to panic. I just had to get out of that dreadful place. I pushed the 'inflate' button on my buoyancy wings; the diving equivalent of the 'up' button on an elevator. Air gushed into my wings and I started to lift up from the seabed.

I can't remember if I signalled to Dave or not that I was going up – in fact I can't remember much about what happened at all after the surge overtook me. I know I headed up at rather too brisk a rate – and the first proper memory I have is of being aware of my surroundings getting lighter, looking at my wrist computer and seeing that I was at 35 metres. I don't know how long it took after I bugged out to get from 58 to 35 metres – a rise of about 80 feet – but it was pretty quick. It was as though I had come round from being unconscious. I wasn't entirely sure where I was or how I got there. But a large velvet curtain had been lifted from me – and I realised that any narcosis had completely disappeared. One minute I was in a blind panic at 58 metres – the next I was back in control at 35 metres.

I halted my ascent by dumping air from my suit and buoyancy wings and hung motionless in mid-water. Dave appeared beside me – how he had kept in touch with me I'll never know. The dive was over and I gave the signal to ascend. We made sure that we carried out some extra decompression stops on the way up, over and above the stops shown as required by my dive computer. We wanted to try and minimise any decompression consequences from the depth and rapid ascent.

Dave had done a lot of deep air diving at this depth in the past and didn't seem too phased about the bail out. Although outwardly we laughed about what had just happened, the truth is that I had just had a real scare. I had been consumed by panic and seemed in one moment to have suffered nearly all the effects of severe nitrogen narcosis that I'd been taught about in my theory training years before. I had learned a valuable lesson the hard way – I would never venture that deep on air again.

The effects of nitrogen narcosis get progressively more intense the further you descend and vary from person to person and from day to day. For me, I experience the first noticeable effects on air at about a depth of 35 metres – although I am probably affected shallower than that but simply don't notice the weaker effects. By 45 metres however, I know I am well narcosed. By 50 metres – the recommended maximum depth for air diving – I am only operating with a fraction of my usual mental powers. That's why the British Sub Aqua Club (BSAC) set the 50-metre depth limit. Venture deeper than this and you are getting into very serious and dangerous territory. To make matters worse, by the time you get to 80 metres or more – apart from being narked out of your skull – the increasing amounts of oxygen in your body (from the large volumes of compressed air you are breathing) reach very dangerous toxic levels.

Throughout my deep air diving days I had been constantly battling against the effects of nitrogen narcosis and as the depths to which we were diving in search of new wrecks increased so did the narcosis on each dive. The *Cushendall* bail-out was a wake-up call that put a depth limit on my diving for a number of years.

And then in the mid 1990s everything changed when sport divers gained access to the Holy Grail – helium. Suddenly deep diving would never be the same again. I'm not sure if any of today's generation of divers do the sort of deep air diving my generation of 80s & 90s divers did. I suspect not – deep air may well be as dead as the dinosaur.

Helium is an inert gas, which unlike nitrogen has no narcotic effect on divers at great depths. It has been used in the offshore oil diving industry for a very long time but had never been made available previously for sports divers like myself.

A number of training agencies immediately embraced the opportunities the new helium regime allowed. It revolutionised diving, but had its own peculiarities and required specialist training and gear. It wasn't just a case of sticking some helium in your breathing mix and diving as before.

I trained in 1995 with Technical Divers Incorporated (TDI) and along with my regular dive buddy Ewan, we were the first TDI Trimix divers in the UK to become qualified to dive on a helium mix of gases. We carried out our training over a number of weekends diving deep into Loch Ness, which offered easy shore access for kitting up and a gently shelving bottom which ended abruptly at a sheer wall of rock. This wall dropped off vertically into its murky depths for a very long way and allowed you to get deep quickly. It was a good safe training spot with no dangerous currents to complicate the technical training.

Suddenly, with a large part of the dangerous nitrogen being replaced by inert helium, the old 50-metre depth limit for air diving was swept away overnight. I found my first training dive with helium to 50 metres in Loch Ness a real eye opener. At 50 metres on air I would be very narcosed and clinging on – well disabled. When I first got to 50 metres on a helium mix under the careful instruction of the Aberdeen Watersports' excellent TDI instructor Dave Gordon, I was staggered at how clear my mind was. It felt like I was just walking around in a park. I didn't feel narcosed at all and was able to pick out features on the bottom that I would never have noticed on air. A door had just been opened (there's a lot more about my training and early Trimix dives in my last book *Into the Abyss*).

As well as being inert and having no discernable narcotic effect on divers, the helium molecule is very small compared to nitrogen and seems to flush more easily out of the body tissues. The chances of a rogue bubble becoming trapped in the body and causing a bend were reduced. We were taught the maxim 'helium is your friend – nitrogen is your enemy'.

Helium is however extremely expensive, but as Aberdeen is the oil capital of the world it imports helium in huge quantities for offshore commercial diving. Consequently the helium costs in our area are some of the cheapest in the world. Technical divers elsewhere (not fortunate enough to live in the immediate environs of Aberdeen) had to pay the full going-rate.

To keep costs manageable per dive, the concept of using a 'Trimix' of oxygen, helium and a small amount of nitrogen was conceived. This would keep the percentage of nitrogen at a low enough level to keep narcosis at a minimal level, whilst keeping down the cost by not using unnecessarily high levels of helium. Commercial divers offshore use heliox – a straight blend of helium and oxygen with no nitrogen at all. But they have sophisticated and hugely expensive gas-reclaim systems not feasible in sport diving.

For shallower dives in the range 40–60 metres, we started using a standard Trimix of 19% oxygen, 34% helium and just 47% nitrogen (as opposed to the usual 79% of nitrogen in regular air). For deeper dives in the 60–80 metres of seawater (msw) range, we used a Trimix with a lower oxygen level of 16%, a higher helium constituent of 45% and the balance of 39% being nitrogen.

But even these reduced levels of nitrogen still had an increasingly narcotic effect the deeper you went. So, to work out what level of narcosis a diver would suffer (compared to air diving at given depths) the concept of Equivalent Narcotic Depth (END) was born. This allowed us to know in advance what comparable air narcotic effect we would feel at any given depth on any given mix of gases. For example, at a depth of 65 metres diving on a Trimix of 16% oxygen, 45% helium and 39% nitrogen a diver would experience a narcotic effect (END) equivalent to diving on air at a depth of 27 metres – where there is hardly any nitrogen narcosis at all. On that same Trimix (16/45) at the seriously deep depth of 85 metres the END would be 37 metres – where a diver is only just starting to feel the first real effects of nitrogen narcosis.

Almost overnight – after 15 years of air diving up to depths of 50 metres or just beyond – we found ourselves able to dive to 60, 70, 80 metres and beyond. This in turn meant that we could extend our range far further offshore. Whereas on air, we quickly reached the 50-metre depth contour in the North Sea a few miles offshore, we now found we could range 10–15 miles offshore before the water got too deep for us at about 100 metres. And this in turn meant that wrecks previously too deep and too far offshore suddenly became diveable. New undived territories were being opened up virtually overnight.

The new style of diving was christened 'technical diving' and as it was in its infancy, it soon started to evolve – it was to prove a quantum change from air diving.

In our air days we just used to dive with a twin set of two 12-litre tanks on our back and a simple air diving wrist computer that calculated how deep we had been and how long we had stayed there. It continuously worked out what decompression stops were required, at what depths and for how long, to allow us to surface with all the dangerous nitrogen bubbles flushed safely from our bodies. Things had suddenly got a lot more complicated – and our air computers were redundant overnight.

In addition to our usual twin set of two back-mounted 12-litre tanks, we now carried two additional tanks slung one under either arm and secured to our back plate harness with stainless steel D rings and shackles. These side mounts held our decompression gases, designed for use only on the shallower parts of the dive – known as our 'deco mix' for short.

Our back-mounted twin 12-litre tanks now held only our 'bottom mix' – the helium rich / low oxygen mix tailored for the deep part of the dive; high in helium to reduce nitrogen narcosis and the chance of getting the dreaded bends.

Divers being divers, we were soon experimenting with all sorts of bottom and deco mixes. Some dived with a bottom mix of 17% oxygen and 70% helium (abbreviated to 17/70). Other divers experimented with reducing the oxygen percentage further from the 21% (as on the surface) to 16% or even 10%.

Oxygen, the very stuff that keeps us alive on the surface (and underwater) becomes increasingly toxic in the larger volumes breathed in by divers as they venture deeper. The risk of an oxygen toxicity hit becomes a very real danger. This starts off with twitching and spasms but rapidly develops to uncontrollable convulsions where a diver will (amongst other things) rip off his mask and spit out his breathing regulator. They nearly always result in drowning unless the diver is wearing a full-face mask. But all this was experimental diving: we were, in a sense, guinea pigs developing the sport as we went along and like anything new, we learned lessons the hard way. Some leading technical divers sadly 'ox-toxed' and died of the uncontrollable convulsions, so deadly underwater.

Other divers mistakenly breathed their decompression gases at too great a depth. These are only suitable for the shallow part of the dive and if breathed at depth can quickly bring on a fatal oxygen toxicity hit.

Marshalling your different gas tanks and making sure you had systems to avoid breathing from the wrong regulator at the wrong depth became hugely important. Some divers dived with a round plastic ball held by a bungee in the mouthpiece of their deco regulator – the bungeed ball had to be physically removed from the mouthpiece before they could breathe from it.

Others dived with their deco tanks completely turned off, to avoid breathing from the wrong one by chance at the wrong time. But there are problems associated with doing that.

What if there was a problem with your back tanks and you have to ascend rapidly (say, having lost your bottom gas) to a depth where you can breathe your deco gas? Turning on your tank then could result in an unstoppable free flow where you lost all your deco gas as well. What if your buddy diver had run out of gas and swam over to you, his mouth filled with water, panicking and desperate for a breath of anything? If he grabbed for your deco regulator and tried to inhale from a closed off regulator then he'd get a lungful of water, which could be the end for him. If your buddy diver was in an out-of-gas situation, he may in his panic grab any one of the regulators on your tanks. If he started breathing from a regulator attached to one of your deco tanks then he'd be breathing the wrong gas at the wrong depth and could very quickly start 'ox-toxing'. To get round that possibility we were taught that in an out-of-gas situation, always to take the regulator from your buddy diver's mouth – he'd be breathing the right gas and would know which of his other regulators was the correct back up gas to grab hold of.

It became extremely important to personally analyse the gas in your dive tanks once a dive shop had filled them. Although we never had any incidents locally of the wrong gas being put in a diver's tanks, stories abounded elsewhere of tanks being presented with the wrong gas – a potentially fatal mistake. It was your life – the ultimate responsibility was yours. You analysed your own gas to make sure you *personally* knew what you were breathing.

As we have seen, surface air has about 21% oxygen in it – too much for really deep dives. So where too much oxygen (and hence toxicity) was a real problem, some divers reduced the oxygen in their bottom mix as low as 10%. This was fine at depth when you're breathing huge volumes of compressed gas – you are getting more than enough oxygen to sustain consciousness and life. However, it was quickly found that if you reduced the percentage of oxygen to about 14% or less and breathed it on the surface, say as you surfaced after ascending, then you could black out. If you're slightly too heavy on the surface and black out, then you're going to sink, faster and faster. These low-oxygen mixes can only be used once you're well into the descent and you should switch off them and onto a deco gas with a higher oxygen level as you get back to the shallows on your ascent.

The concept of a 'travel mix' also appeared. This was an oxygen-rich mix (with no helium), used to travel down from the surface to a depth where it was safe to swap over to your high helium bottom mix. It also helped preserve your bottom mix gas for the deeper part of the dive – when gas is used up very quickly. Often a travel mix would be something like 34% oxygen with the balance nitrogen, and would be slung in a 7 or 9 litre tank under one arm.

For the decompression stages of an ascent, you want a mix with a very high oxygen constituent and with no helium at all, to let the huge volumes of helium you have breathed at depth flush out of your body. So the fourth tank we carried would be a 7 or 9 litre deco mix tank slung under the other arm. We evolved to use a deco mix with 50% oxygen or more in it, the balance being nitrogen. Some divers favoured a deco mix of 80% oxygen or even 100% oxygen. What to use as a deco mix became a hot topic of debate amongst tech divers, and something of a balancing act. One of the issues was that the higher the percentage of oxygen, the shallower you have to be before you can switch over to it. So that brings in issues about gas management for your bottom mix – you'd be breathing your bottom mix all the way up to the shallows before you could change to deco mix. What if you ran out of bottom mix? You might be too deep to breathe your deco mix. But also with very high oxygen levels at the end of the dive you needed to work out your total exposure to oxygen for the whole dive (or series of dives) to keep it within safe limits. We were taught about Central Nervous System percentages, and Oxygen Toxicity Units (OTUs). You can see why it was called 'Technical Diving'.

Tech diving developed a language of its own, unintelligible to the ordinary man. Our decompression gases with no helium in them were known as 'Nitrox' – that is, nitrogen and oxygen. A deco mix was also known as 'enriched air Nitrox' – so it was also often called 'EAN'. One of our favourite Nitrox mixes was 50% oxygen and 50% nitrogen, known as 'EAN50'. It could only be breathed safely from a depth of 20 metres up to the surface. Breathe it deeper than 20 metres and you risked an oxygen toxicity hit with its convulsions and possible death. 'EAN80' (80% oxygen) could only be breathed upwards from a depth of 12 metres. 'EAN100' (pure oxygen) could be breathed upwards from a depth of 9 metres.

Whereas the bottom mix Trimix we were now using allowed us to venture into previously unthought-of depths for sport divers of up to 100 metres (or more for some brave folks), the decompression gases we now used also had tremendous advantages. For one thing, by stripping away a large part of the dangerous nitrogen in air and replacing it by hugely beneficial oxygen, we were being kinder to our bodies and lessening the risks of decompression illness – the bends. But also, by getting rid of a large percentage of nitrogen (which is slow to flush from our bodies) the use of these high oxygen/no helium mixes ('Nitrox') reduced the length of our decompression stops. The effect became known as 'accelerated decompression'.

But Nitrox wasn't only about shortening massively the decompression stops traditionally associated with deep air diving. It also had tremendous benefits for shallow diving. A comparison may illustrate this. A diver breathing compressed air could remain at a depth of 25 metres for 25 minutes before being required to carry out decompression stops as he ascended (i.e., a 'no stop' dive). On a Nitrox mix of 40% oxygen ('EAN40'), that same diver could spend more than 50 minutes at that same depth without requiring any decompression stops. He would still be on a 'no stop' dive. His time on the bottom had been doubled without the need for any deco – a great boon for underwater photographers. Likewise, on a dive to 45 metres for say 21 minutes on air, a diver would require to spend 29 minutes decompressing on the ascent (following the prevailing Buhlmann air tables). Therefore, after spending 21 minutes on the bottom, a diver would be able to safely get out of the water after 50 minutes. By using 'EAN60' for the decompression stops for the same dive profile of 21 minutes at a depth of 45 metres, the total dive time was shortened to just 30 minutes. The ascent decompression stops were reduced to just 9 minutes – compared to the 29 minutes diving on air. The leap forward in decompression was staggering.

The 'Deep Frontier' had been thrown open up to us, but we were solemnly warned that if you walk the frontier, you *will* meet Indians.

CHAPTER SIX

TRIMIX – FIRST BEGINNINGS

Our first ventures into deeper water with the new wonder gas Trimix, as we started searching for undived virgin wrecks far offshore, soon had us realising the enormous change that was sweeping over diving. But although we had been formally trained, we were still novices in the new black art with a lot to learn at the coalface. The new kit we had to embrace was complicated and cumbersome – the theory behind it all needed thinking through. It was a time of becoming familiar with the new kit and techniques and putting into practice and adapting what we had learned during our training.

In other parts of the world, the new wave of technical diving was taking off, popularised by pioneers like Billy Deans in Florida who led the way there for years before it was introduced here in the UK. The BSAC had safety concerns about mixed gas diving and did not at first embrace it within its training regime. As they couldn't offer what I wanted, I trained under the American-based Technical Divers Inc. (TDI) regime and left the BSAC at this time.

Tech diving itself soon started to evolve as more understanding and knowledge was brought to the sport. And over time, as we ourselves experimented with gas mixes and decompression software, we found that some things that had been taught to us as pillars of wisdom could be improved upon.

Our first real Trimix virgin wreck dive was off Peterhead in 1995. Ten years earlier I had painstakingly plotted on my Admiralty Charts all the latitudinal & longitudinal positions for the wrecks listed in the print-out I had bought from the Hydrographic Department. Soon I had linked names of vessels with the corresponding bare wreck symbols on the charts. But it became clear that nearly all the undived charted wrecks were well outwith the range we could dive to on air. The printout was consigned to accumulate dust in a drawer in my study.

With the dawn of the Trimix era I soon had my charts out and dusted off, poring over the wrecks listed to see what would be the most likely candidate to search for. The Rattray Head area between Fraserburgh and Peterhead soon had my undivided attention. This area was a favourite Second World War hunting ground for German aircraft flying from air bases in occupied Norway.

Merchant vessels from all over the world that were bound for the large east coast ports of England would congregate in the relatively safe west coast of Scotland deep-water anchorages such as the Oban Roads. Large convoys would be assembled which, with naval protection, would run up the west coast of Scotland, wheel past the Orkney Islands before running the gauntlet of German planes as they passed down the exposed east coast of Scotland and on to England.

To offer protection from U-Boat attack and German mines, a wall of steel nets and mines called the Northern Mine Barrage was constructed. Initially it ran from London all the way up the east coast of the UK to Fraserburgh on the northeast tip. It was a stupendous effort of construction and lay some five to 10 miles offshore. It is impossible to conceive of such a feat nowadays – but the desperate times of World War II brought desperate deeds. Later in the war, the Barrage would be extended all the way up to the Orkney Islands.

On the inside or landward side of the Northern Mine Barrage, a channel for shipping about half a mile wide was laid out and marked by buoys every half a mile. The channel was regularly swept for mines and all merchant shipping would travel up and down the east coast in this Swept Channel, protected from U-boat attack by the mine barrage. The exposed deep water around Rattray Head however, just a few miles south of Fraserburgh became a happy hunting ground for attacks by both German planes and U-boats and around this area some 52 Allied vessels were sunk in World War II alone. In fact there were so many wrecks that the Admiralty declared the whole Rattray Head area unsafe for navigation for two miles offshore.

Growing up in Fraserburgh in the 1970s my family would often go for a walk at low tide out over the exposed flat sands. I can remember at the strongest low water tides seeing brown rusted parts of ships engulfed in sand, sticking out of the exposed sandy seabed. According to the charts the seabed here was almost littered with shipwrecks, most undived other than in commercial post-war salvage operations.

Very soon we had selected an area some five miles north east of the prominent Rattray Head lighthouse. Here there was a cluster of three wrecks charted in relatively close proximity to each other, but all three being on the shallow side of the 50-metre depth contour on the chart. We knew that those depths were the least possible depths, measured at what is called the 'lowest astronomical tide'. To that figure had to be added the tidal range, which varied throughout the month from 3.4 metres to 4.6 metres. There was a very good chance that the depth to the seabed would be well over 50 metres.

All three wrecks formed an equilateral triangle with sides of about a mile. The known clearances over the wrecks were shown in the dotted circular wreck symbols as 28, 37 and 40 metres. Although when I first started looking at wrecks as a youngster I had wrongly assumed that that was the depth down to the wreck, I now knew that these figures meant that the wreck had been swept, and no obstruction found, down to that depth. The actual depth down to the wreck could in fact be much further. With three wrecks in a one-mile triangle we thought there would be a very good chance of finding at least one of them.

Ewan had recently purchased a magnetometer to help in our wreck-finding forays. This clever gadget is a box of electronic tricks that sits in the boat with a long cable attached to a torpedo-like transponder, which is towed behind the boat. It can detect variations in the earth's magnetic field caused by lumps of metal on the seabed. Large lumps of metal like wrecks can be detected on either side of the sweep for up to 1,000 metres – that's two thirds of a mile either side of the boat. With the magnetometer and a 1 square-mile box to search, we thought there was a very good chance of us picking up something.

We arrived at Inverallochy (the nearest good harbour to Rattray Head) to launch *Stonehaven Diver* early one Sunday morning – all tooled up for a search. Slack water, when we would dive if we were successful, was many hours away. We hoped to carry out our search and find a wreck, all in time to dive at slack.

By this time Global Positioning Systems (GPS) suitable for small boats such as my 5.5m RIB were now on the market at affordable prices. We punched in the coordinates for the first and closest wreck of the three, 57 41 30N, 01 49 18W and set off. We knew that this was just a rough position, probably from the dead reckoning of the master of the vessel at the time it sunk – and that it could be a mile or two out.

We were very conscious that when these ships were lost during World War II, they didn't have the sophisticated navigation tools available nowadays. Seamen navigated by dead reckoning: taking sightings of the sun, taking bearings on fixed land points, tracking time on a given course and measuring distance through the water with a ship's log. If visibility at sea was poor they could be well off with their navigation and simple human errors also confused the position.

We had found however, that where the Hydrographic Department had a wreck symbol marked, there would usually be something around in the rough vicinity of the mark. If the wreck symbol had a line under or above it, that meant that the wreck had been wire swept or surveyed in modern times and this meant that the position would be pretty accurate. If the wreck symbol had PA for 'position approximate' marked in it, then the wreck was sometimes up to a mile or two away from its reported position. A mile is a lot of water at sea – but with Ewan's magnetometer we could home in on the target wreck.

In addition to *Stonehaven Diver*, Dave Gordon of Aberdeen Watersports (who had trained us in Trimix diving) had come along in the shop's own RIB as well. Two divers would go down from each boat leaving one cox in each.

Ewan and I got our boat organised first and motored out of Inverallochy harbour into the wide expanse of Fraserburgh Bay. I throttled *Stonehaven Diver* up onto the plane and turned to the southeast, to run the five or so miles along towards Rattray Head. We punched in the coordinates for the first target wreck site into the GPS and hit the 'GO TO' button. The GPS screen changed to simulate a highway – as if on land – which would lead directly to the wreck. I manoeuvred the RIB onto the centre line of the highway and settled down for a steady cruise down to the site at 20 knots.

As we skipped along on an oily, calm surface, to the south of us I could see the tall masts and flare of the St Fergus Gas Terminal. Dimly, in the distance beyond that, I could make out the fishing port of Peterhead. Sticking prominently up from the golden sliver of beach that is Rattray Head was the brilliant white of the famous lighthouse.

As we motored south, Ewan sat behind me on the double console seat giving me directions from the hand held GPS. It was so new that we hadn't had time to fix a bracket on the boat's console for it yet. Steve Collard, an air diver, had just returned from working abroad in the Gulf and having heard all the fuss about Trimix diving had come along to cox our boat and see tech diving in action. I wanted to get out of the harbour and down to the site as quickly as possible to give us a chance of locating the wreck in time to dive it at slack water.

A magnetometer search of a box zone would be time consuming and slack water waits for no man. There was every chance we might not find any wreck at all.

Once we got down to the precise location of the Hydrographic Department position, there was nothing showing on the seabed but a flat undulating sandy bottom. Dave Gordon's boat hadn't come into sight yet to the north of us. Ewan plopped the magnetometer transponder fish over the side and paid out its cable as I motored forward letting the fish fall some 50–70 metres behind us to avoid it getting interference from our engine. Soon he had the magnetometer calibrated and we were off searching.

Ewan sat on the starboard side tube of the RIB watching the LCD of his magnetometer closely, as it read out the information from the transponder fish. I started doing a grid search pattern from the GPS – 'mowing the lawn' as the professionals call it. Ewan was able to guide me, as the strength of the readout got stronger or weakened. Within about 15 minutes, the magnetometer's beeping started to get more and more intense and the LCD graph on the instrument box started to give a large sine wave. We were very close to something very large and metallic. I stared at the readout on my console-mounted echo sounder until suddenly the bottom trace jumped up, marking the presence of something large directly underneath. With the magnetometer going ape noisily around us, we knew it was metal.

Fixing the position with the MOB ('Man over Board') function of the GPS, we got Steve to drop the anchor once we were right over the largest part of it. The anchor snagged on something solid and the GPS showed a ground speed of 0.0 knots. Although the tide was still pushing water past us – creating ripples around the anchor-line and a wash down the side of the boat – we knew we were fixed solid in position relative to the seabed. The outline of the wreck stayed fixed on my Echo Sounder. I switched off the engine and checked my watch. The whole search had only taken 15 minutes; far less than I had expected. We were way too early for slack water, so we had time to relax, to fiddle with our gear, eat some food and hydrate for the coming dive. As I looked to the north I saw the bow splash of Dave Gordon's RIB heading our way.

When Dave Gordon arrived he was mightily impressed, as were we too – all our new toys had worked. I casually remarked the wreck trace looked big enough for it to be a 4,000-ton ship. The echo sounding trace had jumped up from a seabed of 60 metres to a least depth of 50 metres. These were the same dimensions as our local favourite further south, the MS *Taurus* and she was about 4,000 tons. So we christened her 'the Four Thousand Tonner' for the time being, until we established her identity.

An hour or so later and the current sweeping past us had noticeably dropped away. Slack water was approaching and it was time to get ready to dive.

Ewan and I sat opposite each other on the tubes of the RIB, as Steve helped us rig up in our technical gear. It was still new to me, and I felt ungainly, complicated and heavy. Once I was rigged, I had my twin set on my back, a stage nitrox tank under either arm, four regulators hung at different parts of me, two torches and my deco reel stowed on me. My chest looking like Spaghetti Junction with the hoses for my four regulators and back up regulators as well as the direct feeds for my suit and buoyancy wings running all over the place. I felt as though I couldn't move. And here I was away to drop over the side of a boat about five miles offshore. I had to be mad.

But then, Ewan was shouting over: "You ready, Rod?"

"Yes" I replied, "Let's get it done." This was still a 60-metre dive and I was breaking all my ingrained taboos about the depth I could dive to. It was also my deepest dive to that date. The thrill of the chase, the search for and successful finding of the wreck was still with me, but a feeling of unreality overcame me. I had one of those moments when you feel that you are outside your body – it seemed I was high above the boat observing myself below getting ready for the dive. But the blood was up and I was on the dive treadmill, intent of getting my kit on and sorted – nothing would stop me now. When I was rigged up I swung one leg over the side of the tube and sat there resting my twin set on the tube.

Ewan rolled into the water and I followed his lead. As soon as I was in the water my apprehension disappeared, the buoyancy in my wings and suit instantly supporting the weight of my ungainly kit. The water looked crystal clear and I could see a good 20 metres or more down the anchor line. The good visibility and bright blue underwater seascape instantly calmed my beating heart.

As we started the descent, a few metres beneath the surface I rolled over and looked up at the RIB – I could see every detail of its hull. I could also see Steve's face staring over the side of the boat down at me. I gave him a wave, not knowing if he could see me, turned over and finned across to the downline – our guide into the depths.

I travelled down breathing from my oxygen-rich, travel mix 7-litre stage tank under my left arm, which was filled with EAN32. Once I got down to about 35 metres I took that regulator out of my mouth, stowed it under its bungee and stuck my bottom mix regulator of 16/45 Trimix (16% oxygen, 45% helium) into my mouth and took a few long deep breaths.

Above me the bright sunshine illuminated the anchor line all the way up to the surface, where I could still see the outline of *Stonehaven Diver*. Something special was going on here. I gave Ewan an 'OK' signal and got the 'OK' reply back. I turned and headed downwards again.

As I approached 40 metres I thought I could see a brown coloured seabed about 10 metres beneath me. I started to fear that the current might, after all, have pulled our anchor off the wreck. But as I pressed on downwards, the brown seabed slowly parted like a pair of curtains and I found myself passing through a huge shoal of fish. As we passed through it, the shoal closed again above us.

I looked down, and was staggered to see a huge shipwreck resting on a clean white sandy seabed. I could easily see down to the seabed at 60 metres, and could see perhaps 25 metres laterally either way, fore and aft along the ship. Three huge boilers sat amid a scene of devastation and loose portholes lay scattered everywhere.

We swam up to one of the boilers and Ewan drew my attention to some copper piping coming out of one of them. We could see where it had been neatly hack sawed off by a commercial diver aeons ago when the engine room had been plundered for its precious non-ferrous metals. The ship had clearly been blasted to pieces here, to allow access for salvage divers – hence the loose portholes that had been sprung from their mounts.

Of the roof and sides of the engine room and indeed any of the usual superstructures above, there was no trace. This was a method favoured by the famous (and since 1981, defunct) salvage company Risdon Beazley Ltd, who salvaged nearly all of the accessible war wrecks around the British shores in the post war years. Divers would set charges on the hull around the engine room area and then return to the surface. Once the charges were blown, a large grab would be deployed which would lift off the entire upper section of the engine room and superstructure and dump it at the side of the ship.

I finned up to the side of the hull and stared out across the sandy seabed bed at either side - but there was no sight of the superstructure. I knew it must have been lying there somewhere, tantalisingly out of sight. It would probably hold endless clues as to the identity of the wreck, as here in the engine room, the salvers would have removed anything that may give a clue to the ship's identity.

We finned forward and very soon were rising up at the end of the blast area as the ship's hull, which sat on an even keel, reformed before our eyes. We finned aft past an open hold and then were at the very stern.

Intent on having a good exploration of the ship, we then headed forward along the other side of the hull at a depth of about 50 metres, the seabed easily visible 10 metres beneath us. If we stayed at this height we reduced our decompression stops, which had been worked out for the worst-case scenario of a full dive at 60 metres and built in a safety factor.

Passing beyond the blast area again, but in the other direction, first one, then a second open cargo hold appeared before us. There was no sign of any bridge superstructure and I realised that the whole superstructure had been removed and dumped, not just the engine room deckhouse.

I finned over the open holds, and looking down saw that they contained neatly stacked steel railway tracks and piles of coiled warps of steel cable. The fo'c'stle was intact but the hull had cracked just aft of it, causing the fo'c'stle to roll slightly backwards until the deck was at an angle of 45 degrees. Two open black, aft facing doorways offered easy entry into the fo'c'stle, but because of the cracking and collapsing, they were near the seabed well beneath my present depth of 50 metres. I didn't want to go deeper again, and load up on decompression requirements at this late stage of the dive, even though there was the tantalising prospect that the bell – if not taken by the salvers – might lie somewhere down there in the debris. That unmistakeable clue to the wreck's identity would have to wait for another day.

Ewan and I called the dive here and made our way back to the anchor line for the slow ascent. I always preferred the security of the anchor line on these new technical dives – it was something fixed to hold onto if I suddenly found myself too light and taking the elevator to the surface.

As I made the slow ascent to the surface, I went over what I had learned about the vessel on this one dive. She was a single-screw steamship, some 400 or so feet long with a beam of about 45 feet. She was carrying a cargo of railway tracks and warps of steel wire and – from her layout and generally good condition – was clearly a World War II loss. I couldn't wait to get back to the Hydrographic Department print-out to see if I could identify her from this information. That night, Ewan and I pored over the print-out. This vessel was just too large to be the ship charted as being lost in that position. The wreck of the SS *Port Dennison* fitted the bill size-wise, as did a few other ships lost in this area. It was a bit of a muddle and no one ship leapt out as a positive identification.

I have been back to dive this wreck on a few occasions since but we have never found anything on her that would categorically establish her identity. The *Port Dennison* is in fact charted as having been sunk far further out to sea. It was possible that she drifted in towards shore after being abandoned, before sinking – so I hadn't ruled her out yet.

However, in Moya Crawford's compelling book *Deep Water*, she mentions that her husband, the famous commercial salver Alex Crawford, actually located and identified the wreck of the *Port Dennison*. She reports that it was intact with its bridge in situ – and that they conclusively identified it by ROV when, on the hull at the bow, they found the ship's name *Port Dennison* in large ornate brass letters. So, we know that the fabulous wreck we had found and dived is not the *Port Dennison*.

A far better candidate would be the Second World War loss, SS *Anvers*. She was bombed and sunk by German aircraft on 13 November 1940 whilst en route from Philadelphia to London.

The *Anvers* was a 383-foot long steamship with a beam of 52.1 feet. These are very close to the dimensions of the wreck we had dived. She was built in Belgium in 1908 and weighed in at 4398 gross tons. She was charted as lying some two miles further north at position 57 43 00.00N, 001 49 00.00W – but that was just an approximate position and it's possible that the master's dead reckoning could have been a few miles out at the time of the sinking. Further research revealed that the *Anvers* was carrying a cargo of 6,000 tons of scrap steel, which was consistent with the railway track like girders and warps of coiled steel wire we had seen stowed in the foredeck holds.

In 1974 commercial divers from the Northern Shipbreaking Co. had reported the wreck we had dived to be complete and estimated the vessel to be 3,500–4,000 grt (gross registered tonnage) with some explosion damage to the port side, and that she was laden with a cargo of steel. The wreck we had dived had been commercially worked and our best bet is that it is indeed the *Anvers* – just lying a couple of miles away from the reported site of its sinking.

In the late summer of 2008 Jim Burke, Mike Rosie and Roger Mathieson from the Peterhead contingent of our group located a large undived wreck, which appears to be sitting on her keel (as described in *Deep Water*) in the approximate position of the SS *Port Dennison* in 95 metres. The wreck rises up for 10 metres from the seabed so is a substantial vessel. In that sort of depth, so far offshore, a dive on this wreck requires a lot of careful planning, back up, support divers – and fine settled weather. We haven't as yet managed to get organised and dive it – but it remains high on the agenda.

CHAPTER SEVEN

INTO THE CORRYVRECKAN WHIRLPOOL

In amongst this great rush to find new virgin wrecks in deeper waters there were also gems of occasions where our Trimix diving didn't involve a new shipwreck at the end of it. To practice our skills we would sometimes dive deep down sheer rock walls on the west coast of Scotland, Ewan and Chris Allen being the first of our group to reach the magical 100-metre depth.

On one occasion in 2000 we used our newfound skills to dive the Corryvreckan Whirlpool – the stuff of legends. As a child I grew up hearing romantic tales of boats and ships being caught in it and sucked down with their unfortunate sailors into the depths of the monster. Although the name was familiar, my only idea of it was a childhood memory of a hand drawn colour image in *Look & Learn* magazine. A small boat was being spun round and round as it was sucked down into a perfect whirlpool. For most of my life I had had no idea where it was – and certainly never envisaged that one day I would dive into its heart.

As my involvement with the sea grew throughout my diving career, I became more aware of the Corryvreckan Whirlpool. It is the third largest whirlpool in the world and takes centre stage in the Gulf of Corryvreckan, a small channel of water just over half a mile wide that separates the Isle of Jura from the smaller island of Scarba on the West Coast of Scotland, south of Oban.

The Corryvreckan Whirlpool is perhaps the most feared strip of water around Britain. When the whirlpool is in full motion, the half-mile wide gulf is a very dangerous place to be. Tales abound of boats and ships being caught in it and sucked down into oblivion. Such is its danger that the Royal Navy has classed the channel as unnavigable and the lifeboat has been called out to over 50 emergencies there in recent years. Currents can reach 16 knots and its roar can be heard 10 miles away. Standing waves ten feet high breaking endlessly reveal that there is some massive obstruction on the seabed.

To the west of the Gulf of Corryvreckan is the Atlantic – open water all the way to America. To the east of the gulf is the Sound of Jura and then mainland Scotland.

It seems as though the whole of the Atlantic tries to funnel through this small half-mile wide channel, pushing colossal amounts of water on the flood towards Scotland. This tidal action has scoured out a massive chasm in the gulf more than 200 metres deep. In the middle of this chasm, trying to block the might of the Atlantic stands a pinnacle of solid rock that reaches up from a depth of 200 metres to just 30 metres short of the surface. The top of the pinnacle is about 100 feet wide and it widens as it drops down towards the bottom of the chasm 200 metres below. The standing waves visible on the surface are caused as the onrushing tide is forced up and over the Pinnacle before dropping instantly back down into the chasm. An underwater waterfall is created with fierce down currents.

A story – now part of Scottish diving folklore – tells of how many years ago, a brave diver tried to dive the pinnacle. He made it down to the pinnacle all right, but the down-currents got hold of him. He inflated his buoyancy jacket – normally enough to send a diver to the surface like a rocket – but he kept going down. He dropped his weight belt gaining more buoyancy – but still he kept going down. The current took him down to the incredible depth of 75 metres before he broke loose and reached up to the surface. The pinnacle has only rarely been dived.

Scientists had been keen to study the pinnacle but were denied permission to dive under HSE regulations because of the great depths, and the great currents. As sport divers, we were not bound by those rules – so when an Edinburgh TV director (who had trained Ewan to dive in his early days) wanted a team of experienced divers to dive the pinnacle for an *Equinox* documentary entitled *Maelstrom* (part of the *Lethal Seas* series), Ewan got the call.

Ewan was very quickly on the phone to me asking if I'd be interested. My initial reaction was that this was a crazy thing to do, but he persisted and eventually I agreed.

Very shortly after that I found myself arriving at Oban on a Saturday morning to meet a team led by the experienced Trimix diver Graeme Bruce, which was made up of Ewan, myself, Jim Burke, Dave Hadden, David Ainsley and Jack Morrison.

The plan was to do a work-up dive in the Falls of Lora, almost directly underneath the Connell Bridge in Oban itself. The Falls of Lora take centre stage in a tight bottleneck channel, which separates Loch Etive from the open sea. The seabed at the Falls is scoured with hundreds of canyons and gorges, which lead to a massive pit or hole where the seabed drops off to about 45 metres.

I had seen the full might of the Falls in action on many occasions. The name is a wee bit of a misnomer as there is no actual waterfall or series of rocky rapids – just the tight bottleneck channel. But that channel is a special place, for a raging torrent of white water and standing waves reveal the presence of the underwater canyons and waterfalls.

On previous visits to Oban I have looked in awe at the Falls. On one occasion I saw a motor yacht trying to make its way up through the Falls in an effort to break through into the upper reaches of Loch Etive. Each time the yacht took a run at the Falls, engine roaring, it failed and was driven back. This was going to be some shake-down dive and I must admit to feeling apprehensive about this dive itself – let alone the Corryvreckan Whirlpool the following day.

We were dropped into the water up-current to seaward of the Falls on the flood tide and descended some 20 metres into an area of canyons scoured by the currents. We found ourselves drifting at speed up river as we approached the main event – the Falls of Lora themselves. Here the water plunges over an underwater cliff invisible from topside – which drops off from a depth of 20 metres to in excess of 40 metres. We had been told that once we went over the edge of the cliff there was no way we could break free from the current. We just had to go with the flow, literally. Once it bottomed-out we would be able to rise up and would find ourselves in calmer water. I wondered if Corryvreckan could be worse than what I now expected to face.

Abruptly the canyons petered out and I thought this meant that the cliff was imminent. I don't like being out of control on a dive and had a strong sense of foreboding about the cliff. But mercifully the cliff never appeared and quite suddenly the current just started to ease off and drop away. We had passed by on the southern side of the cliff and were now past it and into calmer water. We had got off lightly.

That night we headed down to a small pub at the Bridge over the Atlantic – a small bridge that connects the mainland to a small island and so bridges the Atlantic. We had agreed to meet there to conduct the briefing for the next day's dive into the whirlpool, and the ever-present TV director would be there to film.

As we went into the pub we found that the locals had been ushered along to one end of the bar to make way for a number of bright TV lights on stands. They eyed us quizzically as we entered. "Here's the mad divers away to dive the whirlpool", you could almost hear them muttering quietly.

Shots were taken outside of Ewan arriving in his car at the pub and then we moved inside to film the next sequential shot of Ewan entering the pub. In between shooting the outside shot and coming into the bar however, Ewan had taken off his jacket. Once the interior scene had been shot this lack of continuity was noticed and so he had to put it on, go outside and do his big walk in scene again.

We all sat around a beaten circular copper bar table, bought in some beers and laid out charts of the Gulf of Corryvreckan to study. David Ainsley, who runs the hugely respected charter dive boat *Porpoise*, was taking us out to the gulf the next day. He knew the waters there well.

David went on to brief us on the latest weather forecast – and it wasn't looking good. The wind was already gusting strongly and a Force 8 was now expected the next day, which might well put paid to the dive on the whirlpool.

Nevertheless, although there was a real chance that the dive would be off, we still went through the motions of the dive briefing for the TV camera. There was a sense of unreality about the whole thing. Here we were, planning to dive the most dangerous dive in British waters and now there was a Force 8 forecast to boot. Surely the dive would be called off.

Waking on the day of the dive, I was immediately struck by the noise of the wind whipping around our B&B. Getting up and throwing on some warm clothes I went outside, to be joined by Ewan. As the force of the wind buffeted us both we looked at each other and agreed that the dive would most probably be off.

Ewan phoned the TV director who told us to go down to the small harbour where the *Porpoise* was berthed – a decision about whether the dive was on would then be made. As I ate breakfast I was feeling a little relieved at the thought of the dive being called off.

After breakfast we collected our gear from our room and made the short drive down to the harbour. There, all the divers were arriving and loading their gear into the *Porpoise*. The wind howled about and I was by this stage absolutely convinced that the dive would be called off. I suspected that we were just not being told as yet so that the TV director could film the actual disappointment (or relief) on our faces as the announcement was made on the quayside. Nevertheless I loaded my gear into the boat and got changed in the lee of a stark concrete fish house into my warm diving undersuit.

Once all the kit and divers were aboard we were filmed as the *Porpoise* cast off and we headed out to open water. The wind still howled around and I thought that if the dive was going to be called off, now was the time, but the *Porpoise* kept going – and kept going. Because of the lie of the surrounding islands the skipper felt he could find shelter and run all the way to the Gulf of Corryvreckan without getting into the stormy weather, which would be found in exposed waters.

After being convinced in my own mind for the last 12 hours that the dive was not going ahead, I had to come to terms with the fact that after all, I was now about to be pitched into the heart of the Corryvreckan Whirlpool. Perhaps it was just as well it turned out like that – at least I had slept well the night before.

The *Porpoise* left the small harbour at about 9.00 a.m. and, although sea conditions were fairly lumpy, we had a surprisingly comfortable two-hour ride out to the gulf.

At first there was a lot of nervous gallows humour as we headed out across the Sound of Jura. The divers busied themselves setting up their dive gear and doing the usual round of kit checks. It was in the back of all of our minds that if the down-currents got hold of us, we could be pulled quite some distance down the side of the pinnacle.

As you have heard endlessly from me by now, the maximum recommended depth for air diving is 50 metres. The depth to the bottom of the pinnacle was 200 metres. If we were to dive it on compressed air and got pulled down the side of the pinnacle to such great depths, the very air we breathed would become toxic and kill us.

As a result I had chosen to dive using a Trimix of 16% oxygen, 45% helium and 39% nitrogen as my bottom mix in my back tanks. This would allow me to survive being pulled down to more than 100 metres. Ewan was going a step further still. He had rigged his much-cherished Inspiration closed-circuit rebreather, now known as Kato, with an even higher helium mixture, which would allow him if necessary to be swept to the bottom of the pinnacle at 200 metres – and survive. No one was intending going below 50–60 metres – but it was comforting to know that if the worst came to the worst, and things went wrong, Ewan could actually stand at the bottom of the pinnacle, look up and at least witness the rest of us casting off this mortal coil.

As we arrived in the Gulf of Corryvreckan everyone on the boat fell silent. The gallows humour petered out as an apprehensive and nervous silence enveloped the *Porpoise*. This was a special place – one of the most foreboding and eerie places I have been in my life. The gulf simply seemed filled with doom, broken only by the cries of a few seagulls. We could see the much-fabled standing waves marking the spot where the pinnacle stood, ominously hidden in the depths.

David Ainsley manoeuvred his boat above into position above the pinnacle and a very heavy shot, made up of two old iron railway grips, was dropped over the side and plunged down into the depths. Once the shot had landed and snagged, the current whipped the rope tight. White water broke around the buoys as the current worked on them, leaving a huge rippling wake as though they were being pulled through the water at speed.

The *Porpoise* would not be tying up to the downline, for even at the weakest tides of the month, there is never a period of absolute slack water on the pinnacle. There is only a short window of about ten minutes of relatively slack water that comes about every six hours as the tide turns. The rest of the time, the force of moving water would work on the hull of the boat with so much strength that even our heavy shot would be easily dragged off. To get the ten minutes of slack water for the divers down on the pinnacle we would have to start the dive before slack water – when the tide was still running.

Once all the divers were prepped the first two took their positions on the gunwales of the boat. David came out from the wheelhouse to give us a final briefing on the conditions and how the dive had to be run. He told us that the tide was now starting to drop away towards the ten minutes of slack water. After the short period of slack, the tide would pick up fiercely in the opposite direction – and it would be time to get out of there and start the ascent.

We were told that a warning sign that the tide was about to turn would be when all the small crabs which we would see on the pinnacle, darted for cover. They presumably had learnt through experience that if they didn't get tucked away in some nook or cranny that they would end up being swept over the side of the pinnacle for a long 200-metre fall into the chasm. No doubt that would be a long climb back up for a wee crab.

We were ominously told that when the air bubbles we breathed out started going downwards we should get the hell out of there – that would mean that the current was escalating dramatically. We were told to put buoyant gas into everything we could, by bleeding air into our drysuits, into our buoyancy wings and by sending up our deco bags on our reels – together that should be sufficient to support us and get us clear of the down currents. Finally, David added a sobering warning: "Conditions today are not ideal – no one is forced to go in on this dive. There is no pressure on anybody to do so." But we were all now committed and psyched up for the dive. There was no going back – none of us were going to wimp out at this stage.

David took the *Porpoise* up beside the buoys and was able to assess the tidal flow at that time as being between 2.4 and 2.9 knots (a diver can only swim against ½ knot of current at best). He then took the boat about 30 feet up-current to where he would drop us. By the time we were in the water and had righted ourselves we should be drifting up to the buoys.

It was time to go – the dive was on.

The first two divers rolled backwards into the water on David's signal, righted themselves and grabbed hold of the shot-line as they drifted with the current. A quick round of 'OK' signals to each other and the boat and they slipped under the water and started the descent to the pinnacle.

Once they had cleared the buoys it was time for Dave Hadden and myself to go. I pulled myself awkwardly up from the bench where I had got kitted up and made my way to the gunwale. It was hard work in a pitching boat carrying two heavy 12 litre tanks on my back, two 9 litre tanks of deco mix, one under either arm, my weights and all the other paraphernalia necessary to survive down in the depths. I sat down on the gunwale and Dave Hadden clumped down beside me. The skipper gave the signal that we were in position again and, hearts racing, Dave and I rolled over backwards, dropping over the side of the boat heavily into the water a few feet below.

As the usual explosion of white water and bubbles that greets a diver on entry disappeared, I righted myself quickly and looked down-current, searching for the buoys and line. All my earlier fears and foreboding had disappeared. I was preoccupied with the mechanics of the dive, of getting to the shot-line and not missing it. Sure enough, I was drifting towards the buoys and could see the shot-line leading down from them into the abyss. The underwater visibility looked good – at least 25 metres – and I could see the bubble streams rising up from the two divers ahead of and below me.

As soon as I grabbed the shot-line, the current that had been my friend in drifting me onto the rope, became my enemy and swung me round so my legs streamed out down-current. I kept a firm grip on the rope – if I let go of it I would be off very quickly towards America. I dumped excess buoyant air from my suit and wings and started to laboriously make the descent, hand over hand, inch by inch.

It took Dave and I just a few minutes to haul our way down to the top of the pinnacle and we found that although the top of the pinnacle is at a depth of 30 metres, the shot had snagged down one side of it at about 40 metres.

Initially I thought that the pinnacle was devoid of life, seemingly scoured clean by the current. But on closer examination however, I could see that there was a fine mat of tiny filter feeder organisms such as anemones, sponges and soft corals. All were noticeably smaller than their counterparts elsewhere in Scottish waters. Larger specimens are perhaps swept away by the current, or perhaps they have just evolved to be smaller to enable them to survive in this unique habitat. Because of the depth, the top of the pinnacle was clear and unobstructed by any kelp forests. Kelp fronds usually peter out at about 15 metres.

Large smooth potholes 4–5 feet across peppered the surface of the pinnacle where small stones had lodged in cracks or crevices and were then remorselessly ground round and round by the currents. Over a long period of time these small stones had carved out 6-foot deep potholes.

There seemed to be no fish life noticeable, perhaps because there was no prey or food worthy of eating here. A few small crabs went about their business here and there.

Dave and I circumnavigated the pinnacle at a depth of about 45 metres and then headed up as planned to its top plateau. We were conscious of trying to avoid spending too long at depth, as that would rack up lengthy decompression stops for the ascent. We kept a careful eye on our dive computers as the minutes ticked away.

In glorious 25-metre visibility all three pairs of divers gradually collected on the top of the pinnacle. It was an odd feeling to see all six of us there and I imagined how it must have looked if you could somehow have stripped away the water. Six tiny specks of humanity, standing on the 100 feet wide table top, of a 200-metre high pinnacle.

As we collected on the plateau, I noticed a perceptible change in the direction of the current – it felt as if someone had thrown a big switch. One minute the tide was dropping off gently in the one direction. The next minute you could feel it starting to pick up rapidly in the other direction. There are titanic forces at work here.

I looked down at the rock I was resting on and sure enough, as if on cue, the one or two small crabs around my feet just made their way into little crevices, braced out their claws and seemingly disappeared. In fact, all life seemed to disappear from the pinnacle simultaneously. The all too brief moment of calm had passed and the residents of the pinnacle were preparing themselves for the next six hours in the maelstrom. If the locals were getting worried, I thought, our team of six divers should be getting out of there.

Dave and I however couldn't resist the temptation to fin over to the edge of the pinnacle and look over the side, down into the 200-metre deep abyss. Of course, in the limited visibility we could only see about 25 metres down the side – deeper than that was just an ominous uniform black. The bottom was well out of sight.

As we held onto rocks and peered over the side of the pinnacle I became aware that my exhaled bubbles had stopped rising upwards – as they had done throughout the whole of my diving career. For a second or two, some bubbles were held motionless in front of my face. With my next exhaled breath the bubbles started to slowly sink downwards over the side of the pinnacle. As I continued to breathe out my bubbles started going downward more and more vigorously. It was a very surreal experience and it was certainly time to get out of this dangerous place.

I looked at Dave and gave the thumbs up hand signal – which was returned with an 'OK' signal from Dave. We prepared ourselves by pumping gas into our suits and wings until we were almost positively buoyant. We then each inflated our deco bags; the reels spun and chattered, paying out their thin line as the bags sped to the surface.

Once the bags hit the surface and the reels stopped paying out, it was time to go. Pumping even more gas into suit and wings we let go of our rocky handholds, stood up and basically let the current get hold of us. We were swept instantly off the pinnacle and out over the chasm of the Gulf of Corryvreckan. Our exhaust bubbles were still going downwards.

We had been warned that the first 10 metres of the ascent would be difficult, and right enough, as I stepped off the top of the pinnacle it was as though a thousand invisible hands were clutching at my legs and trying to pull me down. It was quite an unsettling feeling and initially I had to fin hard to make any headway upwards. The task of managing the ascent however soon absorbed me as I kicked my legs and simultaneously wound in the slack on my reel, essentially winching myself up towards the surface.

Once I got 10 metres up from the top of the pinnacle, the current had already carried us so far downstream and away from the pinnacle that we were starting to come out of the whirlpool. As I rose higher and got further away, the water seemed to settle down – and soon we were just into a regular free hanging ascent on our deco bags and reels. We drifted free in the current, seemingly motionless but in reality speeding over the seabed at several knots in a fixed column of water.

As we all broke the surface and clambered back into the safety of the *Porpoise* a sense of euphoria overwhelmed us. There was much manly banter and slapping of backs – a complete contrast to the silent gallows mood that had overcome the team before the dive. We had successfully carried out perhaps the most challenging dive in British waters, into one of the last great, unexplored habitats on earth. We all realised that it had all gone so smoothly largely due to the professionalism and know-how of David Ainsley and team leader Graeme Bruce. They had made a potentially terrifying dive manageable.

We had stood on the pinnacle and peered into the abyss.

CHAPTER EIGHT

HMS *HAMPSHIRE*

In 1997 for the 3rd edition of *Dive Scapa Flow*, our group of technical divers had arranged a week's diving in Scapa Flow. Scapa Flow is normally associated with the remaining seven colossal wrecks of the World War I German High Seas Fleet. The entire fleet of 74 warships scuttled on 21 June 1919 after seven months of internment in the great natural harbour. It was – and still is – the single greatest act of maritime suicide ever.

The majority of the sunken warships were raised and scrapped in the decades following the scuttling. Economic factors however stopped the original main salvers lifting all the wrecks – and seven complete wrecks were left unworked. These seven all went on to suffer further smaller-scale salvage works as selected areas were blown open to allow removal of valuable engine room fitments, torpedo tubes and the like. Today, these seven badly scarred giants still slumber in the depths, slowly collapsing and falling to pieces as the ravages of their long immersion take their toll.

The purpose of this weeks diving however, would leave little time for exploring the classic German High Seas Fleet wrecks. I had to survey two wrecks that had largely been undiveable on air before – but which now fell within the ambit of technical diving.

The first of these was the boom defence vessel *Strathgarry*, which sunk following a collision in Hoxa Sound in 1915 – and was completely forgotten about until she was re-discovered by sport divers in the late 1980s and early 1990s. She sits on an even keel in 58 metres and had been dived occasionally by a few brave souls on compressed air – but I suspect that on air it must have been a case of get down, touch it and get up again.

The second wreck to be included in the new edition was HMS *Hampshire* on which Lord Kitchener died en route for Russia on 5 June 1916. The *Hampshire* lies in 68 metres in difficult waters 1½ miles west of the towering cliffs of Marwick Head. Of Lord Kitchener, his staff and the ship's crew of 655 officers and men, only 12 lucky souls would survive.

The *Hampshire* was so deep that she had effectively been beyond the range of air divers – although again a few deep air divers had dived her in the 1980s. There had been several commercial salvage attempts over the decades since her sinking to recover the rumoured (but never officially admitted) two million gold sovereigns aboard, which were allegedly being taken to Russia to help with the Russian war effort. In the 1930s, hard-hat divers in standard dress, breathing air had worked her – with the loss of a diver. In the 1980s, modern salvers using North Sea oil field technology had a go at recovering the sovereigns – if still there, or indeed if they ever existed in the first place.

With the advent of technical diving techniques she had now become a very diveable wreck, lying in a perfect depth in the crystal clear oceanic waters of the Atlantic and complete with a huge history.

In the first two editions of *Dive Scapa Flow*, I had (in my air days) recounted the story of her loss but never surveyed her nor had a painting of her wreck on the seabed made up. For the 3rd edition I was going to extend the book to have a full description of the essential information required for diving her remains.

HMS Hampshire *sunk off Orkney in 1916 with the loss of Lord Kitchener. (IWM)*

The *Hampshire* was a 10,850-ton armoured cruiser launched on 30 April 1904. She had performed a variety of roles before seeing action in World War I, when early in the War in 1914 she captured a German merchantman. She also took part in the famous hunt for the German light cruiser *Emden*, which was harassing Allied shipping in the Indian Ocean after having ingeniously passed through the Dutch East Indies by adding a false fourth funnel to make her look like a British cruiser.

Hampshire subsequently joined the British Grand Fleet in December 1914 and fought as part of the 2nd Cruiser Squadron at the Battle of Jutland on 31 May 1916. Shortly after the battle, she received fresh sailing orders on 4 June 1916 to take Lord Kitchener on a voyage to Archangel in Northern Russia; a journey of 1,649 nautical miles.

Initially, she was to depart the following day (5 June) and pass up the east side of the Orkney Islands along a route that was regularly swept for mines. She would be provided with

The famous World War I recruiting poster of Lord Kitchener. Watch the eyes!

a protective screen of two destroyers – *Victor* and *Unity* – as far north as latitude 62° North. From there *Hampshire* would proceed alone, zigzagging at 16 knots to avoid torpedo attack.

The following day however, on 5 June, the weather worsened and by the afternoon a gale was blowing from the northeast. A heavy sea was running along the east coast, making mine sweeping difficult. The heavy seas would also make it difficult for the two smaller destroyers to keep up with the far larger and more seaworthy 10,850-ton cruiser. The plan was therefore changed and at the last minute the small flotilla was ordered to proceed along one of the routes up the west side of the Orkney Islands, where it was felt that the land would give some protection against the easterly gale.

The flotilla left Scapa Flow and started to battle up the west coast of Orkney. It soon became clear however that the weather forecast was inaccurate, for within just an hour of the group's departure the storm centre had passed overhead. The easterly wind backed to the northwest and the seas started to mount from that direction, building in intensity and starting to crash against the rugged cliffs and rocky bays of the west coast of Orkney. The conditions that the *Hampshire* and her escorts faced were now exactly the opposite of what had been intended.

Soon, the two smaller destroyers started to struggle in the rising seas to keep up with the larger *Hampshire*. A predetermined speed of not less than 18 knots had been set to allow the group to outrun any hostile U-boat, which would be far slower. It was imperative to maintain that speed despite the seas.

Victor then signalled *Hampshire* that she could only make 15 knots. Just a few minutes later *Unity* signalled that she could only make 12 knots. Shortly after that *Unity* signalled that she could now only make 10 knots. The group could not be allowed to slow up because *Unity* could not keep up – *Hampshire*, the *raison d'être* of the group, would be placed in danger. Accordingly, *Hampshire* signalled *Unity* that she should return to Scapa Flow.

Another ten minutes later and *Victor* was facing the same speed problem. She signalled that she could not maintain any speed greater than 12 knots, and she too was ordered to return to Scapa Flow. *Hampshire* now struggled on alone up the west coast into the full fury of the north- westerly gale.

An hour later and *Hampshire* herself was now only able to make 13.5 knots. She dipped and crashed in the raging seas, her bow burying deep into the oncoming walls of water as she fought and struggled up towards the northwesterly point of the main island, Marwick Head. The bow splash billowed high up over the bridge and green water surged across the weather deck.

Suddenly, at 7.40 p.m., a rumbling explosion shook the whole ship and a huge hole was rent open in her keel, between her bows and bridge. The helm jammed and the lights below deck went out as the power faded. With no power, she had lost the ability to make radio contact with shore to call for assistance. *Hampshire* immediately started to settle into the water by the head and as she did, clouds of brown suffocating smoke started to billow up from the stoker's mess forward, making it difficult for those on the bridge to see.

The crew streamed aft away from the onrushing water and an officer was heard to call out, "Make way for Lord Kitchener!" Kitchener passed by, clad in a greatcoat, and went up the after hatch onto the weather deck. This was the last sighting of this legendary soldier and statesman.

The cruiser was by now sinking quickly by the bow, whilst the crew frantically did what they could to salvage the situation. But with the ship's power gone there was no power to work the lifeboat derricks and so none of the larger boats could be hoisted out. Smaller boats were lowered into the water but these were smashed against *Hampshire*'s side by the force of the storm. Not one single boat got clear intact.

A number of men took their places in the large boom boats (which also had not been launched due to the loss of power) hoping that as the ship went down these boats would float off. The suction created by *Hampshire*'s passing however would pull these boats and the unfortunate souls aboard under with her.

At about 7.50 p.m. – only 10–15 minutes after striking the mine – *Hampshire* went down, bows first, heeling over to starboard. Smoke and flame belched from just behind the bridge. Her stern lifted slowly out of the water and her two mighty 43 ton phosphor bronze propellers were seen clear of the water, still revolving slowly as she went under.

Only three oval, cork and wood Carley rafts got away from the sinking ship, one of which held only six men. The desperate survivors in it faced severe sea conditions as it was bitingly cold and they were soaked through. The wind chill cut right through them and they were soon suffering from exposure. The raft was flung over twice, pitching its human cargo into the seas, before it was finally washed ashore in Skaill Bay. By that time only two men in it were still alive.

Forty-five to fifty men clung grimly to the second larger Carley raft. When it made the shore more than five hours later at 1.15 a.m. only four of them were still alive.

The third raft had about 40 men in it when it got away from the sinking ship. By the time it was finally washed ashore on rocks north of Skaill Bay, there were only six men alive in it.

The legendary story of the sinking of the *Hampshire* and the loss of Lord Kitchener is now part of the folklore of Orkney and is still very close to the hearts of many of the islanders. As it is a sensitive war grave, we treated the wreck with tremendous respect for our 1997 expedition and were given formal permission to survey it from the Ministry of Defence. It certainly helped that we had a number of military personnel amongst our group.

We managed to get two dives in on the wreck of the *Hampshire* – which we found to be lying completely upside down, its superstructure crushed and driven into the seabed by the colossal weight of the ship bearing down on it.

On the first dive on Day 1, our shot had landed on the seabed beside the midships area. We explored this area and worked aft until we came across the one remaining massive propeller still *in situ*. I was hugely concerned that I had not managed to make my way to the bow area of the wreck some 400 feet away, but it was just too far in one short bottom time of 20–25 minutes. I simply had to see the bow area the following day or I couldn't have a complete image of the wreck made up for the new edition.

Day 2 saw fine conditions again as we motored up the west coast of the Orkney from Stromness. On this occasion, we tried to place the shot-weight on the seabed right beside the very stern of the vessel. There was a slight current running from stern to bow over the wreck and we felt the drift would help us see the whole wreck.

We arrived down on the wreck at the stern, close to the rudder, which had fallen off and was now lying flat on the seabed. We let ourselves be drifted gently forward along the wreck, noting what we saw and sketching where we could. Our allotted bottom time of 20 minutes ran out just as we arrived at the bow. Here I could see how the bow had been damaged by the original mine blast – but the main damage to the wreck seemed clearly as a result of the wreck being almost surgically blasted and cut open in the vicinity of the strong room, by salvers no doubt looking for the fabled gold sovereigns. The upturned bottom of the bow right back to the front of the bridge superstructure had been cleanly and professionally removed as though cut off with a large knife. As I started my ascent and rose up from the wreck I caught a glimpse of the barbette of the main forward 7.5 inch deck gun, now fallen on its side in the midst of the blasted devastation of the bow.

The weather unfortunately broke overnight with strong winds from the west – the wind direction that had originally caused all the difficulty for the 1916 flotilla. The *Hampshire* is a very exposed site and the benign calm conditions we had had over the preceding two days suddenly turned into a churning, inhospitable seascape speckled with white horses. Any further diving on the site was ruled out for the rest of week and we retreated to dive the wrecks inside the shelter of Scapa Flow itself.

From our survey of the wreck, I was able to have a local marine artist who lives near me – Rob Ward of Illusion Illustration – paint the wreck as it lies on the seabed. This was the first time this had been done and his haunting painting immediately reveals at a glance how the wreck looks today.

In 2000 we planned a return expedition with the aim of checking how much the vessel had deteriorated in the intervening three years. We chartered the superb hard boat *Three Sisters* from Keith Thomson, the dive charterer at Scapa Flow who I had used since the mid 1980s. Keith is a tall, immensely strong man with a beguiling sense of humour. He came to Orkney a long time ago after living in South Africa and like many folk, just stayed. He has worked the waters around Orkney for more than 20 years and knows them like the back of his hand. I was always immensely confident when Keith was skippering a trip for us.

The first day after our arrival in Scapa Flow, the sea conditions were perfect. We motored out through Hoy Sound to the west before heading north along the western shores and cliffs of Orkney up towards Birsay.

On the steam up the west coast, the seas were calm, glistening like oil in a slow languid, gentle swell. As I stood at the gunwale of the *Three Sisters* I saw a group of seagulls floating on the surface. Suddenly a grey seal shot up from below and grabbed one of the seagulls in its jaws. An enormous flapping of wings followed as the seagull bravely tried to fight off its attacker to no avail. The seal pulled the seagull under and that was it, all over. I'm told that sea gulls are not tasty birds – even for seals – and aren't part of their usual food. Keith remarked that that must have been a very hungry seal to take a sea gull.

The *Three Sisters* continued its voyage up north towards the last resting place of the *Hampshire*. Soon, a few dolphins had joined us and started playing in the bow surge, flashing from one side of the ship to the other, seemingly right under the bow, before giving a little jump from time to time. The seas are busy today, I thought.

Further on, and we saw a couple of minke whales. I was very familiar with them after seeing one at close quarters off Fraserburgh earlier that year when it surfaced and crossed right in front of my RIB whilst we were doing about 20 knots. I had to swerve frantically to the side and just missed running over it.

As we neared the wreck site, Keith pointed out a school of pilot whales a mile or so off, their white water spouts dazzling in the bright sunlight. Extremely busy seas today, I thought.

Finally after a run of a few hours we were on site and Keith had picked up the wreck on his echo sounder and dropped a shot-line and buoys. He then backed off and we finalised getting dressed into our dive kit. Once we were all ready, our eight divers clustered around the starboard gunwale as Keith took a final run in towards the shot-line for drop off.

As he approached the buoys, four large black and white objects surfaced beside us. Water cascaded off their smooth backs and there was the unmistakable tall dorsal fin of orcas screaming danger to us. A pod of four orcas – also known as killer whales – was passing by us just as we were away to jump in the water. If we'd gone in just a minute or two earlier we would have been right in amongst them. Orcas are seen from time to time in Orkney waters and in the North Sea offshore. They can get aggressive with divers and it is unsafe to be in the water with wild orcas. As I looked carefully I could see that one of the pod of four was quite small – an infant sticking close to its larger parent, dipping and diving in unison. All of us froze in our tracks at the gunwales and although nothing was said, we all just sat down simultaneously on the side benches. No one was going in the water when these guys were around.

We kept an eye on the pod of orcas as they moved away from the *Three Sisters* heading towards the shore a mile or two off. Once they were about a mile away Keith turned the boat and took us back in and we all jumped into the water for the dive.

I had thought nothing more of the incident until a later trip to Scapa Flow in October 2005 when I had had dinner with a group of divers diving off John Thornton's well-equipped technical hard boat, the *Karin*. That day in 2000 we had seen John's *Karin* coming down from the north and approaching another part of the wreck. He dropped a shot-line, as we were getting ready to dive. In the Ferry Inn over dinner, John and I started reminiscing about that day and the orcas we had seen. We recalled how our team had already been kitted up and so were the first of the two boats to dive. Once we thought the orcas were far enough away, we clustered at the gunwales as Keith made his approach. Three of our divers splashed into the water and swam over to the buoys and started their descent. Ewan and I had then jumped in and motored over to the downline on our Aquazepp underwater scooters, just as the first three divers ahead of us disappeared below us into the inky depths.

But then what John told me next that night in the Ferry Inn sent a shiver down my spine. For although it was some 30–40 minutes since the pod of orcas had cruised past, as Ewan and I rendezvoused at the downline buoys, John told me that a large male orca had passed between us and our dive boat, the *Three Sisters*. Neither Ewan nor I had had any inkling that this had happened – and it was probably just as well we didn't see the male orca at the time. I feel sure the orca would have known we were in the water close by – perhaps it was the noise of our scooters that put it off a morning snack of one 6'2" skinny Scotsman and a second slightly shorter and more circumferentially challenged Scotsman. Or maybe it was just scared of the sight of Ewan in the water – I know I am! Only kidding, Ewan.

Other than the killer whales, the most memorable event from our dives on *Hampshire* was a stupid mistake I made. Ewan and I were on the seabed just in front of the bow of the *Hampshire* in 68 metres when our planned 20 minutes of bottom time elapsed.

Signalling to Ewan that it was time to ascend, without thinking I unclipped my deco reel from my harness, unfurled the bright red 6 foot long deco bag and cracked open the small air cylinder, which fills the bag and sends it rocketing to the surface to mark our position. The line paid out more and more quickly as the reel spun, trying to keep up with the bag that was accelerating from our depth of 68 metres towards the distant surface. The air in the bag would expand eight times in volume during the journey back up to the light. The reel whipped round and round as plastic chattering noises muffled by water came to me – it was going so fast I swear I almost saw smoke coming from it. As it chattered faster and faster I suddenly realised that I'd forgotten that there was only 50 metres of line on the reel – and we were standing in 68 metres. Now this would be interesting, I thought.

As the last of the 50 metres of line paid out, the reel stopped turning and my arm got a severe jerk upwards. As if in a cartoon, my right arm seemed to extend to about three times its normal length, as the bag sought to drag me up the last 20 metres or so until it reached the surface. The buoyancy of the bag then overcame my inertia – and I was off. The lifting power of the bag just picked me off my feet and I went shooting up from 68 metres to 50 metres when the bag reached the surface and stopped. In an optical illusion, Ewan who had been standing beside me on the seabed seemed to disappear straight downward getting smaller and smaller until I was suspended 20 metres above him. As technical divers we like to get up to our first planned deep decompression stop fairly quickly but this was going a bit too far. Ewan arrived beside me shortly afterwards and I detected a wry smile on his face as his lips twitched upwards. He knew fine what I'd just done.

The *Hampshire* is a magnificent wreck – certainly one of Scotland's greatest. She lies completely upside down and her colossal 10,000 ton weight has crushed her superstructure and driven it into the seabed to such an extent that none of it is now visible at all on either side of the wreck.

The wreck of HMS Hampshire *lies in 68 metres, 1 ½ miles off Birsay, Orkney.*

The whole bow area has been removed down to the underside of the weather deck, partly as a result of the original mine explosion and partly in the decades following her sinking by the various salvage attempts. In the 1980s a consortium of German businessmen put together a salvage attempt and hired at great expense, an oilfield diving support vessel. Blasting by this succession of salvers hunting for the strong room and the gold has all but completely (and very neatly) removed the entire bow.

Her upturned hull retains its ship shape from the strong room area all the way to the rounded stern. Here the most photogenic aspect is the magnificent three-bladed 43-ton phosphor bronze port propeller. The *Hampshire* was a twin-screw vessel – that is, she had two propellers. The starboard propeller is missing, the shaft blasted and cut away from the hull. The remnants of its A-frame support bracket still bear the tell tale scars of this salvage work.

Along with other artefacts from the wreck, the starboard propeller was lifted in the 1980s from the wreck under the guise of a commercial 'survey'. The salvage vessel berthed at Peterhead where the authorities got wind of what was happening and went to inspect. There are rumours locally of artefacts being dropped through moon-pools in advance of the inspection.

The propeller became a problem and sat on the pier at Peterhead for some time (coincidentally whilst I worked there as a young lawyer in the 1980s). Eventually, the propeller was repatriated to Orkney and is now on display at the Naval Museum at the old naval base at Lyness on the island of Hoy. We must be one of the few groups of divers who have dived the wreck in the morning and seen the port propeller and then gone to the Lyness Naval Museum and seen the starboard prop the same day.

During our 2000 re-inspection we noticed that a fissure is forming in the hull, running almost the full length of the hull where the keel meets the side of the ship. This is the point of greatest stress on the hull and eventually the keel will collapse downwards flattening the wreck.

Although we were given formal permission from the Ministry of Defence to dive and survey HMS *Hampshire*, she has since become a protected wreck under the Protection of Military Remains Act 1986 and no diving on this important and historic wreck is now permitted.

Above: Ewan Rowell sits at the bows of the Jane R *on the approach to the Norwegian Horse © Author*

Below: Phil Hodson approaches the twin rudders of HMS Audacious, *North Channel on his scooter © Grainne Patton*

Above: Rod approaches the side armament of HMS Repulse, South China Sea © Guy Wallis

Below: Ewan Rowell at the summit of the Norwegian Horse © Author

Above: Heinkel 111 *in northern Norwegian waters* © Gordon Wadsworth

Left: Sherman tank deck cargo on the SS Empire Heritage, *North Channel, Irish Sea* © Grainne Patton tanks

Below: Sherman tank deck cargo, SS Empire Heritage, North Channel, Irish Sea © Grainne Patton

Above: Rod in Stonehaven Diver *heads south from Stonehaven followed by Jim Burke in* Buchan Diver © *Tony Ray*

Below: The massive boilers of the SS Empire Heritage, *North Channel, Irish Sea © Grainne Patton*

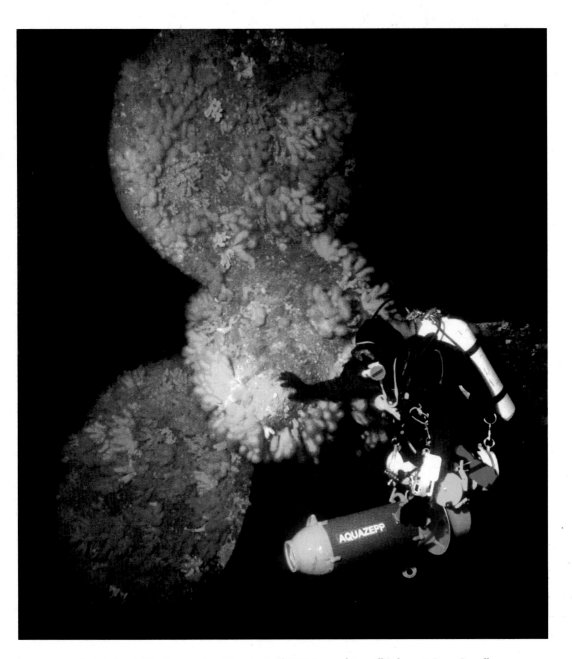

Rod is dwarfed by the massive 43-ton prop of HMS Hampshire, *off Orkney © Ewan Rowell*

Above: Twin 15-inch gun barrels of B turret, HMS Repulse, *South China Sea, half buried in the sand © Guy Wallis*

Below: Stonehaven Diver *returns from another wreck dive © Paul Haynes*

*Above: Ready to dive
aboard* Stonehaven Diver *© Tony Ray*

*Left: Rod beside the Tri-Services ensign just
flown on HMS* Repulse *© Guy Wallis*

Below: The Jane R *tied up in crystal clear
waters at the foot of the Norwegian
Horse © Author*

Twin rudders of HMS Audacious, *North Channel, Irish Sea © Grainne Patton*

The Russian cruiser Murmansk, north of Tromso © Gordon Wadsworth

On the afternoon of the HMS Hampshire *dive the team visit the Naval Museum at Lyness on Hoy where the salvaged prop of HMS* Hampshire *is displayed.*

CHAPTER NINE

THE WRECK OF THE LINER *REMUERA*

A small number of other divers locally were now qualifying as Trimix divers and, hearing of our exploits some got in touch. Aberdeen Watersports (our local dive shop) was offering mixed gas training courses along with all the equipment you needed and became a focus for technical diving. Divers came from all over the UK to train here.

A group of about half a dozen or so tech divers was loosely formed to share knowledge, experiences, boats and beer. When, in 1998 Dave Gordon – the Aberdeen Watersports technical diving instructor – said he wanted to try and find the liner *Remuera* about eight miles off Fraserburgh later that summer, we all said we were up for it.

Dave chartered a fishing boat out of Fraserburgh for an evening dive. The target, the liner *Remuera,* is the largest ship lost off the northeast coast of Scotland. Photos of it show an elegant vessel with massive superstructures rising up amidships and at the stern for several deck levels.

After a full day of legal work at my office, I picked up Ewan and together we drove the hour or so up to Fraserburgh, rendezvoused at the harbour and started loading our kit aboard the fishing boat. By this time Steve Collard, who had been blown away by the *Port Dennison/ Anvers* dive, had got himself qualified as a Trimix diver. A Royal Marine commando John Quinn, who had recently qualified as a tech diver, also joined us.

Once loaded up the boat ambled gently out of the harbour and set off on an hour-long

The liner Remuera *located and identified by the Stonehaven Snorkellers 8 miles off Fraserburgh.*

journey out to the site as we all set about rigging our kit. The skipper assured us he could drop us on the *Remuera*.

I knew that the *Remuera* was possibly the most exciting wreck on the northeast coast of Scotland and was very interested in finding it. She was a large twin-screw vessel, 502 feet in length with a beam of 62 feet built in 1911 in Dumbarton, on the Clyde, by the well-known ship builders W. Denny, for the New Zealand Shipping Company – for service on their UK to New Zealand round-the-world run. She weighed in at 11,445 tons and had 60 first-class berths, 90 second-class berths and 130 third-class. Her construction cost was £176,102 9s 4d.

Initially she operated eastwards around the Cape of Good Hope and then back around the Horn on the homeward leg. This was a tough voyage through difficult seas and there are lots of archive photographs and souvenir postcards around showing icebergs seen from her decks on these voyages through the southern Pacific.

The Panama Canal opened in 1914 and almost overnight this cut out from the voyage the need for the often-horrendous passage around the Horn. *Remuera* was the first New Zealand ship to transit the Panama Canal two years later in 1916. She subsequently saw service in World War I as a troopship and in the inter-war years served as a migrant ship running from Southampton to Wellington, New Zealand, calling at Pitcairn (of mutiny on the *Bounty* fame) on the Pacific leg.

On 26 August 1940 on a return voyage from Wellington, four Heinkel 115s and eight Ju-88 German aircraft based in Norway attacked her. She took a fatal hit from an aerial torpedo and her fate was sealed.

The photograph we had of her showed her massive midships superstructure rising up for five deck levels and a similarly large second superstructure at the stern. Both were liberally dotted with portholes. If she were sitting upright, exploring her would keep me happy as a diver for the rest of my career. I imagined drifting through a latticework of encrusted rooms – and entering an intact liner's bridge with everything still *in situ*.

By the time the engine slowed as the skipper reached the site, we were all sitting rigged up in our twin sets waiting to pop our masks on and leap over the side. It was almost slack water and if we didn't get in the water soon we would find ourselves working in a current.

The skipper started searching for the wreck – and he searched… and searched. And as he searched we all sat waiting, fully rigged. Forty minutes later there was a total air of despondency aboard as we realised we had missed slack water and were not going to get a dive on the fabled *Remuera*. Time and tide wait for no man.

Stern view of the liner Remuera.

By now it was getting on in the evening and the first hint of nightfall was hovering over the eastern horizon. Eventually the skipper admitted he couldn't find the wreck and turned his boat to head for home. About 15 minutes later on the run ashore however, the engine note suddenly changed and the boat slowed. Dave Gordon came running out of the wheelhouse and threw a large shot-weight, line and pink Dhan Buoy over the side exclaiming: "We've just run over another wreck – it's a bit away from the *Remuera* site but who wants to dive it?" I had already learned that fishermen are good at avoiding wrecks by large margins with their trawl nets, but sometimes accurately pinpointing them was not their forte. It was still just possible that we had run over the *Remuera* by chance. We all jumped at the prospect of getting a dive in after all.

Ewan was unable to dive this evening and so would be staying topside. Although I was sorry he couldn't dive, I was relieved to have him topside, as I didn't know anything about the skipper or his sea-craft. It was good to have an experienced diver like Ewan staying aboard to let the skipper know what we were doing. I was paired to dive with John Quinn and we both quickly got our kit back on. Once ready, the skipper took his boat in beside the shot-line and we jumped from the gunwales, splashing heavily into the water.

With the sun low on the horizon there was not much light penetrating down from above and as I reached a depth of 25 metres we were enveloped in a shroud of darkness – completely reliant on our torches. My eyes strained into the darkness looking for snagged trawl nets suspended on buoys that would be a danger to us.

At 50 metres down my torch picked out the keel strip of an upturned vessel five metres beneath. Although I was thankful to have got on a wreck, as I swept my torch to either side, I could see immediately that this was the keel of a sleek, narrow vessel, far smaller than the *Remuera*.

John and I landed on the upturned hull just forward of the rudder and I settled down astride the keel strip as I adjusted all my kit and got comfortable. After that, picking the starboard side at random, we headed over to the side of the ship and dropped down the vertical, rusted steel wall of its hull until we landed on the seabed at 64 metres.

The sheer side of the hull disappointingly disappeared straight into the seabed on this side so John and I finned forward just above the seabed, which seemed to slope downwards. Our depth steadily increased to about 68 metres but we found little of interest – just a flat wall of rusted steel disappearing into the silt bank that had built up against it.

As we neared the bow, the flat expanse of the hull however abruptly ended. The whole bow was gone, as though someone had simply sliced off the front 30–40 feet of the bow with a giant knife, giving an aeroplane hanger effect much like the *Hampshire*. The whole inside of the ship gaped black and ominous, enticing us to explore further inside.

I swept my torch around and as its beam cut through the darkness of the interior it briefly lit up piles of spare porthole glasses, still neatly stacked and gleaming: the porthole locker. I roughly measured the beam of the ship and made it to be around 35 feet – a far cry from the 62 feet beam of the *Remuera*.

By this time our allotted bottom time was gone and it was time to ascend. John and I rose up from the bow area to about 45 metres and then fired off our delayed deco bags to show our position to the boat above. Slack water was long gone and as we ascended we came out of the shelter of the wreck and found ourselves in an accelerating current drifting down the length of the wreck. We actually passed our start point and the anchor line, which was visible in the distance off to one side and unattainable in the current.

Just short of an hour later, John and I had completed our scheduled inwater decompression stops and our heads broke the surface. I could see the fishing boat, which seemed about a quarter of a mile away in the distance. It was picking up other divers who had ascended via the shot-line.

As John and I bobbed in the water, waiting to be picked up, I was struck by the immensity of my surroundings. The land, some eight miles away, was just a sliver of darkness far in the distance and it disappeared from sight as each swell passed over us. It was very dusky to the east of us and over the land to the west, the orange glow of the setting sun lit up the horizon. A pair of seagulls flew in and landed in the water close to us and simply sat there beside us, staring at us and trying to make out what we were. The surface cover in the boat should have seen our delayed deco buoys and be aware that we would be drifting down current but they would be looking east into the fast approaching darkness of night. Perhaps they wouldn't be able to see our fashionably black wet suit hoods and kit in the swell.

I inflated my suit and buoyancy wings as far as I could to lift me as high as possible out of the water. Then a large rolling swell came towards us and as we crested its languid top, I switched on my large dive torch and pointed it directly at the boat. I traced a large 'O' – the diver's low visibility 'OK' signal. I immediately got a corresponding 'OK' signal back from the boat and was hugely reassured that someone was looking in our direction and knew where we had ended up. I knew it would be Ewan.

About ten minutes of bobbing in the water later, the fishing boat turned and started coming towards us. Soon it was alongside and welcoming hands were helping us up over a makeshift ladder of tyres at the stern. This was a fishing boat after all and not a well-equipped dive boat. All the other divers were there aboard safe and well.

My post dive euphoria was dampened when Ewan took me aside and told me that the skipper hadn't had a clue about how our diving worked. He had no idea that we would drift downstream and that we would be hanging free on our buoys for about 45 minutes. When it was time to pick us up he had headed off in the wrong direction, upstream. I wondered what would have happened if Ewan had been in the water with us and not on board to guide the skipper. A short unplanned holiday in Norway would have been a distinct possibility.

Having established that our wreck wasn't the *Remuera*, I started looking at possible identities for it. Tracing our route in from the charted site of the *Remuera*, a wreck symbol at 57 45 17N, 01 57 04W was charted with a clearance over it marked as 50 metres. Looking up my records for this vessel gave a possible name for it: the 1369 grt World War II loss, SS *Trsat*.

The more I looked at the information on this vessel, the more I became convinced that this was in fact the wreck we had just dived. The *Trsat* was built in 1919 by the Forth Ship Building Company. She was 235.6 feet in length with a beam of 36.2 feet. Her proportions fitted our rough approximation from our dive – she was in the right place and had the right measurements.

A search of the historical records revealed that in September 1941 the she had set out on a journey from Reykjavik in Iceland to Hull, with a war cargo of 845 tons of fish. After safely navigating the dangerous Atlantic waters she had passed by the Faeroe Islands and then the Shetland and Orkney islands, before running down the very northeast tip of Scotland into the

Moray Firth. No doubt she was seeking the protection of the Swept Channel for the last and most dangerous leg of the journey – down the east coast to Hull. Although the wall of steel nets and mines of the Northern Mine Barrage would provide some protection from U-boat attack, the greatest danger for her was from air attack by German planes flying from Norway. Like all other shipping along the east coast she was hugely exposed to air attack at this most critical stage of her voyage.

Suddenly, late in the evening of 7 September at 8.54 p.m., the quiet dusk of the evening was rudely shattered as a German aircraft swept down on a bombing run. One bomb scored a direct hit, causing massive and fatal damage to her bow. Not surprisingly having seen the damage to the wreck, she sank quickly – her whole bow had been blown off.

Coastguards on watch ashore at Kinnaird Head reported seeing flares and alerted the Fraserburgh lifeboat *John and Charles Kennedy* a few minutes later at 8.57 p.m. The lifeboat was launched at 10.07 p.m. and was soon on the scene of the reported attack. They initially found an empty lifeboat drifting freely and then started to encounter wreckage before they came across a waterlogged boat with 13 men in it alive and one dead.

The lifeboat coxswain passed the waterlogged boat and body on to *HM Trawler Ebor Abbey*, which had also now arrived on the scene. The lifeboat then continued searching for the missing three members of the *Trsat*'s crew of 17. The missing three could not be found and the *Ebor Abbey* picked up a body the next day.

Although we were pretty sure the wreck we had dived was the *Trsat*, the *Remuera* remained high on our list of wrecks to find. In 1999 (the year after the *Trsat* dive) Ewan and I took a week off work to dive our local wrecks and on one of the days decided to have another go at finding the *Remuera*. This time we would work from our own boat and find it the old fashioned way by an echo sounder and magnetometer search.

On a blisteringly hot summer's day we towed *Stonehaven Diver* up to Fraserburgh and launched from the small slip there. We had worked out our own search area from the approximate positions shown on the Admiralty chart and had set up waypoints for our search area in our GPS.

With the two of us in red and yellow sailing gear and *Stonehaven Diver* filled with pink Dhan buoys, magnetometers and coiled lengths of weighted rope we headed out on an oily calm under a hot sun. The target area was about eight miles off Fraserburgh, but in these perfect conditions and the boat lightly laden for once with no heavy dive gear, the miles flashed by.

As we skipped across a millpond sea I switched on my Lowrance echo sounder. We were going too fast for my old Lowrance to give me a proper bottom trace but it still gave a good digital read out even at these speeds. I focussed on reading the navigation information on the GPS to home in on our first search position as we sped along at about 25 knots, bang on-track on the GPS LCD Highway. Ewan stood behind me with an eye on the echo sounder.

"About a mile to go, Ewan", I called above the din of the outboard engine as we closed on the first waypoint marking the perimeter of the GPS search box. Ewan had his eyes glued to the echo sounder, peering over my shoulder, and when we were still about half a mile short of the search box, he suddenly called out: "Wait a minute, Rod, turn and go back – we just went over something big."

I had been focussed on the GPS and hadn't noticed anything, but I immediately throttled down the boat, turned and retraced our steps along our wake. The bottom trace of the echo sounder kicked in now that we were off the plane – scrolling out a good trace at about 65 metres. Suddenly, the trace leapt up to about 55 metres. There was indeed something big down there rising up for about 30 feet. I punched the MOB ('man over board') button on the GPS to mark the position forever and then slowed to a stop.

We threw over one of our pre-weighted coils of rope with a large pink Dhan buoy on it. The weight plummeted downwards and soon we saw that it had snagged on the wreck. A gentle ripple from it betrayed the current working on the line.

We motored slowly around the wreck site punching in a couple of other high points into the GPS. We dropped another couple of weighed Dhan buoys at the opposite ends of the wreck. The orientation of the buoys revealed the line or direction that the wreck was lying in as though it were floating on the surface. She lay north east/south west and was very, very large. Using the GPS to measure her distance we traced along the top of the wreck between the buoys. She was in excess of 500 feet long. This could only be the *Remuera* and we had found it by chance, right on the southern most limit of the box we were going to search in, without even having to put the magnetometer in the water.

We tied off to one of the buoys and ate some lunch, the long sought after *Remuera* lying hidden from view more than 200 feet beneath us.

The following weekend we had three boatloads of enthusiastic technical divers (almost our whole team) zipping out to the site, gases laboriously mixed during the week. We had Chris Allen and his new Tornado RIB, my Humber Destroyer RIB and Richard Colliar who had bought my last RIB from me. We had about nine divers in total.

The North Sea is a very exposed place to be and the very northeast tip of Scotland around Fraserburgh is particularly exposed to bad seas and wind from most directions. This day the wind seemed too much and the seas just a bit too big, but with three boats and nine divers all keyed up for the biggest dive of the year, it was going to take something more than a Force 5–6 to stop us.

Our small flotilla of orange dive boats set off from Rosehearty and bumped and bashed the nine or so miles along to the wreck site. The journey wasn't too bad at all – my Humber Destroyer seemed to devour seas like this. I was probably making about 15 knots, bouncing from wave to wave and looking ahead to read the seas, when the black back and fin of a minke whale surfaced right in front of my boat about 15 feet ahead – it was cruising directly across our path. I had to do a quick slow down and swerve to avoid running right over it.

Once we got out on site above the wreck we anchored into it. As we all wanted to dive it, and we had only one bespoke boat handler out, we were going to divide the dive into two waves. The first wave would dive whilst the second wave gave boat cover. Once the first wave was up and back safely in the boats, then the second wave would go in.

The sea conditions were rough with a big swell running – probably no more than a Force 5 but exposed eight miles offshore out there, this was right at the limit of small boat diving. It wasn't going to be pleasant for those left in the anchored boats. We discussed the situation and agreed that the first wave would go in and then we'd review the position and make a call after they were out of the water. If the conditions worsened then we might have to abort. As Ewan and I had found the wreck, we were going in on the first wave along with Dave Gordon and Jim Burke. The others stayed topside pitching about in our boats, Dave Hadden handling my boat.

As ever, no matter how rough sea conditions are, as soon as we were under water the topside traumas were forgotten about as the dive unfolded. The surface conditions only really affect you down for the first 5 metres or so.

We started the descent to the wreck in crystal clear, greenish water and at about 50 metres I saw the wreck materialising out of the gloom, reaching up towards us and beckoning us down.

We were however, immediately disappointed – we had hoped for a Hollywood-style wreck sitting on its keel. Instead we got a wreck lying almost upside down on one side – the upmost side of which had largely collapsed downwards. We could tell we were on the collapsed side of a great ship, but even in the crystal clear visibility of some 25 metres (which meant no lights were necessary), it was so vast that as there were no obvious immediate clues, we couldn't tell which way was forward and which way aft.

Ewan and I finned along the gunwale of the wreck looking upwards at the crumpled ship's side, which looked like a mountain range beyond and above us. We finned for about 150 feet or more but still didn't manage to find one end of the ship. It was big indeed and the side we were swimming along was lined with rows of portholes, many with their glasses still in them.

We had agreed topside, to return to the line to ascend because in these poor sea conditions with such a large swell, there was a possibility that our surface cover might not see our deco marker buoys if we did a free hanging, drifting decompression. So we turned and finned back to the starting point – the downline with its strobes flashing away being an easy marker in the good visibility. Jim Burke and Dave Gordon had gone to explore in the opposite direction and as we returned to the line they arrived back as well. We spent the last few minutes of our bottom time exploring the wreck around the foot of the downline before making our ascent.

Forty-five minutes later our heads broke surface and from our subsea calm and tranquillity, everything changed in an instant. Topside was a raging maelstrom, as large surging waves washed past our anchored boats lifting us divers and the boats together in one seamless movement. And worse – there were only two boats.

"Where's Richard gone, Dave?" I asked, concerned.

"His boat was getting swamped and he decided to bail out and head for Rosehearty. Conditions too bad for him mate – and it'll be a bugger getting you guys and your kit in."

Dave was right. As mountainous waves swept past us, my RIB was rising and falling considerably, the bow lifting out of the water before slamming back down heavily. If I got drifted under the hull I would be in serious danger.

"Cast off Dave and we'll drift – it'll be easier."

Dave untied us from the Dhan buoy as Ewan went to one side of the RIB and I the other. Free from the anchor, conditions were a bit easier for us to de-kit. One by one we got our stage tanks off and then our back twin sets, but it was still very difficult getting them into the boat.

Once Ewan and I were safely in the boat we motored back to the anchor line. Dave and Jim were already in Chris's boat and it was clear the second wave wasn't going to dive – caution being the better part of valour. I tried pulling up the anchor line but it was snagged solid on something. No wonder – it had had all four of us ascending on it and a boat tied to it in these conditions. Chris motored over in his Tornado asking: "Did you guys see the minke down there? It surfaced right beside my RIB whilst I was tied off – I leaned over and could touch it." Dave Gordon chipped in: "Sorry, Rod, you're not going to get that anchor back I'm afraid.

Seeing the conditions, to make sure we didn't pull it off the wreck on our ascent and to fix it for the second wave, I popped the anchor through an open porthole. There is no way that anchor with its open flukes is coming back up through that porthole – sorry, but it's gone."

I wasn't aware he'd done that down on the wreck but could understand his logic. He didn't know the second wave would abort. I took out my knife and cut the rope and pulled the Dhan buoy inboard. We'll find it easy enough on our next dive, I thought. In fact it took five years before my now-rusted and rather frail anchor and chain was recovered by Mike Rosie and returned to me. I lost it on another wreck shortly afterwards!

In the event, we didn't return to the *Remuera* until 2002, when we had a couple of fantastic dives on her in glorious visibility. By now we had all purchased our Aquazepp underwater scooters – long, thin bright orange torpedo like scooters with a propeller at the stern and a headlamp at the front. The scooter clips to your harness and can drag you through the water very comfortably at just over 2 knots. On our Zepps we were effortlessly able to tour the *Remuera* and get a feel for her layout. We found she lies on her port side with her bows facing to the west. Her hull is collapsing but some large sections remain intact around her boiler room.

As we have explored this wreck, our initial disappointment at her somewhat collapsed remains has been replaced with wonder – we have become familiar with her over the course of some 20 dives. She is truly one of Scotland's finest wrecks.

Although the wreck lies on its port side, the front bow section, for some 50 feet back from the stem must have sheared and twisted (but not detached) as she sank. The bow section now lies in the same straight line as the rest of the ship – but it is lying on its starboard side, i.e. the opposite side to the rest of the ship. Only catastrophic torpedo damage during the air attack could have led to this dramatic result. The uppermost portside anchor is still held snugly in its hawse.

The uppermost starboard side of the main section of the wreck has collapsed down so that the starboard guardrail is now only a few metres from the seabed. Around the vicinity of the boiler room however, the hull has kept its shape creating a large cavern, which can be safely penetrated. On one dive in 2005 Ewan and I found that our shot-line had snagged right beside the boiler room and in good clear visibility of 25 metres we could see an easy access right into the room. We gunned our Aquazepp scooters and moved forward into the opening in single file. As we moved from the brightness of deep open water into the dark confines of the hull we could see, far to our right towards the stern, shafts of bright green light marking an exit route. Four massive boilers lay tumbled on top of each other on the seabed and above us the rotted ship's side seemed to be lying directly on top of them.

> We moved into a gap between the 25-foot high boilers and started to thread our way astern in the darkness through the boilers. As we moved astern, the bright green opening of our planned exit point loomed larger and larger, until finally we were able to move through a rotted piece of collapsed ship's side and into the now exposed engine room, where her large engine lay covered in soft corals and anemones.

We moved further aft on top of collapsed hull plating intent on getting to the very stern and finding out if the rudder and propellers were still visible, our underwater scooters dragging us gently through the water at a steady 2 knots. As the keel of the ship to our left, swept back towards the stern, we came across a three-bladed and rather delicate starboard propeller standing high and proud of the seabed. As I stared at the propeller I saw the tip of one of the blades of the lower port side propeller sticking out of sand; the prop being almost completely buried in the seabed. The rudder itself lay flat on the seabed nearby having fallen there as the ship collapsed.

Moving round the very stern of the crumpled wreck I looked up: silhouetted against the light of the distant surface were fishermen's nets, snagged on the wreck aeons ago, straining on their buoys as they tried to reach for the surface. I wouldn't want to surface under them by mistake in poor visibility.

The very stern itself originally had a superstructure that rose up for many deck levels and was lined by dozens of portholes. A lot of this superstructure has now rotted away or been crushed beneath the wreck but (like the *Trsat* not far away) the porthole locker is still recognisable, with neatly stacked spare porthole glasses still secured for transport.

The top of the wreck is at about 55 metres and if we're not making our way back to the shot-line to ascend we swim up to the high part above the boiler room and then fire off our delayed deco bags as we fin upwards from there. On one dive I made the same bad move that I had done years before on the *Hampshire* by firing off my bag with its 50 metres of line from a depth of 55 metres. It was a short but dramatic elevator ride up to 50 metres. Evolution is a slow process.

Even though we have dived this wreck many times over the years, we have struggled to understand it completely. The whole hull is there, canted over on its port side so that it is almost upside down. But there is no trace of the vast central midships deckhouse rising up five deck levels and fronted by the bridge. Perhaps it lies crumpled and buried beneath the hull itself. Perhaps the aerial torpedo that sent the liner to her grave destroyed the massive superstructure. But of the five-deck level high superstructure, lined with hundreds of portholes there is just no obvious trace.

One dive on her in 2008 found us sitting over the wreck with two RIBs and six divers getting dressed to dive. We had high hopes of getting good visibility out here, eight miles off the land, as the visibility in the harbour had been crystal clear and out here it should be even better. As I finished getting all my gear on – my rebreather, stage tanks and all the paraphernalia needed – I looked over the side of the RIB and could see the shot-line heading down into the depths for some way. The underwater visibility did look exceptionally good.

I rolled over backwards into the water and started heading down the shot with my buddy Paul Haynes. I had met Paul and dived with him a couple of times about ten years earlier when he had just come out of the Royal Marines and was taking up a sales position with Divex (one of the world leaders in supplying commercial and military subsea equipment) at a crucial time for the Stealth Clearance Diver Life Support System rebreather (SCDLSS), which had been under development by Divex for many years. Paul had served 13 years in the Royal Marines, over half of which were spent in the Special Forces, but he was now heavily involved in marketing the Stealth to navies around the world as it took over from the older American Mk16. He also provided the training for it.

I hadn't seen Paul after those few dives years before until, by chance, he came along on one day of a weekend's mixed gas dive trip my group had set up out of Fraserburgh on Bill Ruck's

Dive buddy Paul Haynes, ready for a South China Sea dive.

boat *Top Cat* in 2006. I invited Paul to join our group and very soon he had become a very valuable and skilled member of the team. Working in the commercial dive world, Paul had acquired an intricate technical knowledge of practically every piece of dive equipment ever invented. He also was the BSAC technical diving advisor and his understanding of delicate medical diving aspects was unparalleled. Like most service personnel I have dived with, Paul was sound in the water, extremely capable and versatile in dealing with any challenge. A shade under 6' tall, an extremely fit man now in his early 40s, he was a black belt in three martial arts and pretty handy on the guitar.

But the good topside visibility quickly got poorer as we descended and by 20 metres down it was getting cloudy and really dark. Come 30 metres down, I was cocooned in darkness – all I could see of him was the beam of his powerful torch.

We were both using our Aquazepp scooters, so I switched on the headlamp and gunned the throttle and allowed it to pull me down beside the shot-line into the darkness. Periodically I swept the beam from the small torch I keep on my mask strap over my depth gauge. The numbers were scrolling by: 35 metres; 45 metres; and 55 metres. Still complete darkness – it was hard to see the hand on the end of my arm. This wasn't going to be the grand tour on scooters in beautiful visibility I had promised Paul.

And then the nose of my scooter suddenly hit metal – I hadn't seen the wreck coming up in the darkness and had bumped into it before I saw it. Worse, even though the nose of my scooter was touching the wreck I still couldn't see it in front of me. But I did recognise the dim curl of steel high up beside me to my right – it was the section of hull that is crumpled down over the boilers. At least I still knew where I was.

Paul landed beside me – this was his first dive on the *Remuera* so I knew he would have no idea where he was. He told me later that he landed in silty sand and put his hand down to steady himself. He felt something smooth in the sand under his hand and shone his torch downwards. White bones were sticking out of the sand. Oh no, he thought: human remains. As he looked at the bone it dawned on him that what he was looking at was far too massive to be human – it was the big bone of a beast like a cow. He had in fact landed in the refrigerated hold, which had been filled with a cargo of refrigerated beef on the bone. As he swept his torch around he could see other cattle bones sticking up here and there from the silt.

Once I realised I was kneeling on the sand at the gunwale just forward of the boiler room I knew that to take Paul up towards the bow we could just follow the gunwale to our left. We gunned our scooters and started off.

But very soon my headlamp beam started to yellow and dim, the tell tale sign of the battery dying. As I lost power I saw the halo of light surrounding Paul on his scooter disappearing forward to the bow. I had no way to attract his attention or of catching up with him. In an instant we were separated – alone in poor pitch-black visibility, more than 200 feet beneath the surface.

The motor on my scooter quickly got so weak that it was struggling to turn the prop at all and had completely stopped pulling me through the water. I gave up with it and started swimming back along the guardrail towards the boiler room and shot-line, laboriously dragging the dead scooter. As I finally reached the line, Paul arrived beside me having turned and retraced his steps when he realised I was no longer with him. In the poor visibility I was relieved to eventually see our strobes blinking away on the downline to lead us back up to the surface – at least we would be away from the nets which billowed unseen above us somewhere in the darkness towards the stern.

Our group of divers contacted the *Remuera*'s insurers who had paid out following her loss during World War II. They were still the legal owners of the wreck and were quite happy to sell the wreck to us. A deal was easily and quickly agreed and ownership passed to our group.

The *Remuera* is the largest and most important wreck in the area and part of our purpose in buying the wreck was to make sure that it is preserved for the future. The propellers and engine would be valuable salvage material and might attract the attention of salvers. We will make sure that does not happen and that the wreck will remain the way it is for future generations of divers to enjoy. We are happy for other divers to dive our wreck but would simply ask that nothing be removed from it.

In any event, lying eight miles offshore in 65 metres of water in an extremely exposed section of the coast she is not easily dived and will seldom be visited.

CHAPTER TEN

STONEHAVEN SHIPWRECKS

Directly out towards Norway from Stonehaven harbour there is a cluster of four deep-water shipwrecks which local fishermen call the 'five mile wrecks'. We had dived one of these – the SS *Cushendall* – on air to 58 metres in the early 1990s. Although some of the team had got onto the wreck, I had been overcome by narcosis and fooled into thinking that I was having a buoyant ascent. I have no recollection of what happened between leaving the bottom at 58 metres and the return of awareness at 38 metres. But now we had virtually narcosis-free Trimix we wanted to find the other local wrecks and dive them. The wreck we had found, dived and identified as the sizeable 626-ton *Cushendall* was listed in the old Hydrographic Department print-out I had, as the small 158-ton British steamship *Matador* lost on 9 October 1924 at 56 59 24.00N, 002 04 22.00W. To add further confusion, local fishermen called it the *Gowrie*. The *Cushendall* herself was listed by the Hydrographic Department as lying at 56 57 39.00N, 002 04 00.00W – the closest inshore of the three wrecks charted and some two miles south of where she actually lay: an understandable error from the days of dead reckoning.

The 689-ton SS *Gowrie* was a World War II loss listed by the Hydrographic Department as lying two miles further south of the *Matador* (now confirmed as the *Cushendall*) and just over a mile further east to seaward at 56 57 24.00N, 002 01 42.00W. When I checked Bob Baird's reference book *Shipwrecks of the Forth* (1st edition, 1993) he suggested that the *Matador* was in fact a 395.7ft long steamship weighing in at a mighty 4,761 gross tons and gave the same date of loss as the Hydrographic Department: 9 October 1924. I suspected that that reference was incorrect, as if there was such a large vessel lying so close to Stonehaven, then the local fisher-men would know all about it. Nevertheless, if Bob Baird was correct and there was a 4,761-ton steamship right on our doorstep then we would be happy divers for a very long time.

The vessel we had dived, the SS *Cushendall* (charted as the *Matador*), was the northmost of the triangle of three charted wrecks. She had been built in 1904 to an old design and was a distinctive, Victorian era style vessel. She had been easy to identify on subsequent Trimix survey dives. As a complete contrast, the SS *Gowrie*, although built just six years later in 1910, had been built along far more modern lines for the Dundee Perth & London Shipping Co Ltd – a shipping line still alive and well today. She was the DP&L's only loss during World War II. The photographs I sourced of the two vessels showed two ships that couldn't look more different. In fact, the *Gowrie* was such a modern ship that she wouldn't look out of place tied up in a port nowadays. Try as I could I couldn't trace a photograph of either the Hydrographic Department's 158-ton SS *Matador* or Bob Baird's 4,761-ton SS *Matador*.

Our group determined to try to locate and dive the other two wrecks of the shipwreck triangle. As they were too deep for air diving, to the best of my knowledge neither had been dived at that time. We set up a dive on the inshore southmost wreck of the triangle – erroneously charted as the *Cushendall*. Which vessel would it be?

Once we got ourselves out to the right area for the charted wreck, after a brief search we soon passed over a sizeable wreck, which clearly showed up on our echo sounder. Six divers splashed into the water from two RIBs and made the descent in poor visibility – and by the time we got down on the wreck it was a uniform pitch black. The anchor lay on the sand just a few feet from the very tip of the bow of a large ship, which was lying on its port side. I swept my torch around the seabed looking for the lucky sight of a bell, fallen from the fo'c'stle to lie on the seabed. But there was no sign of a bell – only scattered pieces of coal littering the seabed.

Ewan and I were the first of our group to get down on the wreck and we started to move aft from the bow. We passed by a large open hold on its side like a rectangular cave, black and ominous inside. Like the *Cushendall*, here too was a vertical column of trawl nets spun hard and still suspended on their buoys. As I swept my torch upwards, the column rose up beyond the limit of my beam.

I moved up to the upper starboard side of the hull and started to see the very characteristic gunwales and scuppers of the *Gowrie*, straight out of a black and white 60 year old photograph I had of her. There was no mistaking this wreck.

We moved beyond the foredeck hold and arrived at a now horizontal bridge superstructure. The upper levels of this superstructure had largely rotted away however the helm was still *in situ*, its spokes – some bent, others broken – radiating outwards. The telemotor pedestal was still firmly bolted to what would have been the bridge floor but now projected outwards on its side in open water, the walls and roof of the bridge having long ago completely rotted away.

The SS Gowrie *– the wreck in Stonehaven Bay is perhaps one of the most beautiful wrecks on the east coast of Scotland. (World Ship Society)*

Behind the bridge deckhouse was a circular funnel opening and then the pitched roof of an engine room. Shining my torch in through the fanlights of its small, pitched roof, I easily picked out the complete triple expansion engine still projecting out horizontally above the ground on the centre line of the vessel with catwalks ringing around it.

There seemed plenty of room to move around inside the engine room, but the fanlights – which make entry to engine rooms on bigger vessels easy – were too small to allow entry in our bulky technical rigs. I vowed to return another day and find my way into the engine room – but it would be several years before I managed to do so.

After making it round the whole wreck, Ewan and I made our way back to the anchor line, led there by the blinking of the strobe we had velcroed to it. Each pulse of its rhythmic flashing lit up the inky darkness momentarily. As I grabbed hold of the line and started to make my way up, with my night vision now well kicked in I could make out the silhouette of almost half of the wreck lying there in the darkness. Once I was 15 metres up the line, I spotted in the distance below me the other four divers slowly making their way back along the wreck to the anchor line, their torch beams flashing around in the dark. Stonehaven wreck number 2: identified.

The last of the charted 5-mile wrecks was the outside wreck of the triangle. We had now identified the *Gowrie* and *Cushendall* – so this must be the *Matador*, which was either a 158-ton or 4,761-ton steamship. Either way it would be an exciting dive we thought. We started to plan a dive, but life intervened, time passed and it was a few years later before I got organised enough to dive the suspected *Matador*.

One fine evening in 2000 our dive group of two RIBs with four divers arrived over the *Matador* and we anchored into it in about 68 metres. Disappointingly, the trace on the echo sounder revealed a small wreck – not the promised 4,761-ton steamship. But it was still a virgin wreck dive.

We had with us Chris Allen – a former Chairman of the BSAC and experienced technical diver who had returned to Stonehaven after living abroad for some time – and a new younger diver, Tony Ray – who had just qualified as a Trimix diver and joined our group. Tony was more than ten years younger than me and had come into diving not that many years previously. With a quick mind and an intricate technical ability from his work in the oil world, he had quickly and easily progressed to become a scuba instructor before moving to technical diving. This was his first non-training, Trimix dive – and his deepest to date. And a virgin wreck was getting thrown in to boot.

Although Ewan and I had located this new wreck, we asked if Chris and Tony wanted to go down in the first wave and be the first divers to see and touch it. They jumped at the chance – it was to be Tony's first virgin wreck dive. When they came back an hour later, they reported a small shipwreck sitting upright.

Ewan and I then dived and found that it was an old steam ship, possibly a trawler and about 125 feet long at most. The small wheelhouse had completely disintegrated and we were left with the simple hull, deck stringers and ribs. It was a pity we hadn't found a big steamship, but at least the final part of the jigsaw had been added ... or so we thought.

In the summer of 2004 the underwater visibility along our east coast had improved to an average of 20 metres. It was chalk and cheese compared to the usual five-metre pitch-black visibility we get in the winter and spring months. We decided to get in as much diving as we could on our local deep-water wrecks and high on the list was a return to the beautiful wreck of the SS *Gowrie*. Completely intact and lying on her port side in just over 60 metres of water, she had turned out to be a jewel of a wreck: one of the finest on the east coast of Scotland. Our first dive on her six years earlier and the few subsequent dives we enjoyed on her had all been explorations around the outside of the wreck. This dive would be different.

After arriving in our boats above her wreck, five miles offshore in a languid swell, we managed to snag into her with our shot-line. I was diving in a threesome with Tony Ray and Jim Burke. Dave Hadden would be staying topside to boat handle. An experienced deep air diver, I was always happy when Dave was boat handling – you knew there wouldn't be any complications topside.

The three of us splashed into the water and finned over to the shot-line for the descent. As I looked down the line I could see it disappearing a long way below before it merged with the underwater background.

As we made the slow descent into the darkness below our eyes adjusted to the fading ambient light from above. At about 35 metres down I saw the top of the five-foot thick column of spun nets that rises up from the bow. The nets are now covered in sea life and rock hard – they are little danger to us. But at least I knew where we were in relation to the wreck, which was still far below us and out of sight.

As we pressed on down my depth gauge scrolled out the increasing depth. As I got to about 45 metres the dark blurred outline of the uppermost starboard side of the wreck started to materialise out of the gloom. Straight man-made lines and sharp angles contrasted with nature's smooth rounded shapes.

I slowed my descent and landed on the hull near the guardrail. Tony and Jim arrived beside me and after a round of 'OK' hand signals we moved out over the now vertical deck and started to drop the remaining 10 metres to the seabed. We were right beside the massive single hold, now long empty of any cargo.

The *Gowrie* was a simple ship. A single massive refrigerated cargo hold forward and all the superstructure and engine room right at the very stern. So aft it was for us this day.

We finned along the seabed past the familiar small delicate pitched roof of the engine room. Looking inside through the fan lights I saw the triple expansion engine still sitting there on the centre line of the vessel – still defying gravity just as it had been when I had seen it first six years earlier.

We passed the now horizontal helm, with its bent and buckled spokes, the bridge walls and roof that would have surrounded it, long ago disintegrated and disappeared. As I looked downwards from the helm, I was staggered to see the unmistakeable outline of the ship's telegraph head and pedestal lying flat on the seabed – the white circular face stared up me with bold black letters ringing around it. I had never noticed it in that spot on previous dives; perhaps it had been buried and only now exposed by the continuously shifting sand of the seabed.

I dropped down to look at it more carefully and could easily read the lettering on the faceplate: 'Mechans Limited, Scotstoun, Glasgow'. The brass pointer was at 'stand by' – just as it had been following the attack by German planes 60 years earlier.

Beside the telegraph was the unmistakeable shape of a compass binnacle half buried in the shale, hard under the deeper port side of the vessel. The bridge superstructure, which had projected outwards here, had apparently collapsed aeons ago, spilling its innards onto the seabed.

Scattered here and there were 2-inch thick slabs of reinforced concrete. Like the bituminous bricks on top of the bridge superstructure of the MS *Taurus* these concrete slabs would have been layered on top of the bridge superstructure as a cheap but effective form of armour plating against machine gun fire from aircraft.

Moving on, I passed the large 4–5 foot wide circular opening where the funnel had once stood. Funnels are always made of the lightest of steel and don't usually stand up well to long immersion in seawater – they usually rot away fairly quickly. There was no trace of the funnel itself, only the black circular opening into the hull.

Moving further aft we arrived at the very stern where there was quite a scene of devastation with parts of ship lying all over the place. I was puzzled because there was only a small section of plating missing from the very tip of the stern of the *Gowrie*. It seemed to me that there was just too much wreckage lying around here – but more of that later. I swept my torch over the stern and saw that there was a vertical opening in the hull some 8 feet high by about 3 feet wide. There had been no obvious sign of any damage from the bombing attack elsewhere on the vessel, but the missing bit of the stern allied to the general mess of wreckage lying around the stern seemed a clear indication that a bomb struck near here. 'What's inside the wreck here?' I wondered.

I motioned to Jim and Tony that I was going to have a look inside and swam over until I hung in front of a diver sized entry point into the hull. It was a neat fit but I felt I could easily pass inside. I moved closer and swept my torch around inside the hull, lighting up the cavernous space of the whole engine room. It seemed in good condition with no visible snags to worry about, other than some ancient encrusted electric cabling hanging down. I squeezed through the gap and was immediately inside the engine room.

A diver who enters a wreck that is not sitting on its keel must conceive of space differently than he would do simply walking around a ship topside. The *Gowrie* lies completely on her port side. So to try and understand where you are inside a wreck orientated like this, you have to think in three dimensions. You look at what you're seeing and then try in your mind to rotate it 90 degrees. The port side steel wall of the hull had become the floor. Decks were now impenetrable vertical sheets of steel rising from the seabed all the way up to the starboard side of the hull (now the roof).

Once you penetrate a wreck you must remember everything you do – every little nuance of a turn in direction – for every movement you make has a consequence. A number of small movements can throw off your sense of direction and prevent you finding the way back out. You remember every turn, every movement: up, down, along to the right, to the left.

The scene unfolding before you confuses your mind. It's hard to take it all in when your normal frames of reference are all skewed out by 90 degrees. You try to memorise every obvious or recognisable piece of metal you see, to allow you to retrace your path through the twisted innards of the wreck to the illusive 'safety' of clear open water outside. It may be safer outside but you are still more than 200 feet beneath the surface of the water and in great danger.

Serious wreck penetration requires ropes, reels and cave-diving techniques. For those divers who don't reel in and just wing it, danger lurks close at hand. Without ropes or reel, if you lose your bearings and sense of direction inside a wreck you will become disorientated, perhaps searching for the way out in the wrong direction. If your navigation slips; if your memory gets confused or falters – problems loom. As soon as the worm turns and you think: "Was it right here – or left?" you are in difficulty. One simple wrong turn takes you into an unrecognisable part of the ship where you haven't been before. With nothing you recognise it's simple to make yet another wrong turn, hopeful of seeing something familiar, but you just become even more lost deep inside the rotting carcass of a ship forgotten for 60 years. The futility of your situation flashes across your mind, the first flush of a panicked desperation courses through your body. You are lost inside the pitch darkness of a shipwreck.

A diver lost inside a shipwreck is in grave danger. Even when not lost, a diver is aware of a potential wave of panic lying just beneath the conscious. You may be in control, buoyancy nicely adjusted and all your equipment working – but you know that panic is never far away. And it just takes one small thing to start off a chain reaction that can lead to disaster. The mind – even whilst you are in control – plays an insidious game with you when you are alone in the bowels of a rotted shipwreck.

Closed-circuit rebreather divers worry constantly about a possible build-up of carbon dioxide that can lead to a potentially lethal carbon dioxide hit ('CO_2 hit'). Rapid breathing (when you never seem to be able to draw a proper breath to fill your lungs), racing heart rate, erratic behaviour, tunnel vision, disorientation and death are all never far away when you get a CO_2 hit. In diving we say you are always only three breaths from death. Once you start getting a bit paranoid inside a shipwreck, it's easy to convince yourself that you are starting to experience a CO_2 hit. Even thinking you are in trouble can cause unfortunate events to start to unfold. You worry about a myriad of potential problems such as entanglement in hanging electric cables or entrapment by some rotted bulkhead falling on you. The worm turns and you feel the first surge of panic rising. Suddenly your veneer of control seems wafer thin. You know the demon is there, waiting to snare you. As panic sets in so your problems escalate. If you're diving on a rebreather, which continuously recycles the gas you are breathing (instead of venting it off in open-circuit), running out of breathing gas quickly isn't such a big problem as it can be if using an open circuit. A rebreather allows you to stay down a lot longer, but even if you find your way out the decompression time to surface stretches out the longer and the deeper you are down. Your heart rate races up to over 120 beats per minute.

A diver inside a wreck also has to contend with visibility issues. In the clear blue waters of the Pacific when you can see for 200 feet it's easy to see the whole room that you are in and see ways out in the distance. But in the North Sea our visibility underwater is often 8 feet – or less. At best in the good months of late summer we can see 10–20 metres. But the *Gowrie* lies in more than 60 metres of water and so at most times of the year all trace of ambient light is filtered out by microscopic sea life and particles held in suspension in the water. No sunlight makes it down to light up our surroundings. It is black – and not black as in walking downtown at night in streetlamps black. I mean *black* as in walking in a country lane at night when there is no moon and not being able to see the tarmac or where you are putting your feet. I mean *pitch black* – and that's *outside* the wreck. *Inside* it always seems even blacker – as if that is possible. In the good months for visibility our powerful torches can light up large swathes of the wreck – but in poor visibility in pitch-black conditions when you can only see 8 feet in your torch beam, it's easy to get disorientated and lost. And what if your torch battery dies…

To make matters worse a shipwreck is filled with silt and debris. The diver's slightest movement; a kick of a fin, banging into a bulkhead in the darkness or even a simple turn to memorise a landmark, can cause what divers call a 'silt out'. Silt billows up to engulf a diver and rob him of the last traces of visibility. If a diver is diving open-circuit his exhaust bubbles (instead of being recycled as with a rebreather) are vented off as he exhales. As the bubbles rush up towards the surface they collide with some force against the roof of the room the diver is in. Silt and particles of rust are dislodged and start literally to rain down on top of the diver. To keep from disturbing the deep silt layering the bottom of a wreck, divers have developed a range of finning techniques – each has his own preferred way of passing through a shipwreck with the least disturbance. Some divers like to get right down on the bottom of the room or corridor they are in and then, without kicking with their fins, take hold of something solid and effortlessly propel themselves smoothly along using only these handholds, their legs and fins floating motionless in the water behind them. Other divers like to fin along well above the bottom of the room to try and let the downdraught of their fin strokes lose some of its power before it hits the silt. Other divers use finning techniques developed by cave divers to stop the down draught of their fin strokes reaching the floor. The cave diver's 'frog kick' forces the propelled water out to the side instead of downwards. Some divers will fin with only one leg making sure that the other redundant fin is right under the moving fin so that it receives and dissipates the downdraught.

The innards of a shipwreck don't look anything like you see at the movies. There is nothing glamorous inside a wreck. It's dark, oily, silty, dangerous and filled with serious hazards. Shipwrecks are rusting hulks and every now and then something falls off them – and it's always downwards. Good wreck divers always have a careful look around with their torches a long way above them, to see what hazards are up there before they venture inside. Whole sections of shipwrecks can collapse – the unlucky diver inside when that happens doesn't stand a chance.

Scapa Flow attracts thousands of divers each year and because of this concentration of diving, has seen its fair share of fatalities from wreck penetration. Several years ago two divers got lost and drowned inside one of the four massive upside down 600-ton gun turrets of the 28,000-ton battleship *Bayern* (the four turrets had not been secured for lifting during salvage operations in the 1930s and when the wreck was accidentally overfilled with air the turrets dropped out of their mounts as the wreck shot to the surface).

A diver was lost just a few years ago far inside the upturned wreck of the battleship *König*, his body only being found by chance two years later despite detailed searches by police divers at the time. Another diver was lost inside the light cruiser *Dresden* a few years ago and failed to surface. A search located his weight belt lying on the seabed inside the wreck and he was then found jammed inside an opening at the top of the room, which was too small to let him through and out to safety. Having lost his weight belt and floated up to the ceiling, he was perhaps unable to get low enough down to allow him to pass out the way he entered.

The armoured door of the fire control tower of the light cruiser *Karlsruhe* fell from its rotted hinges without warning and landed on top of an unfortunate diver passing by below. This was no ordinary door but an armoured door, some 3.8 inches thick of best German steel. It was extremely heavy and pinned the unfortunate diver to the seabed. He was unable to move it himself but thankfully help arrived and the door was moved, the diver living to tell the tale.

On the wreck of the *Taurus* when I first dived it in the early 1990s, I went into the galley at the rear of the engine room superstructure. I moved inside some 30–40 feet and had a good look around. When I went back the next year I could hardly find the doorway as it had been crushed along with the whole of the deckhouse by the immense weight of the 100-foot long, 4-foot thick tubular steel main mast. This mast had collapsed down in the past and now lies on top of the deckhouse. I hadn't seen the mast in the poor visibility the first time I dived it. The galley, from being about 7–8 feet high from floor to roof, was now about 4 foot high – and is no doubt even smaller now. Shipwrecks are falling to pieces all the time – you just need to be in the wrong place at the wrong time.

In the violence of a ship's sinking, bulkheads give way, walls are buckled and large pieces of machinery are thrown about. Once on the seabed, over time the mountings for electric cables and wires rot and the cables fall to hang silent and dangerous, blocking routes through the wreck. Everywhere, bent spars – rusted and sharpened to a knife-edge – stick out at awkward angles offering easy injury or damage to vital life support kit.

Once tangled, the worst thing a diver can do is to thrash around without thinking. A diver should pause, see where the entanglement is and then deal with it slowly and carefully. We were taught to stop, not move and just take three long deep breaths to try to calm down and then assess the situation. If you have been using a reel to lay a guideline in (and back), it may just be that line that has got wrapped round your legs – a simple job to get free if you have a buddy diver with you. A panicking diver looks death in the face – and our evolutionary instinct of fight or flight kicks in. A panicked diver thrashes around, twisting and turning without thinking in an effort to break free. The situation goes from bad to worse. A silt-out is one of the common consequences of entanglement. Blinded, the diver panics even more and the situation gets even worse. Rarely is it the danger that kills a diver – it is the diver's response to the danger that does the job. Badly entangled, wrapped up in wires or cables, there will come a point where the diver gives up the struggle to free himself and waits silently and patiently for his breathing gas to run out. To dive alone inside a shipwreck can be to die alone. But I digress – back to the story.

Before going inside – alone, without ropes and breaking all the rules – I had signalled to Tony and Jim what I was going to do. I was just going to have a wee peak in and wasn't intent on venturing far inside. They gave me an 'OK' signal back and continued with their dive round past the rudder and prop to the keel side of the wreck. As the darkness swallowed them and they hove out of my view I was left alone contemplating a solo penetration into the unknown at a depth of 60 metres – just over 200 feet. If anything went wrong neither of them would be there to help me out. I was on my own.

I moved tentatively inside, squeezing my body and stage tanks slung under my arms in through the rotted metal on either side, avoiding the hanging electric cables. After concentrating on what I was doing to avoid entanglement, I was suddenly through the restriction and into the large space of the engine room, some 25–30 feet high and disappearing ahead of me out of the range of my torch. Directly ahead of me, the triple expansion engine – which I had only seen previously from outside – dominated the room. It projected horizontally outwards from the now vertical floor of the room and was suspended some 3 metres above the lowermost port side of the hull. Catwalks ringed around the engine block. I swept my torch up to the uppermost starboard side of the hull, now far above me. A row of small portholes with their opening glass still in them allowed small weak beams of green light to penetrate into the room.

I moved forward and swam around freely on both the (now vertical) upper and lower deck levels of the engine room, tracing the workings of the triple expansion engine. It looked in pristine condition – as if it wouldn't take much to get it fired up again.

After several minutes exploring inside I had something of a reality check. I was 60 metres down and alone inside the wreck of a small steamship with my allocated bottom time fast running out. The entry point had been quite tight and I didn't want to experience any difficulty getting out. The end of a dive is not a good time to get snagged – it was time to go.

But then, way ahead of me in the distance at the foremost part of the engine room I saw a familiar 4–5 foot wide perfectly circular area of lighter green water – it was the funnel opening. 'I wonder,' I thought: 'could I get out through there?'

I finned over to the funnel – there were no obstructions and it was the perfect exit point, even though it looked a bit of a squeeze to get through. Sweeping my arms backwards to trim in my stage tanks and deco-reel, I finned slowly out through the opening and was once again outside the wreck in open water that seemed bright by contrast to where I had just been. It was magical.

Sound travels extremely well underwater and as divers we often shout to each other or conduct Donald Duck conversations due to the high helium content of our breathing gas. Floating on the deck-side of the wreck, I could hear grunts and whoops of excitement coming from Jim and Tony who were clearly having a great time on the keel side of the wreck having continued their exploration around from the stern. I finned up to the top of the steel mountain of the hull and soon saw Tony's bubble stream shimmering and billowing upwards. I finned towards the bubble stream and met their beaming faces as they finned up over the rounded hull towards me. It was time to leave this beautiful wreck. We had spent 20 minutes on the bottom exploring – and the penalty for that amount of bottom time at this depth would be a mind numbing 45 minutes of decompression stops before we could surface.

A few years later, in the summer of 2007 I was approached by a group of divers as I recovered my RIB at Gourdon harbour. They asked if I knew anything about a wreck of an armed steamer called the *Fernside*. I told them that I had never heard of this vessel. They mentioned that they had tried to dive the wreck known as the *Cushendall* – which by now we knew was in fact the *Gowrie* – and had located the bell. This information caused me a fair bit of self-doubt because although we had dived the *Cushendall* and the *Gowrie* for 10 or more years (and had photos of them both), we had never found a bell on either wreck. Here was a diver telling me they had found a defining bell on a wreck at the position of the *Cushendall*, aka the *Gowrie*. Something was very wrong.

I googled the *Fernside* and found that there was indeed an armed cargo ship of that name weighing in at 269 tons which had been lost during World War II. Its location was unknown.

It had last been seen leaving Hartlepool bound for Wick with a cargo of coal in on 26 February 1942. She was never seen again and a military Joint Arbitration Committee held her as lost on 27 February 1942, possibly bombed by German aircraft. There was no distress signal, no wreckage and no survivors from her eight crew and two DEMS (Defensively Equipped Merchant Ships) gunners.

It appeared that she was not charted as lost in any particular position – her wreck could be lying on the seabed anywhere between Hartlepool and Wick. Was it possible that this vessel had lain undetected in Stonehaven Bay for almost 70 years? Could I have mistaken a 269-ton cargo vessel with a cargo of coal for the much bigger 689-ton, 185 foot long *Gowrie* that I thought I knew every inch of? I had seen a lot of coal strewn across the seabed around the wreck we called the *Gowrie*. I had assumed that was her coal fuel for her boiler, but was it cargo from a hold spilled onto the seabed? Now that I came to think about it, the coalbunkers on the wreck we called *Gowrie* were intact – there shouldn't be coal strewn around the seabed from them.

It seemed impossible – but what were the alternatives? Had the bell of the *Fernside* somehow made it onto the *Gowrie* before she sank – a quick check of the dates of sinking revealed that the *Gowrie* had been sunk more than two years before the *Fernside* on 9 January 1940. So that ruled out that possibility.

I asked local Stonehaven fishermen whether it was possible that there was a 4th wreck 4–5 miles out in Stonehaven Bay in addition to the *Gowrie*, *Cushendall* and the one tentatively called the *Matador*. They said no – the bay was well fished and they would know if there was a 4th wreck out there. One local fisherman mentioned however that an old fisherman and former harbour master had always said that one of the wrecks was broken in two and it was possible to pass between both sections. We had dived all three charted wrecks and all were structurally intact. There was no wreck broken in two. He also mentioned that it was common to find coal in their nets whilst fishing around in the bay. There must be a lot of coal lying around to account for that – not just bunker coal. I started to wonder...

A posting by the divers in question on the Deeside Divers website reported that the wreck the *Fernside* bell was found on, lay on her port side and was quite broken up and still had her DEMS (defensive) gun on it. The hull of the wreck known as the *Matador* sat completely intact on her keel with all her superstructure rotted away. There was certainly no defensive gun on her. The *Gowrie* lay on her port side too – was that her? I thought that impossible – there was no defensive gun. But a niggle of doubt haunted me.

After getting myself thoroughly confused I decided to forget all about the *Fernside* as we moved into the season of 2008. I had promised to take some of our team who hadn't yet dived the *Gowrie* out to her. She is the most intact and beautiful shipwreck on the east coast of Scotland.

Stonehaven's Maritime Rescue Institute (MRI) is known worldwide for its search and rescue (SAR) training under the then leadership of the renowned rough water supremo Hamish McDonald. MRI provides SAR lifeboat cover for the sector from Newtonhill down to Johnshaven out offshore for 50 miles. It sits neatly between the sectors assigned for the Aberdeen and Montrose RNLI lifeboat stations. It's a little known fact that there are 32 independent lifeboat stations such as MRI around our coasts, MRI being the largest.

I had joined MRI as a lifeboat crewmember a year or two previously – and one of my fellow crewmen, Simon Chalmers had said he was keen to come out and be our regular boat handler. So in setting up the dive on the *Gowrie* we agreed to take him out and give him his first boat handling opportunity for us far offshore on a windy, overcast, August day in what turned out to be marginal Force 4–5 conditions.

The GPS led us out directly to the *Gowrie* and after 25 minutes of a bumpy ride out we were sorting out our shot-line and picking up the silhouette of the *Gowrie* on the echo sounder.

It was strong spring tides this day – and slack water would be two hours after Aberdeen High Water. The tide would still be flooding south immediately before slack water when we would dive. As slack water passed, the current would then turn to head north for the ebb. So, to make sure I got a good snag and that our shot didn't end up bouncing off the seabed away down south with the tide, I got Simon to motor slightly up current to the north before dropping my anchor, chain and extra weight. Once our shot was down on the seabed we let the tide drift us south over the wreck until we pulled the anchor and weight into the wreck and got a good snag.

Once we had a good snag I popped my head round the console and had a look at the GPS chart. For some reason, we seemed to be about 50 metres north of the wreck. That's not much on dry land, but underwater, to miss a wreck by 50 metres means you may not find it all in poor visibility. What's going on? Have we snagged a random piece of wreckage on the seabed north of the main wreck?

We tied a large Dhan buoy to the end of the downline and threw it into the water and then motored around the surface between the buoy and my GPS mark. Sure enough we were snagged on wreckage and there was the large silhouette of the hull of the *Gowrie* on the sounder. Maybe we'd just shotted the other end of it.

As slack water was approaching, rather than miss it we gave up trying to work out what was going on and started the laborious task of getting ourselves dressed in and ready to dive.

The seas had been settled for 3–4 days before the dive and we hoped that the visibility would be good far out here in the clean offshore water. Certainly, in the harbour the visibility had looked magnificent.

I peered over the side of the RIB at the downline and could see it snaking into the depths for at least 5 metres. It looked as though we might get decent visibility and my buddy Paul Haynes might get a good overview of the wreck. If the visibility was really good I would take him inside and along the Macdonald Route through the engine room from the stern to exit through the funnel.

We descended down the shot-line into darkness. For the first five metres or so down, the visibility was all right – but not as good as I had hoped for. By 15 metres down the water looked grainy with particles in suspension – in turn these were blotting out the light trying to reach down from the surface. By 25 metres down it was the standard pitch black of an east coast dive. Bugger. We pressed on down through 30 metres, 40 metres and at 50 metres I knew the wreck was somewhere very close to me just out of reach in the darkness. I swept my torch around me hoping for a glint of some piece of rusted metal I would recognise, which would let me know where on the wreck I was and allow me to get orientated.

In one sweep my light lit up a column of old trawl nets spun hard and encrusted with sea life. I assumed this was the column of nets snagged on the bow of the *Gowrie* that rises up some 15 metres. You often see them on ascent or descent – an unmistakeable tell tale marker for where you are. These nets looked different however.

I dropped further down and saw that the shot-line had actually gone through a gap in the column and was wrapped around it a few times. That was going to make freeing it at the end of the dive tricky. I pressed down and found that our anchor and chain were almost exactly at the foot of the column of nets amongst corroded, distressed metal beams that lay all over the place in a jumble. That was unusual as the area around the *Gowrie* bow where the

SS Fernside, *lost since World War II and discovered in Stonehaven Bay in 2007 by Deeside B.S.A.C.*

nets were snagged was intact and always very clear of debris. Never mind, wrecks collapse and decay all the time – maybe something like that had happened here over the winter's storms.

Reasonably confident that I knew where I was, I motioned to Paul that I was taking him up to the bow. We started off into the darkness laying out a line back to the shot from a reel. It was incredibly dark and outside our torch beams you could see nothing. With nets above us I didn't want to have to do a free ascent and get snagged unwittingly in them.

But as I moved forward I was instantly confused again – there was no bow here at all – just a mass of crumpled rotted steel, all jumbled up. Had a fisherman trawled into the wreck and caused some serious destruction? I moved on a few feet further and found myself looking at a rather small boiler. Now the *Gowrie*'s boiler is a scale bigger than this one and when I last saw it the summer before, it was safely housed inside an intact boiler room just forward of the engine at the stern of the ship. How could a boiler have been pulled out of an intact wreck and moved at least 120 feet up here to the bow?

I swept my torch around and lit up a small engine block standing proud and exposed. It certainly wasn't the engine of a sizeable steamship but was the engine of a far smaller vessel, like a steam trawler. And then the penny dropped and all the clues that I had been wilfully ignoring and trying to fit into my preconceived idea of where I was came tumbling together. This wasn't the *Gowrie* – it was the wreck of a steam trawler or collier lying 25–50 metres away from the *Gowrie*. It had to be the *Fernside*.

This wreck appeared to have been dived before as someone had carefully placed a brass gasket on top of a piece of the engine. It wasn't natural where it was and looked out of context. I moved slightly further on – I knew I was heading astern now as engine rooms are usually astern of the boiler room and thus nearer the prop. A few feet more and I was looking at a small delicate stern with rudder and tiny propeller. This had to be the *Fernside*.

I could well understand why the Aberdeen divers were confused into thinking this was the wreck called the *Cushendall* or the *Gowrie*. The two wrecks were sitting almost on top of each other. The chances of that happening in all these square miles of open sea were extremely slim. And I could well understand why the local fishermen were adamant that there wasn't a 4th wreck in Stonehaven Bay. When you looked at the wrecks on a standard echo sounder they were so close that both seemed to merge into one trace. The astute old fisherman who had always said that this wreck was broken in two parts was right. But little did he know it was in fact two separate vessels.

For years I had thought that there was always too much wreckage strewn around the stern of the *Gowrie*. Only about 5–10 feet at most of the deck and the very tip of the stern above the rudder were missing, removed I presumed by the bombing attack. Yet the seabed around the stern is covered by wreckage – it always looked odd. And then there was the coal scattered around on the seabed.

I subsequently stumbled across the Dundee Perth & London Shipping Co's website, which recounted that the bomb that sank the *Gowrie* had exploded in the water close alongside her, almost at midships on the starboard side. The shock of the blast nearby in the water had stoved in some hull plating beside the boiler and allowed water to start coming into her hull. No bomb had struck the stern at all. The ship had to be abandoned and sank sometime later.

So there was no catastrophic bomb impact to blast plates and debris into the jumbled mass on the seabed at the stern. The seabed around the *Gowrie* was littered with coal whereas her coalbunkers were intact. The *Fernside* was a collier and still has a great pile of coal sitting in the flattened remnants of her hold. Perhaps the scattered coal was part of her cargo.

Although we haven't conclusively proved this yet, I'd wager that it's part of the wreck of the *Fernside* that is sitting at the stern of the *Gowrie*. The *Fernside* was sunk some two years after the *Gowrie* and I suspect that part of her clipped the *Gowrie*'s stern as she ploughed down through the depths to crash onto the seabed.

Once Paul and I had explored the wreck we wound in our reel and retraced our steps back to the anchor line, still snagged right through the nets. Its flukes wouldn't get through the net without snagging if we tried to haul it up. So laboriously, we untied the anchor line from the anchor chain and pulled the line through the nets. We then unwound the line from around the nets and then retied it to the anchor and chain. Closing up the anchor flukes, we threw it over the side of the wreck away from any other snags. Once all that was done we started our ascent.

An hour later our heads broke the surface. We clambered back into our RIB and erupted into a torrent of excited chatter, ignoring the wind and waves throwing the boat about. Simon, on his first boat handling expedition for us, had snagged a new wreck right on our doorstep.

We did a few passes of the wrecks with our side-scan sonar and on one pass sure enough there it was – the unmistakeable image of two separate wrecks lying together at right angles, almost touching on the seabed below.

Research revealed that the 269 grt Rose Line cargo ship SS *Fernside* had sailed from Hartlepool bound for Wick with a cargo of coal on 26 February 1942. She never arrived at her destination and her precise fate was never known at the time. Although her eight crew

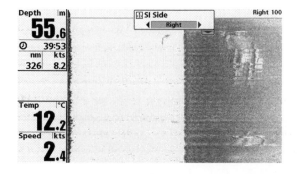

Side scan sonar trace showing SS Gowrie *at the top and the smaller SS* Fernside *not far away at the bottom.*

and two DEMS gunners were lost, a number of bodies were subsequently recovered from the sea, identified and buried ashore but the precise location of the sinking of the ship was never known or recorded. Certainly she was not charted or recorded as being lost in the waters around Stonehaven.

It is hard to truly imagine the terror of the crew as they went into the freezing water five miles offshore, knowing there was little chance of rescue. There have been a few occasions for me when things have been tough or going wrong, when I've been almost hypothermic and suffering. There comes a point when you almost give up and surrender to the immensity of the sea and its power. But nothing I have experienced can really let me know what it was like for the crew here. I think of the pain and suffering of their families – the dread failure of loved ones to return from the sea. My mother lost both her brothers in the RAF during World War II and the loss blighted the family and still haunts her all these years later. It would be just like that for the *Fernside* relatives. Families, wives and children would have clung on in grim desperation to the hope that their loved one was still somehow alive. The sea gave up some of the bodies eventually. Then there would be the sad acceptance of the truth but the pain of the loss, of not knowing what happened, would have haunted families for a generation. At last now however, the story of what happened to them is known – a story that the crew took with them into the sea almost 70 years ago. The crew were:

> ROBERT BAIRD, Second Engineer Officer, Merchant Navy. Age 40.
> THOMAS FLECK, Master, Merchant Navy. Age 38. Son of Mr and Mrs John Fleck, of Island-Magee, Co. Antrim, Northern Ireland; husband of Margaret Smith Fleck, of Burghead, Morayshire.
> JOSEPH SMITH FLETT, Able Seaman, Merchant Navy. Age 23. Son of Alexander & Agnes Flett, Findochty, Banffshire.
> ROBERT HEGGIE, Cook, Merchant Navy. Age 20. Son of William & Annie Heggie, Bo'ness, West Lothian.
> ALEXANDER MAIN, Able Seaman, Merchant Navy. Age 27. Son of Alexander & Jessie Main, Burghead, Morayshire.
> WILLIAM McKENZIE, Chief Engineer Officer, Merchant Navy. Age 33. Son of William & Isabella McKenzie, Peterhead, Aberdeenshire; husband of Lena McKenzie, Peterhead.
> NICHOLAS JOHN RICHARDS, Fireman, Merchant Navy. Age 35. Buried Ashore.
> ALEXANDER HAY, First Officer, Merchant Navy. Age 38. Son of James & Maggie Ann Hay, Buckie; husband of Alexina Hay, Buckie. Buried Buckie New Cemetery.
> DEMS Gunners buried Aberdeen (Grove) Cemetery.

One of our projects for the coming seasons is to simultaneously drop a shot-line on each of the two adjacent wrecks – the two shots should be at worst 100 metres apart. We'll then string a 200-metre warp of rope between the two, put a large noose around each shot-line and weight it. Both weighted ends of the 200-metre rope will then sink down their respective shot-line. Two teams of divers will then go in – one down each shot-line – and once down on the respective wrecks will pull in the 200-metre rope until it is reasonably taught, and then tie it off on a suitable piece of the wreck. The two wrecks will then be linked and divers will be able to see both wrecks in a single dive and understand this unusual piece of maritime history.

CHAPTER ELEVEN

BENT IN THE NORTH CHANNEL

In July 2003 an eagerly awaited ten-day technical dive trip to the fabled wrecks of the North Channel of the Irish Sea was ready to go.

The North Channel is the narrow strip of water much like a bottleneck, which separates Northern Ireland from the west coast of Scotland. Here at the North Channel the gap between Ireland and Scotland reduces to just 14 miles or so. Consequently during wartime, shipping entering or leaving the north stretch of the Irish Sea from major ports such as Liverpool, Cardiff or Bristol was funnelled into this narrow channel – it was a tempting concentration of Allied shipping for predatory German planes or U-boats. As a result, there is a huge volume of World War II shipping lying just outside the North Channel in the crystal clear waters of the Atlantic.

On a land-bound holiday a few years earlier I had stood on the southernmost tip of the small Scottish island of Islay and looked across the North Channel to Ireland, easily visible on the horizon. It was hard to believe that just 70 years earlier, German U-boats had prowled outside its entrance hunting for targets.

Ewan and I drove down from Aberdeen to meet Jim Burke, Mike Rosie, Tony Ray and Chris Allen in Port Patrick in the south west of Scotland, which would be the departure point for our dive boat. An old dive mate of mine from the Aberdeen area – Steve Collard – was driving up from England to meet us there. As the name would imply, Port Patrick on the west coast of Galloway just south of Stranraer, is one of the closest jumping off points for Ireland and is slightly north in latitude from Belfast, just across the water.

After laboriously loading all our heavy kit onto the live-aboard dive boat and getting it all stashed below decks in our cabins, we cast off the mooring lines and headed out of the narrow harbour in a heavy sea fog that limited visibility around us to a couple of hundred feet. The skipper kept a close eye on the radar for danger.

That afternoon saw us steaming up the west coast of Scotland to the Kintyre Peninsula, the long finger of land that runs down from Argyll and points to the south west. The plan was to have a shakedown dive on a new wreck located only the season before in October 2002, and identified in May 2003 as the World War II loss, the 487-ton *HM Rescue Tug, Englishman*. Built by Cochrane & Sons in Selby she was launched on 10 July 1937 and commissioned in February 1940. She would serve for less than a year before being attacked and sent to the bottom.

Just after noon on Tuesday 21 January 1941, a German Condor aircraft raiding a long way from its home base of Bordeaux, sighted the *Englishman* and immediately attacked. On one pass, the Condor aircraft dropped an SC250 bomb, which went straight down the *Englishman*'s funnel. The resulting explosion was catastrophic - the *Englishman* sank straight away with the loss of all her crew.

We steamed north all day from Port Patrick, crossing the wide expanse of the entrance to the Firth of Clyde, which leads up towards Glasgow. We motored round the Mull of Kintyre and started moving along the Kintyre peninsula – all the time trying to work out which house in the distance was Paul McCartney's.

Slowly, we wound our way north along the west side of the peninsula until we arrived about seven miles offshore from Bellochantuy. Our skipper soon had the wreck showing far below us on the echo sounder. It was late in the day and starting to get dusky as we started to get ready for our shakedown dive: a cool 65 metres down onto a wreck we had never seen before.

Once ready in our cumbersome dive gear, we strode off our boat and splashed into dark, foreboding water. This was meant to be a shakedown dive – where all the little gremlins get ironed out – and so it would turn out to be. For as soon as I started heading down the shot-line, my UK800 dive torch beam started steadily dimming, turning from brilliant white to a weak yellowish colour. About 40 metres down it went out completely, the bulb now just a feeble spark of orange yellow filament that was doing bugger-all good. 'What a plonker', I thought; 'I must have forgotten to charge it at home'. On the other hand, perhaps the switch had been accidentally knocked in my kit bag on the journey down or aboard - it could have been switched on and discharged itself. Either way it was fairly academic – I was now 40 metres down in pitch black unfamiliar waters with only the thin weak beam of my small head-mounted torch I use for reading my gauges – and I was leading the dive. I turned round towards Ewan who was above me and as I did so, I noticed that the beam from my head torch wasn't as strong as it should be either. It quickly got weaker and then it too went out. Brilliant – 'what a tosser'.

Ewan came over and worked out the problem – there isn't really an underwater hand signal for 'every single light I've got has gone out'. But as I was in complete darkness he soon got the gist of my universal hand signal of 'finger to thumb' to make an 'O' with the hand being extended in and out from my forehead. If you don't understand it - try it - you soon will.

Rather than turn the dive and head back up, and because we must be pretty close to the wreck we pressed on down. Ewan took over the lead – he had our only torch and I was right behind him on his shoulder hitching a ride in the bright glare of his canister HID light.

We arrived down at the wreck: a small but tough looking tug sitting on an even keel. Ewan's bright torch lit up the wreck beautifully. It was completely covered in white anemones and sea life that glowed white in the beam giving the wreck a surreal appearance, as if covered by a ghostly white carpet.

We finned around the wreck for a while seeing what we could but then decided that our Day 1 Shakedown Dive was over and that we should start to ascend. It had been a bit of a 'Charlie Foxtrot' on the lighting side for me but otherwise all went well. With a firm hand on the line we ascended slowly to the shallower waters where at last some faint ambient light trickled down and I could once again see without the aid of Ewan's torch.

After clambering back aboard our dive boat in the early evening dusk, we ate a fine meal and turned in. Very early the next morning the anchor was raised and we started our steam across the North Channel to the Northern Irish coast.

Once across the Channel we motored along the Irish coastline past Rathlin Island – the large island that guards the very northeast most corner of Ireland, before eventually arriving at Lough Swilly, more than half way along the north coast. Here, just off Fanad Head, lies the legendary wreck of the White Star liner *Laurentic*: a beautiful liner of 14,892 tons launched on 29 April 1909 by Harland & Wolff of Belfast, the builders of the *Titanic*.

The *Laurentic* story is one of drama, mystery, and intrigue. On 23 January 1917 she set out from Liverpool bound for Halifax, Canada carrying – to pay for munitions – 43 tons of gold ingots worth *at the time* £5 million. In today's money that's the equivalent of more than a £250 million. After a brief stop at Lough Swilly on 25 January, just after starting out on her trans-Atlantic voyage, she ran into a minefield laid a few days earlier off Fanad Head by the German submarine *U-80*. A single mine caused catastrophic damage and she sank within one hour. Of her 470-strong crew, 354 were drowned or died from exposure in the cold January waters.

With such a valuable cargo in relatively shallow waters of 23 fathoms the wreck was soon located and a well-known salvage diver, Commander Guybon Damant was engaged by the Admiralty to head up a salvage team. In 1906 he had set a world diving record of 210 feet during Naval endurance diving test. Damant set up a specialist team and one of the divers he hired was an Augustus Dent – a diver who had been aboard the *Laurentic* when she sank and who knew the way to the bullion room.

By September of the same year (1917), Damant and his team had recovered £800,000 of the £5 million of gold. It would however take a full seven years – and an incredible five thousand dives – before the bulk of the remaining gold was recovered. His team recovered 3,186 gold bars. A subsequent salvage attempt in 1932 by the Mallet Salvage Company recovered a further five gold bars. Twenty gold bars of her cargo have never been reported as recovered – worth a cool £10 million at today's prices. I wonder what happened to them – are they still on the wreck, or has someone kept quite a secret for a great number of years?

By the time we arrived at the *Laurentic* wreck site, the weather was blowing up and it was marginal as to whether we could dive. But since the wreck lay in a relatively shallow 39 metres of water we decided to go for it. The forecast looked as though the approaching gale would only get stronger and if we didn't get in the water now there was no telling when we might dive again.

Once in the water, the rough waters above us were forgotten about as we finned over a wreck site, which although completely devastated by the actions of sea and salvers, still had lots to see. Large pieces of machinery lay on the seabed *in situ* and allowed you to follow through the layout of the wreck despite the devastation. The magnificent bow section lay on its side easily recognisable and one of the most photogenic images from the wreck.

On surfacing well over an hour later the sea had changed and the dive boat was being rocked from side to side quite violently. It was going to be hard to get back onto the ladder securely without getting bashed by the boat or being dislodged on the climb up the ladder. To fall onto another diver below was extremely dangerous given the combined weight of diver and technical kit.

The skipper took the dive boat deftly up beside us and used the boat to screen us from the worst of the sea. But she rocked heavily from side to side – one minute the rungs of the ladder were almost completely submerged and the next, as the boat rolled away from us, the rungs would clear the water. Somehow, one by one, we all managed to get ourselves securely wedged onto the ladder and at the right time as the boat rolled upwards, climbed slowly, rung by rung, up the ladder and onto the deck of the pitching boat.

We stripped off our gear and gathered in a group on the foredeck – still in our dry suits – as Jim Burke produced a bottle of Isle of Jura malt whisky. We clung grimly onto the guardrail as the deck rolled from side to side almost to a 45 degree angle, passing the bottle around and swigging the whisky from the neck. Spray billowed up from the bow splash requiring a canny hand over the neck of the bottle from time to time to avoid spoiling the whisky with a splash of seawater. The feeling amongst the group was fantastic – good camaraderie and Isle of Jura. The forecast was for a gale to set in for the next couple of days. As we knew there would be no diving tomorrow, the Isle of Jura got a good seeing to as we motored back to the safety of Lough Swilly.

The gale blew for two days solid and we were forced to remain tied up in port. But as soon as it was over we left the Lough and headed out to dive the wreck of the King George V class battleship HMS *Audacious*, which has the dubious honour of being the first British battleship to be sunk during World War I on 27 October 1914. The story of the loss of HMS *Audacious* also involves another famous White Star liner, RMS *Olympic*, which would carry out a dramatic rescue attempt.

The White Star Line decided in 1914 that as a result of the outbreak of war *Olympic* would complete only one round trip from her base in Greenock to New York. On her return to British waters she would be sent to Belfast to be laid up for the duration of the War. *Olympic* left Greenock for this final voyage on 9 October, maintaining a high speed and following a zigzag course to confuse the enemy and outrun any predatory U-boat. She arrived safely in New York seven days later. On 21 October she departed New York for the homeward leg and during the six days of the return Atlantic crossing there were no enemy sightings or alerts. By the morning of Tuesday 27 October *Olympic* was off the north coast of Ireland.

As a result of the Admiralty's concern about the vulnerability of the U-boat defences at the British Grand Fleet's main base at Scapa Flow, the 2nd Battle Squadron of the British Grand Fleet had spent the first few months of the war based at Lough Swilly whilst frantic works were carried out to make Scapa Flow secure. The Germans were aware of the Grand Fleet's deployment and sent the converted liner *Berlin* to lay a minefield in the shipping areas outside Lough Swilly. This minefield was intended to strike at British merchant shipping as well as the Grand Fleet when on manoeuvre. The *Olympic* was unknowingly steaming directly towards the minefield.

At 8.50 a.m. that morning, 27 October, the brand new 23,000-ton British battleship HMS *Audacious* struck one of the *Berlin*'s mines off Tory Island. Fearing a possible torpedo attack on the other ships of the Fleet, Admiral John Jellicoe ordered the Grand Fleet to leave the area and ordered the light cruiser HMS *Liverpool* and a number of smaller vessels to remain on the scene to assist the damaged battleship.

At 10.30 a.m. *Olympic* was sighted by the captain of HMS *Liverpool* and ordered to assist in the evacuation of the crew of the *Audacious*. Two hours later, all but 250 of the battleship's crew had been taken off and after the boats had been safely recovered, arrangements were made to take the damaged battleship in tow to safety.

The small and nimble destroyer HMS *Fury* set up a cable between *Audacious* and the larger and more powerful *Olympic* and by 2.00 p.m. the tow was ready to start. Initially progress was encouraging and as the *Olympic* slowly pulled the sluggish weight of *Audacious* westwards towards safety (flanked by the other ships of the rescue party), the situation looked to be well in hand. But when *Olympic* required to alter course to SSE to head towards Lough Swilly, things began to unravel. The seas were starting to rise and as the steering gear of *Audacious* was no longer operational – she became increasingly unmanageable. Eventually she sheared off into the wind and parted the towline.

Another tow attempt was made at 3.30 p.m., this time by the light cruiser HMS *Liverpool*. HMS *Fury* once again succeeded in attaching another cable, but after only 15 minutes it became fouled in the cruiser's propellers and it too parted. By 4.00 p.m., *Audacious* was visibly settling into the water as HMS *Fury* took over a third tow cable for yet another attempt. But as it was being tightened, this cable also gave way. Once again *Olympic* was ordered to stand by and be ready to make another attempt. But time was remorselessly running out for *Audacious*.

By 5.00 p.m. the quarterdeck of the *Audacious* was awash and the decision was made to evacuate the majority of the crew who had remained on board. During the crew evacuation – due to the heavy weather and deteriorating conditions aboard *Audacious* – it was decided to abandon her completely until the next morning. By 6.30 p.m. the entire crew of the stricken battleship had been safely taken aboard *Olympic* and HMS *Liverpool*.

The decision to abandon *Audacious* would turn out to be fortuitous, for at 8.55 p.m. there was a massive explosion aboard her in the vicinity of the forward magazines that served A and B turrets. Within minutes the battleship turned turtle and sank stern first.

Olympic steamed back to Lough Swilly that evening, ready to disembark the rescued crew of *Audacious*. But for security reasons, she was ordered to remain out of sight of the Grand Fleet, so that none of her paying passengers – with perhaps pro-German sympathies – would be able to observe the Fleet's activities. There were quite a number of German-born Americans aboard *Olympic* who had witnessed *Audacious* sinking, and it was felt that they could not be relied upon to keep quiet.

British military authorities then refused to permit *Olympic*'s civilian passengers to disembark and refused to allow the ship itself to leave Lough Swilly. The only people permitted off the ship were the rescued naval crew of the *Audacious* and *Olympic*'s chief surgeon Dr. John Beaumont, who was being transferred to the *Celtic*.

The White Star Line was understandably reluctant to risk moving their flagship, *Olympic*, whilst there was such danger at sea. But finally, on 2 November after ship and her civilian passengers had been incarcerated for six days, *Olympic* was allowed to leave Lough Swilly and complete her voyage – not to Greenock as originally planned, but to Belfast. She finally disembarked her passengers the following day.

In recognition of his outstanding services, the *Olympic*'s Captain Haddock was appointed by the Admiralty to command a squadron of merchant ships that were being fitted out to resemble British warships, in a covert operation to mislead German intelligence about the Fleet's whereabouts.

For security reasons, the Admiralty tried to cover up the sinking but despite their best attempts, speculation about the possible sinking of the *Audacious* got into the public domain. In an effort to hide the disaster, the Admiralty went as far as modifying the SS *Mountclan* to resemble the lost battleship. But the large number of witnesses to the sinking and the inevitable loose tongues made the task of keeping the secret all but impossible. It proved difficult enough to persuade the neutral passengers who had been aboard the *Olympic* during the attempts to save the battleship to keep silent, but some of the crew themselves also let the cat out of the bag. *The Daily Mail* published a letter proclaiming that a masseur from the *Olympic* had openly boasted to his barber that he had seen *Audacious* sink – and that the authorities had ordered everyone to say nothing. The publication of this letter led to the Admiralty being deluged with enquiries from anxious relatives of the *Audacious'* crew. If the deception were to be maintained then the fears of the families would have to be assuaged.

None of the crew of *Audacious* had been lost during the sinking, so when an enquiry was received the Admiralty could reply with a reasonable degree of truth: 'According to the latest information, 85 is well and serving with the Fleet.' All enquiries about *Audacious* itself were ignored.

The only casualty during the entire momentous incident had been the unfortunate Petty Officer William Burgess on HMS *Liverpool*. He was sadly killed while standing on the deck of the cruiser *Liverpool* (some 800 yards away) when he was hit by a 2 foot by 3 foot fragment of armour plate as *Audacious* blew up. The decks of the cruiser had been crowded so it was perhaps fortunate that no one else was killed or injured.

◆　　◆　　◆

Far out in the Atlantic above the *Audacious'* grave, Ewan and I got rigged up to dive, striding off the dive boat and dropping down into languid blue water. The sea was calm and the sun, already high in the sky, beat directly down. A lot of light would be pouring down onto the wreck far below.

Ewan was diving his closed-circuit Classic Inspiration rebreather – I was diving open-circuit with two 12-litre tanks on my back holding a huge amount of a 16/45 Trimix (i.e., 16% oxygen, 45% helium and the balance of 39% of nitrogen). Under each of my arms was slung a 7-litre stage tank each holding EAN50; a mix of 50% oxygen and 50% nitrogen.

Once in the water I looked around me and was staggered to be able to see for at least 100 feet in any one direction. The visibility was fantastic – a stunning opposite to the dark, cloudy waters of my usual east coast dive sites. This wreck was going to be a joy to dive today.

We dropped down slowly beside the shot-line, peering below as we descended. The uniform deep blue beneath us started to acquire a form – loose, ragged lines. Something man made lay beneath us.

We pressed on down, feeling the squeeze of the water pressure on our ears, on our body – our dry suits compressing and nipping at our skin until we bled some air into them.

After a few minutes descent we passed through a visibility horizon and there beneath us lay an upturned World War I battleship. It looked magnificent – a massive man-made island set on an underwater desert of clean white sand and shale.

Our shot-line had landed amidships – the wreck was so big I couldn't tell initially which way was forward and which way astern. So, picking one direction at random we gunned the motors of our Aquazepp underwater scooters and headed off. Soon it became clear we were heading to towards the bow. I checked my depth gauge – it read 63 metres. There was more than 200 feet of water above us – it was a long, long way back up to the surface.

As we made our way towards the bow, the ship suddenly petered out – the whole bow was missing. Something terrible had happened here to detach a section of a heavily armoured battleship like this. Not far away – almost separate from the wreck itself – lay an upturned barbette of one of her main twin 13.5-inch gun turrets. Barbettes are the huge armoured columns that run down from the gun turret on the deck nearly all the way to the bottom of the ship and which pass through the internal armoured decks. The turning system for the gun turret is housed inside the barbette and shells also travel up to the gun turrets from the magazines, which are situated in the bowels of the ship beneath the armoured deck. The cylindrical walls of the barbette would have been about 10 inches thick at their maximum tapering to 5 inches or less where armoured decks gave some protection. This barbette appeared to be about 10–15 metres across and rose up for about 10 metres or more.

Although I hadn't read the historical account at the time of diving the wreck, it was still obvious that something catastrophic had happened here at the bow – the structure of the hull had been devastated and the barbette cast out from the body of the wreck like a toy from a pram. As I swam over and into the barbette, I felt a slight wobble of narcosis wash over me. I suddenly felt a bit light-headed and remote from my surroundings – perhaps I'd been working too hard and was getting a slight CO_2 build-up. I stopped, hung motionless in mid water and breathed deeply – the wave of narcosis passed.

After 5–10 minutes exploring the bow area, we turned our Aquazepps and headed down the starboard side of the upturned hull. The scooters soon whisked us right down to the stern where, like the German battleships of the same era lying at Scapa Flow, we found a small rounded and almost delicate stern – the upturned main quarterdeck sitting flat on the sand.

The stern area is the most visually stunning on this wreck – it just blew both Ewan and I away. Both massive rudders still stood proudly upright with propellers and shafts set around them. For a battleship weighing in at 23,000 tons you'd think the props would be massive – the props on the far smaller 10,000-ton cruiser *Hampshire* at Scapa Flow were huge 43-ton affairs, which dwarfed a diver. But when we got beside the props on *Audacious* I was amazed at just how small they were – just the same size you'd find on an average steamship of a few thousand tons. These were small high-speed propellers, designed for high revs.

As we scootered around the props and rudders I looked across at Ewan and he gave me a hand signal – his hand outstretched, palm downward, fingers spread and rocking from side to side. The signal that says: 'There's something wrong – I'm not too good'. I scootered over to him and he looked extremely unhappy and repeated the signal. I knew the illusory safety of the downline was a few hundred feet away amidships – so I beckoned him to come up beside me and pointed in the direction of the downline. Side-by-side we scootered back to the downline where he gave me an 'OK' signal. Panic over, he looked fine again. We started our hour-long ascent.

Once back aboard the dive boat we discussed what had happened. Ewan felt that he had had a carbon dioxide build-up, perhaps from skip breathing or working too hard – I'd had a wash of narcosis as well at the barbette near the bow. He had felt apprehension, dread and a bit of tunnel vision, but psychologically once he had his hand on the ascent line and we had started up, he had immediately felt OK again. His breathing would have relaxed and his rebreather wouldn't have been working as hard as it was at depth.

That afternoon on the run back to Lough Swilly to overnight, we dropped in past the site of the *Laurentic* for another dive on the ragged remains of this White Star liner. Despite the apparent chaos of the site, from our earlier dive we were now quite familiar with her layout. Amidst jumbled plates and mangled spars it was possible to navigate by following all the large pieces of machinery, which were still in the right place. It was as though the outer skin of the ship had been peeled away to leave all the innards exposed. Prop shafts led to engines and in turn they led to massive boilers.

It was ropes-off early the next morning for a big steam of about 25 miles out from Malin Head, Co Donegal to the site of the 32,000-ton Royal Mail Ship, RMS *Justicia*. This would turn out to be one of the greatest dives in the UK. Think of diving the *Titanic* and you'll get the idea.

In the early years of the 20th century shipping lines competed to offer the largest and fastest ocean liners to discerning and demanding transatlantic passengers. The design of the ocean liner had evolved swiftly during the preceding 25 years or so and the great ships of the era are household names: *Titanic*; *Laurentic*; *Britannic*; *Olympic* and many others. The Dutch Holland–Amerika Line had enviously eyed the dominance of the great British shipping lines and wanted to be part of this glamorous world. The Dutch wanted great ships as emblem bearers, not just for their shipping line but also to represent their nation. They approached the legendary shipbuilders Harland & Wolff of Belfast, makers of the *Titanic,* with an order for a new 32,234-ton liner.

The keel of their new ship was laid down in 1912 – and two years later on 9 July 1914, the new ship was launched and named *Statendam*. Work began on fitting her out immediately for her planned entry into the lucrative North Atlantic run from Europe to the United States. Just 11 days before her launch however, on 28 June 1914, Serb nationalist Gavrilo Princip assassinated the Austrian-Hungarian crown prince in Sarajevo – and ushered in the First World War in all its brutality. The world that the *Statendam* had been conceived and built for had just disappeared overnight, before she had even carried a single commercial passenger. With the declaration of war, the commercial interests of the shipping companies were changed overnight. In September 1914, the Holland–Amerika Line was forced to stop the fitting out and completion of the *Statendam* – and the ship lay idle into the following year. In 1915, the still unfinished and still laid-up *Statendam* was requisitioned for war use and purchased by the British Government, who wanted large fast ships for use as troop carriers. The *Statendam's* immense size and anticipated speed made her a perfect choice.

Harland & Wolff restarted work on the ship but because of wartime material and labour shortages, progress was slow. To save sheet metal, the ship's funnels were made smaller in diameter than originally designed and this gave her a slightly odd appearance. It took Harland & Wolff until 7 April 1917 to complete the *Statendam*. Once she was fully ready for war use as a troopship, able to carry 4,000 troops she was renamed *Justicia*.

Justicia was intended by the British government to be a replacement for the *Lusitania*, which had infamously been torpedoed in 1915 with huge civilian loss of life. Cunard were to manage her during the war and like all their liners, her name would end with 'ia'. It was intended that once the war was won, ownership would be passed outright by the Government to Cunard.

By the time of her completion in 1917 however, Cunard found itself unable to muster a full crew for her. The Admiralty wanted *Justicia* in war service just as soon as possible and could not wait for Cunard to solve the crew problem. Accordingly, the Admiralty offered *Justicia* to Cunard's rival, the White Star Line, for wartime management, as the White Star Line had the crew of the recently sunk *Britannic* available. In 1918, *Justicia*'s grey hull was painted in a dazzle pattern designed to confuse its silhouette for any enemy raiders observing her from a distance. Finally, she was ready for war. After more than a year of war service, on 19 July 1918, *Justicia* had set off on a voyage from Belfast to New York. Not far into the voyage, just 23 miles south of the tiny rocky outcrop of Skerryvore lighthouse (12 miles south of the southernmost tip of the west coast island of Tiree in Scotland), she was attacked and successfully torpedoed by *UB-64*.

Justicia took on a list as seawater poured into her hull through plating torn open by the single torpedo strike. The design of her watertight compartments however successfully contained the water in the one area and stopped her from completely flooding and sinking. Royal Navy destroyers were quickly summoned to escort her to safe waters and she turned to run for the Irish mainland and safety.

UB-64 had not yet however given up on her stricken prey – her captain wanted this massive liner sunk, not just crippled. *UB-64* pressed home her attack despite the protecting destroyers and skilfully manoeuvred into another attacking position. Two more torpedoes were loosed, striking *Justicia*'s side and blowing open two more huge gashes in her hull. But even this additional damage wasn't enough to send the massive liner to the bottom. Again her watertight compartments saved the day and kept her afloat. Most of the crew were now evacuated, with only a small number of essential hands being left on the ship.

Justicia's engines now had to be stopped because of the increased flooding from the two further torpedo strikes. She was taken in tow by the tug HMS *Sonia*, which headed for Lough Swilly, where the waters would be shallow enough to ground her safely. *UB- 64* however proved to be a tenacious foe and continued to stalk the stricken liner, determined to strike a fatal blow. A few hours further into the tow she fired a fourth torpedo into the labouring liner. Royal Navy escort vessels had by this time damaged *UB-64*, and she was finally forced to break off the attack, leaving *Justicia* still defiantly afloat. The tow to Lough Swilly resumed.

UB-64 reported *Justicia*'s position and condition to German command and another U-boat, *UB-124*, was ordered to take over the hunt. *UB-124* would catch up with *Justicia* the following day.

At 9.00 a.m. the next morning, *UB-124* had *Justicia* in her sights and fired two torpedoes. *Justicia* was already severely damaged from the previous day's four torpedoes from *UB-64* – and these two further strikes finally proved too much for her. By noon she had listed well over onto her side and shortly thereafter she finally succumbed to the sea, with 16 men from the engine room lost. *UB-124* was detected and attacked with depth charges by the destroyers *Marne*, *Milbrook* and *Pigeon*. Damaged, she was forced to the surface and abandoned by her crew. German sources reports say that her crew scuttled her, however British sources report she was sunk by naval gunfire. Either way, she went to the bottom with all bar two of her crew being saved and taken prisoner. After just over one year of service – and having never carried a single paying passenger – *Justicia* was gone. Today the 225 metre long wreck of *Justicia* lies on a majestic clean seascape of white sand 28 miles northwest of Malin Head in about 70 metres of water and is justly acclaimed as one of the UK's top technical dives.

◆　◆　◆

Ewan and I jumped off the gunwales of our dive boat into the oily calm waters above the wreck of *Justicia*. As with all the offshore dives we had carried out in the North Channel, I was immediately struck by how clear the water of the Atlantic was this far off the land. As we finned over to the downline the deep blue of the Atlantic surrounded and enveloped us. The downline ran straight down far beneath us until it disappeared into the darkness below. We bled surplus air out of our buoyancy wings and dry suits and started the free-fall descent. Light from the surface seemed to stream down all around us.

By the time I got to about 30 metres down, I started to see the blurred, straight man made lines of a large shipwreck below me. Bubble streams from some of our divers ahead billowed up, being carried away from us in a silvery crescent by the gentle current. Some of the bubbles were a foot across and flat topped, striving upwards and pressing against the water above. Every now and then a large flat-topped bubble would break into two or three smaller segments, each free to carry on its own scurrying ascent.

I peered down into the void, tracing one of the bubble streams below to its origin. The bubbles got smaller and smaller until they coalesced into a single point: a tiny ant of a diver far below me. And then the massive wreck of the *Justicia* materialised out of the gloom below. One minute there were blurry lines below me, the next minute the wreck lay there beneath me set in a desert of clean rolling sand dunes. The dark rotted steel of her remains contrasted starkly against the beautiful white of her surroundings.

I was still suspended some 100 feet above the wreck – a strange feeling for a British diver used to seeing the wreck when you are just a few metres away from it. It was still a long way down to the seabed and I could see the white downline stretching all the way below me to the shot-weight, which had landed just aft of the foc'stle.

The sheer size of the foc'stle took my breath away. I have seen a lot of shipwrecks in my time, but nothing on this scale. It was the foc'stle of a White Star liner – from the era of the greatest ships ever made. It was both huge and majestic.

The shot had landed in a flattened pile of plating – most probably where the remnants of a small hold would have been located. As we arrived down on the wreck, Ewan and I kicked our fins and moved forward. We were at a depth of 70 metres.

We approached the aft-most side of the foc'stle and finned up on top of it into a forest of ventilator tops, anchor winches and two massive anchor chains – one each side of the deck running forward and out through its own hawse pipe. As we approached the very tip of the bow I couldn't stop the image of Kate Winslett and Leonardo Di Caprio popping into my mind. "We're going to America", I almost shouted.

Ewan was carrying his underwater camera and motioned for me to hang at the top of the very bow itself. He turned away and then started to drop down the outside of the stem of the bow until he landed on the seabed far below. I quickly checked my depth gauge – it was reading 55 metres. I knew it was 70 metres on the bottom, so that made him almost 50 feet beneath me. As I watched him, Ewan being Ewan, lay flat on his back on the sand as he manoeuvred to get into the right position to shoot me in silhouette floating, holding the tip of the bow with one hand. From there we explored aft, crossing the collapsed foredeck and coming upon the whole bridge superstructure, which was almost intact but which had fallen onto the seabed to the port side of the wreck as it collapsed. Large square windows still rimmed in green brass and massive portholes kept our attention. We finned further aft beyond the bridge and came across the first of many huge boilers – each one seemed the size of a small house. Fire corridors where the stokers would have passed snaked between the rows of boilers. But with our bottom-time nearly spent, we made our way back to the shot-line to ascend. This was a massive wreck and as we were going to dive it again in a couple of days, we vowed we would take in our scooters and try to get round the whole wreck.

Ewan Rowell lies on his back at 70msw to shoot Rod hanging at the bow of the liner Justicia, *North Channel © Ewan Rowell.*

The next day, the penultimate of our trip, saw us diving the SS *Empire Heritage* in the morning – a large American World War II transport vessel weighing in at 15,702 tons and some 512 feet in length. She had been carrying a cargo of oil fuel as well as a deck cargo of trucks, general war supplies and Sherman tanks in convoy from America. In the dead of night at 4.00 a.m. on 8 September 1944 as she approached Ireland, she was struck by a single torpedo on her starboard side and sank within ten minutes. She now lies in 70 metres of water.

The small Royal Fleet Auxiliary vessel *Pinto* was detached from the convoy and – exposing herself to great danger – stopped to pick up survivors from the *Empire Heritage*. Some of those survivors, whilst in the water, saw 4–10 feet of a U-boat periscope sticking up through the water as it closed on the *Pinto*. As they watched, the periscope passed right through the survivors before submerging as another Allied vessel approached.

Shortly afterwards, at 4.34 a.m. with the survivors now on board, *Pinto* herself was struck by a torpedo on her starboard side directly under the bridge. It was a devastating blow for such a small ship and she is reported to have sunk in 90 seconds. The unfortunate survivors of the *Empire Heritage* who had just been plucked to apparent safety were pitched back into the water for a second time in just 30 minutes. Some of them had in fact been aboard the *Empire Heritage* after their own convoy vessels had been sunk and found themselves torpedoed for a third time. The wreck of the *Pinto* now lies just half a mile from the *Empire Heritage* – a poignant snapshot of the horrors of war.

As we dropped down the line towards the vast wreck of the *Empire Heritage* in the beautiful visibility below us, we soon saw the wreck materialise out of the gloom. Our shot had landed right in the middle of the deck cargo and unmistakeable Sherman tanks were strewn everywhere – some upright, others upside down. When we got down on the wreck we found the shot wedged right in between two of the tanks. I was surprised at how small they were – they had always seemed so big in the black and white wartime footage I had seen previously.

That afternoon we motored towards the second 70-metre dive of the day on *U-155*, which we were told had only been dived twice before us. Most of the team (barring Tony and myself) were by now on rebreathers, which recycle your exhaled breathing gas instead of venting it to the surface. Rebreathers made possible far higher levels of helium on the bottom and oxygen during decompression stops. I was still diving my open-circuit (O.C.) Trimix rig using a fixed deco mix of EAN50 (50% oxygen and 50% nitrogen) for my deco stops. The rebreathers would be feeding the other divers increasing percentages of oxygen in their shallower deco stops as they ascended. By the time they got to their last stop at six metres they'd be breathing almost pure oxygen as opposed to my 50% oxygen – far more beneficial for decompression.

I thought long and hard about whether I should do a second 70-metre O.C. dive in the same day. I knew that in reality I shouldn't do the dive, but here was an opportunity to see a pristine almost undived World War II U-boat. I was in a dive boat right above it with all my dive kit and I wouldn't have this opportunity again. So I determined to dive, but to try and minimise decompression issues I decided to limit my bottom time to 15 minutes.

The dive went flawlessly – a dark, brooding dive on a very intact Type IXC U-boat. *U-155* had entered war service on 23 August 1941 and had proved to be a survivor at a time when in the later stages of the war, the lifespan of a U-boat and her crew had become very short. During her ten patrols she had sunk 25 Allied merchant ships totalling 126,664 tons, in addition to sending one Allied warship and one auxiliary warship to the bottom. She had not been sunk in action but had surrendered to the Allies at Fredericia in Denmark on 8 May 1945 after the unconditional surrender of all German forces on that date marked the end of the European war. On 30 June 1945 *U-155* was transferred to Loch Ryan in Scotland for Operation Deadlight – the scuttling of 116 unwanted U-boats of the 156 boats surrendered. Thirty U-boats were eventually scuttled from Lisahally in Northern Ireland and 86 U-boats from Loch Ryan between November 1945 and February 1946. Whilst some of the U-boats were correctly sunk in their pre-selected locations, many others sank en route due to the bad weather that hampered the operation. *U-155* herself went to the bottom on 21 December 1945. This dumping ground of U-boats had only relatively recently been rediscovered and with the advent of the Trimix revolution, these pristine U-boats were now in a very diveable range. Leading wreck diver Innes McCartney had organised his own operation over the preceding few years to find, chart and explore these historically important relics from World War II.

Once down on the wreck I found *U-115* impressive in scale – its sheer size was far greater than I had expected and I remember being surprised to see the compass head lying on the foredeck just in front of the conning tower.

I kept my bottom-time to the planned 15 minutes and then Ewan and I made a perfect ascent, following my decompression tables carefully and adding in some extra stops in the shallows. We had had two 70 metre dives in one day and I wanted to err on the side of caution.

That night the skipper anchored up our boat 20 miles offshore, not far from tomorrow's planned target, our old friend the *Justicia*. That would be the last dive of the trip – after that dive we would be heading home.

There was a lot of shipping around our night's anchoring spot, so the skipper set the radar alarm for a 20-mile perimeter – we didn't want to be surprised by a large vessel running us down at speed in the darkness. Nevertheless I did feel exposed trying to bunk down and get some kip, anchored 20 miles offshore with that prospect in the back of my mind. I dozed fitfully and then between 2.00 to 3.00 a.m. the radar alarm went off and there was a flurry of activity as the crewman on watch went and roused the skipper. It turned out to be an Irish naval vessel checking us out to see what we were up to this far out overnight.

The next day, after breakfast, we steamed over to the wreck of the *Justicia*. Before long Ewan and I were dressed in and standing at the gunwales of the dive boat with our Aquazepp scooters ready to splash. We were aiming for a last day grand tour of this huge old lady of the sea.

Once down on the wreck, we scootered around the bow before starting to fly aft past the collapsed bridge superstructure. Next, the rows of massive boilers we had seen on our last dive flew past beneath us, as our bottom time all too rapidly ticked away. Once past the boilers, the massive engines loomed up, followed by the prop shafts leading directly astern. And then in the distance we saw the sides of the hull starting to sweep together towards the very stern itself.

We arrived at the stern just as the twentieth minute – the last minute of our planned bottom time – clocked up. It was now time to ascend. There was no time to retrace our steps back to the shot-line, which lay more than 200 metres away up near the bow.

We started our ascent, drifting away from the wreck in the gentle current. When we reached 50 metres we fired off our deco bags on reels to mark our position for the skipper topside. Again we had a perfect slow ascent, following our deco tables to the letter and adding in some extra stops for good measure. It was the last dive of the trip and we knew we had been pushing it.

About an hour later our heads broke the oily surface into a blaze of sunshine. Not far away, silhouetted against the blue sky, sat the dive boat – seemingly motionless and as steady as a rock, silently waiting for us.

Ewan and I were the first divers to surface and we climbed heavily and laboriously up the ladder on the side of the boat. My four tanks and kit had seemed effortless to carry in the water but climbing 6 feet up the side of a dive boat with all that heavy kit on was tough. My arms strained as I forced the power down into my legs to lift me up, one rung at a time.

Once I had got up onto the deck I stripped off my tanks and weights and carried them to the tank storage rack. As I came back to the ladder, the rest of our team was surfacing and clustering at the bottom of the ladder waiting for their chance to climb up. As they came up the ladder one by one, I stripped off their rebreathers, tanks and weights and started ferrying them to the storage rack. As technical divers, we are taught never to exercise after a technical dive and to take it easy for an hour or so. But that mantra obviously went clean out of my head as like a good team player I tried to help out the boys with their kit.

I had surfaced at about 12.30 p.m. and once all the boys were up I got my dry suit off and got changed. I then went to the saloon and sat down for some lunch – and at this point I started to feel unwell. It was probably 30–40 minutes after I had got out of the water – it was just past 1.00 p.m. I thought at first that I was just feeling fatigued by the dive, but just before I left the table I felt a pinprick sensation of pain in my right knee. I thought I must have banged it on something and that it would pass.

I was feeling more tired than usual after a tech dive, so I decided to turn into my bunk and have a power snooze. I told the boys I was going for a kip and didn't let on I was feeling none too good. As I reached my cabin I felt a pinprick sensation in my left knee and then the pain seemed to change. From being a very isolated and identifiable point in each knee, it seemed to spread out to cover the whole of both knees.

Then I noticed that I had the same pinprick sensation in each of my elbows.

Then I realised just how fuzzy my head was. In Scotland we have an expression that your head is 'full of mince'. That's just how it felt.

The pain in my knees was intensifying – it was getting extremely sore. I lay on my back in my bunk and as I did so, I realised that there was a small shelf above the foot of the bunk. I remembered from my BSAC days that in bend cases it was a good idea to get your feet above your head to let bubbles move away from your head. I got my feet up on the shelf pronto.

The pain got worse and worse – it was so bad that there were tears running down my cheeks. I knew that I was badly bent but was already past the point where I could deal with the situation myself. I just thought I would tough it out and that it would pass. I'd had niggles in the past – they always passed – this one would too, wouldn't it?

Two hours passed as I lay there in pain. By now however I felt that I had a bit more clarity of thought, so I decided to try and have a shower in the hope that would freshen me up and snap me out of the situation I was in. I obviously also forgot my training about not taking a hot shower or bath after a tech dive as that can bring on vasodilatation – a swelling of the brain. I wasn't exactly covering myself in glory with the way I was handling my bend.

In truth I should have flagged up straight away to my mates what was going on and got a ride in a yellow helicopter to the nearest recompression chamber. If I had I would be getting treatment by now. But I hadn't told anyone and now was lying in my bunk in some difficulty.

My decision to shower turned out to be academic. I managed to swing my legs over the edge of my bunk – but ended up sitting there for 10–15 minutes, willing myself to get off the bunk and make the short 15-foot trip up the corridor to the head. It may have been just 15 feet but it seemed like 10 miles to me right then.

Eventually I managed to stand up rather shakily and clamber my way up to the shower room. I moved inside and closed the door, but was again in trouble. I stood there shakily for five minutes before deciding I couldn't physically go through with a shower – I gave up on the idea and returned to my bunk and lay down again.

Shortly afterwards Ewan came down to the cabin. Because I had not given an inkling of my problem, he, like the rest of the lads thought I was having a kip. He came into our cabin, saw I was awake and asked me how I was doing. I told him that I wasn't so good and had pains in my knees and elbows. Ewan took me in hand and got me up onto deck and sat me down and rigged me into his rebreather, which would deliver almost pure oxygen to me – hugely therapeutic for a bend.

After 20–30 minutes of breathing pure oxygen I was feeling immensely better – but still far from right. It's fair to say that I still did not let on to Ewan just how bad I had been. I told him that I was feeling a lot better and as I went back down below to my bunk I said 'hi' to the chaps in the saloon without letting on what had happened.

Another couple of hours later and we were approaching the port where we would tie up overnight. Once we were snug against the pier wall, we all went ashore to get some grub. I recollect walking along the pier and across the harbour car park feeling very unsteady on my feet. We had a good meal and a few beers and returned to the boat to sleep.

The next day, Saturday, we made the short sea trip across the North Channel to Port Patrick where we disembarked and loaded up our various jeeps for the motor up north. Thankfully Ewan was driving me up north – I don't think I'd have been able to drive as although my elbows were now fine and there wasn't any pain in my knees, there was still a discernable weakness in my legs.

We reached Stonehaven that afternoon and Ewan dropped me off at my house. I was pleased to see my wife Claire and my kids again – although I probably didn't let on just how bad I had been to avoid alarming them.

The next day, Sunday, we went for a family walk along a local river to a local picnic spot called The Rocks of Solitude. We took along a little portable BBQ and I cooked up on top of a large boulder as the kids, in wetsuits, played in a little pool formed by shale at the riverside. I remember putting my head in my hands and still feeling very out of sorts.

Monday. I was feeling a lot better but not completely right, but I was still back to work at 9.00 a.m. in my legal office. Seated at my desk, I started to try and sift through the backlog of correspondence, e-mails and documents, but I was very aware that my legs still weren't feeling 100%. It was now three days after my bend on the last dive.

As a result of the oil industry centred in Aberdeen, we are very lucky to have the internationally-renowned National Hyperbaric Centre situated adjacent to Aberdeen Royal Infirmary hospital at Foresterhill. The Hyperbaric Centre is widely known as a centre of excellence that provides expertise and services such as commercial diver training, hyperbaric welding and subsea testing to the commercial offshore oil and pressure related industries. It also provides consulting services to customers worldwide. Their state of the art hyperbaric facilities offer a range of specialised medical facilities and treatments, the recompression chamber being operated on behalf of NHS Grampian. If you get a bend in the north of Scotland you will most likely end up in their recompression chamber – the 'pot' as we lovingly call it.

By 11.00 a.m. that morning it was time for a break and whilst sipping a coffee I decided that it couldn't hurt to give them a call and see what they thought of what had taken place and what I was still experiencing. I rang up their number and was put through to a very helpful consultant. I explained that we had spent a week diving to 70 metres each day with two dives on some days to that depth. He sounded a bit shocked. I explained about the bend, the *ad hoc* oxygen treatment I'd had on Ewan's rebreather and the current symptoms I was experiencing. He said I should come in and be seen as soon as possible.

"I'll jump in my car and drive through just now - if that suits?" I replied.

"No, don't do that – you've got a neurological abnormality. You could lose control of the car at any time", he cautioned. "Take your dive computer", he added.

I had one of those 'the penny drops' moments. Until then I guess I'd been largely in denial about what had happened to me – thinking it would just all go away and I'd get better. But here was an expert telling me that I was still possibly seriously ill and shouldn't be driving.

My secretary volunteered to drive me through from my law office and 30 minutes later she was dropping me off in Aberdeen at the National Hyperbaric Centre. Here I was first asked to go through a series of preliminary forms and provide personal and medical information. After that I was walked through smart corridors to an examination room where I was met by a consultant who wanted me to talk him through the diving I had done and the symptoms I was still experiencing. Whilst I was doing that a couple of other people came in and asked for my dive computer which they took away to lift the information in it about my dive profiles.

I was then asked to sit back on an examination bench where they started testing my reflexes by knocking my knees and elbows with a flat round headed medical hammer. All seemed OK. They then did another series of tests designed to check out my balance. I was asked to walk in a straight line, heel to toe, which I didn't appear to be too good at anymore. Then I was asked to stand straight and stretch both arms out in front of me, palms down. Easy enough it seemed. I was then asked to close my eyes. A little bit of a wobble – oops. And then with my arms out and eyes closed, they asked me to lift up one knee so I was standing on just one leg and count to 20 or 30.

I fell over.

The consultant explained that I wasn't too bad but that my balance was still affected – I should have been able to count to 20 in that position easily. They recommended that I should undergo recompression treatment in the chamber.

About 30 minutes later and I was struggling in through a circular opening into the cylindrical steel recompression chamber. A nurse came in and put a circular collar over my head, which had a latex seal onto my neck. It dawned on me that they were going to put some sort of hood or helmet on me to allow a precise high oxygen content gas. The recompression chamber would be pressurised to simulate a dive and rather than wastefully fill the whole thing with oxygen rich gas, which would be very costly and potentially explosive (think of the oxygen fire that killed the Apollo 1 astronauts in 1967) – the remainder of the huge volume of the chamber would be filled with standard air.

As I sat there in the chamber a medical patient on a stretcher was manhandled into the chamber. Then another person was led in – he appeared to be the victim of a stroke as he had lost the use of an arm and leg on the same side. And then the last of the people to be recompressed – a middle aged man – was led in by a nurse and sat opposite me. We nodded to each other but didn't say anything.

Now that the crew were all assembled the nurse came over with a clear semi rigid polythene helmet that she put over my head and connected to the latex collar around my neck. I felt the cool whisper of gas across my face from the tube leading into it. I asked the nurse what I was breathing – interested with my tech diver head on to know what was going on. I thought she said "Fifty fifty", which I took to mean Nitrox 50; i.e. 50% oxygen and 50% nitrogen. Or maybe she meant the flow rate was 50 litres a minute. I wasn't clear.

The circular hatch into the chamber clanged shut and was dogged down. We were ready to be recompressed.

A couple of nurses stayed in the chamber with us to look after everyone. I had heard that high percentages of oxygen at pressure were used therapeutically for all sorts of medical conditions including stroke victims, but I had not previously appreciated that the NHS in Aberdeen are carrying out these therapeutic oxygen treatments on a daily basis.

Once the chamber was secure a steady hiss told me that recompression had started and we were being blown down. Essentially we were being taken on a dive – the increasing air pressure in the chamber would shrink any bubbles in my systems that were still there causing my balance problems. The recompression took place fairly slowly and from time to time I popped my ears as if on a dive to relieve the pressure on my ears and sinuses.

I looked across at my fellow traveller sitting directly opposite me and said hello loudly through my spaceman's helmet. He nodded back – and I shouted over: "What are you in for?" At this he didn't reply – he reached into a pocket and pulled out a little black notebook and with a pencil he pointed to one of a list of sentences already written in it one below the other. It read: "I have had my tongue removed and find it hard to communicate."

I think we were blown down to a depth of about 18 metres – or three times atmospheric pressure – so any bubble would be reduced in size to a third of the volume it was before we started. After staying at that depth for a set time they then started to decompress the chamber extremely slowly – essentially bringing us back from depth to the surface. In all the whole process took almost three hours.

After we finally got back to atmospheric pressure the hatch was carefully un-dogged and everyone was slowly taken out. I was led back to meet the same consultant who had seen me before and put through another brief series of tests. The remarkable test was the one I had fallen over at previously – standing on one leg with my arms outstretched in front of me and my eyes closed. Now when they asked me to do that I was able to stand and count to 20. The difference before and after recompression was remarkable – especially considering it was three days after the dive that bent me.

After I had been checked out, I had a final meeting with the consultant who confirmed their view that the recompression had alleviated my lingering symptoms. He then added that it would be my decision as to whether I continued diving or gave it up.

I took his advice away with me and thought about it for several weeks. I continued in the local running club – and at first I would have sworn that my knees didn't feel the same as before the bend. Although it was probably all in my head, my legs seemed to get stronger week by week as I exercised. I managed to convince myself that I still had a slight residual loss of balance – nothing dramatic, but I felt I couldn't do some exercises, like the one-legged quad stretch, as well as I could before. That's the one where you stand on one leg and pull your other foot up behind you towards your butt to stretch the quad. I seemed wobbly at that one – but then most people who haven't had a bend find that one hard anyway – I just couldn't tell for sure.

After six weeks off diving I made the decision that I would continue diving – although I vowed that I would never dive repetitively to that depth again. I was already starting to think that I should be moving away from open-circuit diving to closed-circuit rebreather diving. That would be far more kind to my body and would minimise decompression issues. Tony Ray and I were the only remaining open-circuit divers in our group and none of the others had got bent on the North Channel trip after carrying out the same dives as me – sometimes with longer bottom times. But evolution is a slow process – and it would be some time before I finally made the transition to rebreather diving.

My first tentative post bend dive was a 50-metre O.C. Trimix dive on a new wreck we had located three miles southeast of Todhead Lighthouse. Once on the bottom we found a small steam trawler from the war era sitting on the seabed on an even keel. Her superstructure was almost completely gone and she appeared to be little more than a hull with exposed deck beams allowing glimpses between them into her innards. Subsequent research led us to believe this was the 117 feet long, 230-ton steam trawler *Repro,* which had struck a mine on 23 April 1917. Her state of decay tied in with her being a World War I loss. The dive went well and passed without incident although for a few hours after surfacing I was almost waiting to feel the onset of another bend.

Next up was another virgin wreck dive on an uncharted snag 6 miles south east of Todhead Lighthouse – the position for which had been given to me by a local fisherman. This was a 60-metre dive – my deepest since my bend – and again I felt comfortable and in control in the water. After the dive, despite being on tender hooks waiting for the slightest sign of a niggle, there were again no post dive symptoms. I fitted in a few further Trimix dives before ending the season with a November weekend based in Lochaline air diving the classic shallower Sound of Mull wrecks, SS *Shuna*, SS *Thesis*, SS *Hispania* and the *Rondo* without incident. It seemed I had got away with my bend lightly. It could have been a lot worse.

With the winter basically a 'no dive' time in the North Sea, by the time the 2004 season started I was itching to get going again. I started Trimix diving again in earnest and the season passed without incident as my weekends were filled with new wrecks such as the SS *Muriel*, SS *St Glen* and SS *Simonburn* up off Peterhead (courtesy of Jim Burke, Mike Rosie and Roger Mathieson), as well as our local favourites such as the tanker *Baku Standard*, SS *Gowrie* and MS *Taurus*. We were able to get out and dive the liner *Remuera* we own off Fraserburgh and I managed to fit in two trips to Scapa Flow to re-survey the German wrecks for an updated edition of *Dive Scapa Flow*. Memory of my bend faded.

CHAPTER TWELVE

IN THE DARKNESS – NETS

In November 2004 Ian Balgowan, a local fisherman from Stonehaven who had been very interested in our diving exploits on wrecks he had fished all his life, approached me with a problem. He had snagged his prawn net on an unmarked obstruction some nine miles off Montrose and wondered if there was anything I could do to help retrieve it.

Ian is an old sea dog who lives down at Stonehaven harbour. He is a genial, mild mannered, lovely bloke who has fished out of Stonehaven and the surrounding ports all his days. His knowledge of the sea, local currents and fishing is immense – and I have learnt a lot from him about the cat and mouse game played out daily in the quest to catch those tricky little blighters, prawns – his speciality. Ian has lost nets on several of the local 'snags' over the years – I'm sure I have seen a few of them.

Like me, he is interested in the history of the local wrecks and is always keen to see our video footage and stills photos of the wrecks. In the past he had just been able to see the wrecks as an outline bottom trace on his echo sounder, or felt them when his trawler came to a sudden stop. The video footage Paul Haynes and Tony Ray have taken of most of our local wrecks is spell binding and often when we come back in from a day's diving, if he has heard us at sea on the VHF he'll be on the phone for an update. Sometimes we get a call from him on the VHF whilst we're sitting on top of the wreck. There's nothing much goes on out on the water that he doesn't know about.

We soon had a chart looked at and Ian showed me where his fishing boat had come to an unexpected grinding halt as his nets snagged on an underwater obstruction. There was no wreck charted within miles of the snag – just flat seabed that should have been safe to trawl. The net was a valuable piece of fishing gear for a full-time fisherman and would be uninsured. It was a big loss for him. Would our group of divers have a go at getting the net back?

Ian still uses the old yardstick of fathoms to measure depth – and he told us that the water depth was 36 fathoms deep. A rough mental calculation put the depth in metric terms as being some 70 metres or more: deep, very deep.

The depth was bad enough for starters but to make matters worse we were now well into November and the underwater visibility around this coast had started to close in with the first winter's storms. The water close inshore looked like – and had the consistency of – a bowl of porridge. It would be bad enough dealing with the depth alone – but to be handling nets that far underwater in poor visibility meant great danger. But Ian had been good to us in the past and the least we could do would be to dive, look at the problem and see if there was any way we could easily free the net.

Ian talked of it being a prawn net – but I had no real conception of what that sort of net looked like. So, to get an idea of the type of net I'd be handling I asked him if there were any other prawn nets around in the harbour he could show me. In fact, it turned out that he had another similar prawn net aboard his fishing boat, the *Harvester*, which was berthed at Gourdon – one of the small harbours we used about 15 miles south of Stonehaven. I arranged to go and have a look.

That evening I drove down to Gourdon and climbed the ladder rungs down the side of the harbour wall and jumped onto *Harvester*'s deck where I shook hands with Ian and his partner in the boat. The prawn net was rolled up on a winch and they carefully unwound it from the winch drum so that I could have a look and see what it was like. The net was about 40–50 feet wide and about 6 feet high and was designed to be dragged along just above the seabed. Steel multicore trawl cables or wires connected via shackles to each side of the net and ran back up to the winches aboard the boat. On one side, a large heavy rusted steel trawl door was shackled in.

We agreed that we would first try to free the net in its entirety, as the problem might only be a simple snag in one area – if necessary we could cut the net free from the snag. If the cables were a problem, perhaps wound up and irretrievably ensnared on the wreck, then there would be no way we could free those underwater by hand. If that were the case then we would try to unshackle the net from the trawl cables at either side and at least save the net. These trawl cables were incredibly strong and even though I had determined to take down a hacksaw to get through the netting if necessary, the saw wouldn't make the slightest impression on the 1–2 inch thick multicore steel cables.

Ian told us that he had a couple of large pink Dhan buoys still keeping one end of the trawl cable afloat and whilst doing what he could to free his nets, he had wound the cable to the net very tight. We could follow it straight down to the obstruction.

We checked the weather forecast for the following day. November in the North Sea can be very difficult – but a dive looked possible with a Force 3–4 from the southwest forecast. This would mean a slight swell or chop to the sea, but nothing we hadn't been out in before.

As the snag lay nine miles directly out from Montrose we decided to launch *Stonehaven Diver* at Gourdon and motor down from there. This would save us a cold and exposed 10-mile leg by sea each way from Stonehaven.

Mike Wilcox – who had just recently joined our group agreed to dive with me – and Tony Ray would boat handle. Mike was a very capable Trimix rebreather diver. Built like an ox and immensely strong, he had very quickly shown us that he had a very good technical mind and excelled at the sort of diving we were doing. Mike had tried his hand at a number of interests and seemed to have done well at them all. A black belt in karate, he was also a very talented rock climber, as familiar making high-grade technical rock climbs as he was diving with us at the very cutting edge of Scottish technical diving.

I agreed to rendezvous with Ian and the *Harvester* out at the wreck site at 11.00 a.m. the next morning. We expected that it would take us short of an hour by sea to get from Gourdon out to the site in *Stonehaven Diver*. Ian in the much slower fishing boat would set off much earlier.

After a fitful night's sleep filled with images of struggling, snagged up in nets in pitch darkness far from the surface, I woke and breakfasted early at 6.30 a.m. We would be out on the water for a long time so I crammed as much food as I could down my throat – fruit juice, cereal, porridge, toast and tea. I then hitched up *Stonehaven Diver* to my less-than-trusty Vauxhall Frontera and towed it down the 10 miles or so to Gourdon where Tony and Mike were already waiting at the slipway.

We soon had the trailer board, electrics and ropes off my RIB and I was reversing the trailer down the slip into the water until the trailer wheels were half submerged. With a few pushes the RIB slid off the trailer into the water and I could drive the trailer out of the water and park up the Frontera and trailer ashore. Once we had the RIB laboriously loaded up with all our tanks and dive gear, I jumped aboard and clambered onto the console seat. Pumping the fuel bulb a few times until it was hard, I turned the ignition key, my Yamaha 90 engine roared into life, guiltily shattering the morning calm of the peaceful small village. Tony jumped aboard followed by Mike.

As I motored slowly forward out of the narrow harbour entrance to open sea, I switched on my GPS and punched in the coordinates for the rendezvous with the *Harvester* nine miles offshore. The signal was strong and very soon the LCD highway display was pointing me in the right direction.

Once out of the main harbour entrance and into open sea I throttled up and the RIB, lightly laden for once, rose effortlessly onto the plane, our speed leaping up within a few seconds from 3 knots to about 25 knots. About half a mile offshore I throttled down slightly and called the coastguard on channel 16 of my VHF radio: "Forth Coastguard, Forth Coastguard, Forth Coastguard. *Stonehaven Diver*, *Stonehaven Diver*."

The reply came back almost immediately: "*Stonehaven Diver*, this is Forth Coastguard. Go ahead."

"Forth Coastguard, this is *Stonehaven Diver* MRMWN6. I have some safety traffic for you. Over."

"*Stonehaven Diver*, Six seven for routine traffic and stand by."

I scrolled the 'channel select' knob on my VHF to channel 67 and waited for the coastguard to call back. A couple of minutes later the radio crackled into life again: "*Stonehaven Diver*, Forth Coastguard – Go ahead, please."

"Forth Coastguard, *Stonehaven Diver*. This vessel is registered under your small boat scheme so you have my details. We have just left Gourdon harbour. There are three persons aboard. We will be diving nine miles east of Montrose, returning Gourdon harbour at 1400 hours. Over."

"*Stonehaven Diver*, that's all copied. Please call us when you have completed your diving operations. Forth Coastguard – out."

The radio safety traffic completed, I then called Ian Balgowan on the previously agreed channel 69. Sure enough Ian was almost at the site – but he was still well out of view for us over the horizon. I told him we were now *en route* and would be with him in about 40 minutes.

With that done, *Stonehaven Diver* throttled up again and our speed leapt back up. With a southwesterly wind blowing off our east coast, the slight chop to the sea we had seen inshore started to increase the further we got offshore. But it was the sort of sea my RIB devoured and we flashed along almost air born most of the time, as we bounced from one crest to the next, the bow dipping into the occasional trough before punching through and upwards in a splash of brilliant white spray. The distance to the target shown on my GPS reduced steadily and about five miles from the site we started to be able to make out the tiny, dark silhouette of the *Harvester* on the horizon.

We flashed in towards the *Harvester* and soon could make out a large Dhan buoy sitting tight in the water nearby, along with another smaller buoy close by. I looked at my echo sounder and saw it was reading a flat sea bottom at 67 metres. We slowed, coming down off the plane, and motored over towards the Dhan buoy. As we neared it, the flat sea bottom line on my echo sounder LCD suddenly jumped straight up for about 5 metres as we passed over the obstruction – and then quickly dropped back down again to the flat seabed. It was the unmistakeable signature of a small wreck rising just 5 metres and obviously narrow in the beam – we had passed from one side of it to the other very quickly. Such a small wreck was most likely to be a fishing boat or steam trawler.

I went through the usual laborious routine of kitting up. Lead weights, webbing harness on first – it's a real pain if you get kitted up then find you've forgotten to put it on. Next, I hauled my heavy twin set of two 12-litre manifolded tanks until it was balanced on the large orange side tube of the RIB. Carefully I reached one arm under the fixed harness on the back plate, wriggled into the harness and then slid my other arm under the other shoulder loop. My primary bottom-mix regulator went over my right shoulder and the secondary bail-out regulator (for use in emergencies) went under my arm to reduce possible snagging, before being held by a bungee close to my mouth. I connected up my suit-inflation hose, which ran from one of my two 7-litre decompression stage tanks, slung one under either arm. The helium-rich bottom-mix in my back mounts was unsuitable for suit inflation – helium is a very cold gas and would chill my body more quickly than air. I clipped my deco reel to a D-ring on my buoyancy wings and then lastly, after getting all my other bits and pieces sorted out, I bungeed my hacksaw to one of my under arm stage tanks.

Once I was fully rigged and sitting astride the orange tube, I did a last-minute double-check on all my kit and then looked across at Mike who was just finishing getting kitted up. Although I was diving open-circuit, Mike was ahead of me kit-wise and had already bought and been trained on a Classic Inspiration rebreather, which recycled his breathing gas and didn't vent it off like my wasteful open-circuit kit did. Most of our group had moved on to diving with rebreathers, leaving Tony Ray and I left as the last of the open-circuit dinosaurs in our team.

Mike and I rolled over backwards from the RIB's tubes and splashed heavily into the water. Quickly righting ourselves we finned up to the front of the RIB where the painter bow rope was attached to Ian's trawl cable and Dhan buoy.

As I took hold of the trawl cable I could feel it was very taught, tensioned by the lifting effect of the large Dhan buoy and its snag 67 metres below us on the obstruction. The water around us had a greenish 5-metre visibility in the shallows – below us was nothing but pitch black.

In this poor visibility, Mike and I started the long descent down into the darkness. I peered anxiously below, straining for a sight of Ian's billowing nets, which might suddenly appear out of the gloom.

By the time we were 10 metres down the taught cable, all surface sunlight had been filtered out and we found ourselves cocooned in darkness – reliant on nothing but the beams from our powerful dive torches and my small head mounted pencil torch which I use for lighting up my gauges. Keeping one hand on the stiff cable we let ourselves drop down beside it, my eyes peering out to the very limit of my torch beam for a shackle set in the cable that would herald the approach of the nets themselves.

Slowly our depth increased: 20 metres down – nothing but blackness surrounded us; 30 metres down – the unyielding darkness revealed nothing but the thick cable plunging below seemingly endlessly. Forty metres down – still the darkness enveloped us like a heavy shroud and still there was no sign of the nets. Fifty metres down and suddenly the trawl cable gave way to reveal a shiny shackle, like the one I had seen topside connected to the net on the *Harvester*. Ian's net was now just below me – just out of eyesight at the limit of my vision.

I pressed on downwards for a few more metres and suddenly the darkness gave way to a blaze of green nylon netting. Staying a respectful distance away from the net in the slack water, I tried to work out how it was hanging. Following the net further down, suddenly the unmistakeable lines of a small shipwreck appeared in my torch beam. Grateful for something tangible to hold onto other than netting, I kicked over to the wreck and settled down on the rotted steel deck.

Mike soon arrived beside me and we swept our torches around our surroundings. The wreck was a small narrow vessel, sitting upright on an even keel. Although it was pitch black down here, the water was quite clear and in our powerful torch beams we could see right across from one side of the wreck to the other. I estimated that the vessel had a beam of just 25 feet or so.

We turned to our left and started moving along the wreck to try and find where Ian's nets were snagged. Very quickly in the darkness, we lost sight of the cable and netting completely. From the layout of the ship's structures it seemed that we were moving forward towards the bow.

There was no superstructure left standing up on the wreck – only plain flat decking, but we soon entered an area of debris and rotted spars with a few sticking upright. This looked as though it was where the wheelhouse had once stood. On a ship this small there would only have been a small wheelhouse, two deck levels high at most. We were seeing the skeletal remnants of the steel framing, the wooden sections long ago rotted away. Just forward of the bridge, suspended high above us, we came across some nets floating on ancient encrusted buoys. The nets were heavily discoloured and well covered with encrusting sea life – not bright green like the nets we had already seen. Perhaps 20–30 years ago another surprised fisherman had come to a grinding halt in this same spot. These were clearly very old nets and not Ian's

Beyond the nets we arrived at the vessel's bow – no sign of Ian's nets here. Realising that we were diving on what looked like a small steam trawler from the war era, we quickly retraced our steps following the port side of the wreck towards the stern. Very quickly (on such a small wreck) we passed the decayed bridge area and then once again the green glare of Ian's nets exploded into our torch beams.

Gingerly we followed the tightest section of netting as it would hopefully lead us to the snag point. Perhaps there would be a simple snag that we could free and allow the whole net to rise up. You never know unless you go look. Not far along past the wheelhouse remains, we came to a section where the net was snagged on a sharp protruding section of wreckage just forward of the stern. I pulled my hacksaw from its bungee on my deco tank and sawed through the tightest strands of the net - keeping as far back as possible from it.

As soon as I had cut through the last strand the whole net started to slowly move further astern, tensioned by something on the other side of the wreck. I could see now that we were at the very stern of the wreck and that the net neatly enveloped the complete stern of this small ship. Looking over the gunwale of the wreck I could see the rounded sweep of the stern under the hull all the way down to the rudderpost.

The whole net, now free from its initial snag, was actually moving slowly round the stern of the wreck, but after a few metres it came to a sharp halt. We kicked off the deck and following the net went down under the overhanging stern to about 65 metres – perhaps the net had caught on the propeller. As we swam under the stern I saw the small propeller just forward of the rudder, but the net was clear of this area. We followed the net further round until we arrived at the other end of it. The trawl cable was draped over the starboard gunwale under tension and well jammed under the keel of the wreck itself.

By this time our planned bottom time of 20 minutes had elapsed and we were now starting to run into lengthy decompression. I knew we had already clocked up almost an hour's deco from this depth – and every minute we stayed hugely increased our decompression time for the ascent.

Mike went down further under the starboard side of the hull and using his immense strength, tried to unclip the net's shackle from its steel multi-core towing cable. I turned my torch onto where he was working to let him see what he was doing better. But it was soon clear that there was so much tension on the net and cable that the shackle couldn't be moved enough to free it.

In a last vain attempt, I took out my hacksaw again and tried cutting through the multi-strand cable, but it was so strong that the hacksaw made hardly any impression on it at all. We weren't going to be able to do anything more down here. But at least we knew how the net was snagged onto the wreck and could tell Ian. He might now be able to use the *Harvester* to rip it off the stern. I hoped that by freeing the worst snag we might have done enough to let the net come up once the powerful engines of the *Harvester* could be brought to bear.

After an exchange of 'OK' and 'thumbs up' signals, I took hold of the cable and started to pull myself slowly up the line towards the surface. Having spent the good part of 25 minutes at depths of up to 65 metres or more, we were now looking at a time to the surface of about 80 minutes. Rising up from 65 metres after that sort of bottom time, is a protracted business. As we reached a depth of 45 metres our bodies started to 'offgas' the gas we had breathed at depth. Even though we were still very deep and breathing huge volumes of compressed gas with each breath, the mass of gas we had already absorbed into our tissues was so great that as the water pressure decreased it was pouring out of our tissues.

We halted at 45 metres for our one minute 'deep stop' and then slowly rose up at a rate of three metres a minute until we reached 27 metres where our decompression stops started to get progressively longer. At 21 metres I was shallow enough to switch over from my helium-rich bottom mix onto my oxygen-rich, no helium deco mix.

The greatest expansion in the size of the bubbles in our blood stream and tissues happens in the shallower depths and the longer shallow stops are designed to give ample time for all these expanding bubbles to pass harmlessly from our bodies. A bubble doubles in size between 10 metres and the surface. There are many competing theories about how decompression works – the dark art of bubble mechanics. Some decompression theories have you rise up from depth quite quickly to spend very long times at shallower depths and at your final decompression stop at 6 metres. But we believe that it is the deeper stops that are the most critical. If you rise up too fast for the expanding bubbles to safely escape and a tiny bubble forms in one of your tissues at depth, it's going to increase in size hugely as you ascend. It doesn't matter how long you spend at your last 6-metre stop – if you get a bubble stuck in you at depth, you aren't going to get rid of it in the shallows no matter how long you stay there.

After a seeming eternity on deco, we were finally clear to break the surface. The eternal silence and darkness of the deep had been left far below, enshrouding the mystery wreck once again.

As our heads broke the surface, Mike and I let go of the trawl cable and finned leisurely away, moving apart from each other just enough to let Tony manoeuvre *Stonehaven Diver* in between us. We grabbed hold of the lifelines on either side of the RIB and started the laborious routine of inwater de-kitting. Soon, Mike and I were back in the boat and cracking open a flask of hot coffee, as we sat and discussed what we had seen. We both agreed that the small wreck looked like a steam trawler from between the wars. It was sitting on an even keel with its bows pointing towards the distant shore – in common, not surprisingly, with a high percentage of wrecks. If you know you are sinking, you're going to turn and run for the shore. Perhaps this vessel had turned to run for shore before the sea overcame it. This wreck was a forgotten human tragedy from years gone by. What had happened to the crew? Had they survived or perished? What ship was this?

Tony gunned the throttle on *Stonehaven Diver* and we zipped over to the *Harvester*, which had been standing a respectful distance off us whilst we had been inwater – so we didn't end up putting deco bags up under it.

We clambered aboard and briefed Ian about what we had seen and how we thought he should try and get his nets off the wreck. The stern of the wreck pointed out to seaward and the net was wrapped neatly round the entire rounded curve of the stern. We had managed to free the net from its primary entanglement on the port side just forward of the stern. If Ian hooked his trawl cable onto his boat and headed directly out to sea then he might be able to drag the net off the wreck.

Ian took the *Harvester* in close to his buoys, hooked his trawl wire and wound it onto his winches. We jumped back into *Stonehaven Diver* and stood away from the action, not wanting to get in the way.

Once hitched up, Ian turned the *Harvester* to seaward and motored slowly ahead as we all hoped for the best. At first, as he moved away, we thought the plan was working as he seemed to be able to winch in his trawl cable – it looked as though the net was coming free. But then the *Harvester* suddenly leapt ahead – the cable had parted down on the wreck. Ian wound in the remnants of his cable and when we looked at its end, it looked as though it had been cut through with a knife. We had seen how the cable had been draped over the gunwale of the wreck under tension. Perhaps it had been rubbing on a sharp piece of ship's side for the weeks since it was snagged and the strain of the final attempt to free the net had parted it. Whatever the reason, the net was now never going to come free and reluctantly Ian had to remove his buoys from the remaining cable and cast it loose. We will return one day to have another go at recovering his nets. They aren't lost forever – just temporarily misplaced.

CHAPTER THIRTEEN

THE SEARCH FOR THE GERMAN
DESTROYER *T6*

For some time we had heard about the 600-ton German torpedo boat *T6* which was sunk on 7 November 1940 during World War II a little way to the south of Aberdeen, after a sortie from Norway to lay mines across the harbour entrance. Ironically she had struck a mine herself and sunk.

T6 was listed as being 267 feet in length, so she was a sizeable vessel and one that would be of historical interest if we could find and identify her. Being one of the few wartime enemy naval losses around these parts, we felt that we would readily identify her because of her construction and armament.

Jim Burke, one of my regular dive buddies, was particularly keen on an expedition to locate her. Jim is a lovely bloke now in his 40s with a lifetime of diving under his belt. Tall and strong, he is a high-flying management consultant by day who thinks nothing of commuting weekly to distant places like South Africa if that is where he is posted. In his time off he is an extremely enthusiastic and capable tech diver with hundreds of tech dives to his name. Like me, Jim loves the sea and diving shipwrecks and although he lives about 50 miles away from me, when the seas are too rough for diving, I am sure I can hear him sobbing quietly – even from this distance. If there is a chance of getting a dive in, Jim will go for it. He will always put himself out for you too if need be.

In 2005 Jim had got in touch with a local fisherman who told him how some years ago another fisherman had hauled up some shells in his net after trawling around an old wreck in the right approximate location for *T6*. The fishermen had dubbed this wreck the *T6* as a result, so this position looked like a good place to start our hunt.

Aberdeen is known internationally as a world centre for oil and gas. Its harbour throngs 24/7 with every type of oil-related vessel you can get, entering and leaving or manoeuvring into tight berths. Dive Support Vessels, stand-by vessels and supply vessels all compete with local coasters, fishing boats and the large ferries that leave daily for Orkney, Shetland and the Faeroe Islands. From a diver's perspective however, Aberdeen is a difficult area to work.

The Harbour Trustees understandably don't want small dive boats like ours interfering with the continual commercial traffic in the harbour and in any event, there is no slip suitable for launching and retrieving a large RIB in the harbour. Indeed there is no suitable slip for 15 miles to the north and 15 miles to the south. So even though the possible *T6* wreck site was just a few miles south of Aberdeen, the nearest available slip was 15 miles to the south in Stonehaven.

Jim Burke and I teed up a *T6* expedition for a weekend with weak neap tides. According to our charts and tide tables, slack water would arrive between 9.00 a.m. and 10.00 a.m., so to give us time to launch and make the 15-mile journey up the coast, we would have to meet at 6.30 a.m. at Stonehaven harbour.

Jim lives about an hour's drive north of Aberdeen but would tow the big 6-metre *Buchan Diver* RIB all the way down to Stonehaven for a 6.30 a.m. launch. He was going to have a very early rise that day – in fact he'd be getting up not long after I went to bed the night before!

I got my own RIB, *Stonehaven Diver*, all set up the day before the exped. Fuel tanks were filled, oil checked and an extra Jerry can of fuel loaded aboard. I hitched the RIB up to my jeep and got all my personal dive kit ready to load quickly the next morning.

I got to bed about 11.30 p.m. that Friday night – and it felt as though I had hardly dozed off when my alarm clock was going off to tell me it was 5.00 a.m. and time to rise. Jim would have been up for an hour already and no doubt was already on the road south to Stonehaven.

I got up, washed and groggily went downstairs in the early summer morning half-light to the kitchen and put on some porridge whilst I made up a flask of coffee, a litre of juice and some sandwiches. It was going to be a long day out on the water.

I loaded my kit it into my jeep and in half darkness towed my RIB down to the harbour slip for just on 6.30 a.m. As I arrived – to Jim's great credit – I found him there already, dressed into his dry suit with *Buchan Diver* already launched and gently rocking in a mirror sea. Jim never failed to impress me with his stamina and zest for diving – he is just that sort of guy, solid and dependable. Nothing is too much for him and he never lets you down.

Tony Ray and I got my RIB launched and loaded and all the team were by now dressed into their dry suits and loading their kit into the boats. The two RIBs bulged with stacked rebreathers, two stage tanks per diver, kit bags, emergency oxygen sets, weights, shot-lines and Dhan buoys, cameras, flasks and accessories.

A June early morning sun was just starting to rise low over the sea on the horizon to the east – a brilliant blaze of orange. The leaden darkness of night still hung over the distant hills inland to the west. Long dark shadows from harbour buildings and the cliffs to the south crept over the harbour as we worked. Other than the hive of activity that was our group, the harbour was completely deserted and quiet save for a few seagulls wheeling around in the blue sky, squawking and screeching their dawn chorus. The calm and idyllic silence however was abruptly shattered as my Yamaha 90 hp outboard engine and Jim's Suzuki 140 hp outboard were cranked into life and left for a few minutes to warm up. Beyond the harbour, the sea was a flat, oily calm. It was a beautiful day for the motor up the coast.

We cast off and reversed out of our loading spot against the old stone pier and both powerful RIBs motored gently out of the harbour. Once out in open sea we turned to the north and opened up the engines. The heavily-laden RIBs pushed against their bow waves, quickly riding up and over the mountain of water onto the plane. Soon both RIBs were up to

25 knots and screaming up the coast – the bows lifting every now and then before slapping back onto the glassy sea and sending a shimmer of spray out to either side. The coastal towns of Muchalls, Newtonhill, Portlethen and Cove sped past on our port beam.

Forty or so minutes later both boats were approaching the possible wreck site and soon we had picked up a small wreck on our echo sounders – in an area where there was no wreck charted. The trace however looked disappointingly small – it rose only a few metres off the seabed and apparently was not the wreck of a 267-foot long torpedo boat. We reckoned however that such a boat would have been designed for speed and fairly lightly built, so perhaps she hadn't stood up to well to 70 years immersion in the storms of the North Sea. Only a dive would tell – you never know until you get down there.

The depth to the seabed was about 65 metres and the wreck seemed to rise up for about 5 metres at the most. We had a planned bottom time of 20 minutes. As the first two divers got ready to splash from each RIB, it was just coming up to 8.30 a.m. It seemed like it had been a long day already.

Tony and I were to be first divers inwater from my boat and we busied ourselves getting our gear on. Once rigged, we rolled backwards off the tubes into the water, righted ourselves and headed off down the shot-line. The water round and about us was dark but crystal clear.

We descended slowly – our minds occupied with the mechanics of the dive – from time to time pumping air into our dry suits to relieve the squeeze and pumping a little air into our buoyancy wings to stop us sinking too fast. We checked our gauges and computers to monitor how we were doing – and in between all that we fell relentlessly into the darkness, our eyes straining for that first glimpse of what lay beneath.

At just over 50 metres down, the uniform darkness started to acquire a form – and then a small shipwreck materialised out of the gloom. It was immediately apparent that we had a small steam trawler here – and not a German torpedo boat destroyer.

The shot-line had landed conveniently just behind the bridge wheelhouse superstructure. We fixed a strobe onto the line just above the wheelhouse and then we were free to start our exploration. We spent a few minutes having a good look around the wheelhouse superstructure and simultaneously both of us spotted the head of the ship's telegraph lying amidst the debris. The brass rimmed compass head lay not far away, still filled with damping oil. The floating circular white compass face was clear as the day it was made with the compass points easily discernable. In the middle of the face the legend read 'W.A. Johanneson, Grimsby'.

Old-fashioned steam trawlers are great deep wrecks to dive – I love them. They ruled the seas for 70 years and only stopped being made in the 1950s. They are completely different from modern trawlers – put the notion of any similarity out of your mind. These are proper *bona fide* small steamships, with fo'c'stle, bridge superstructure, helm, telegraph, boiler and engine room and are usually around 125–145 feet long. So even at depth, it's easy to do a complete circumnavigation in one dive and spend time on the interesting bits. Diving on a big deep wreck, you only see a small part of it in one dive.

As we completed our circumnavigation we spotted a defensive 3-pounder gun at the stern and realised that it was most likely shells for this gun that fishermen had trawled up, and which had given rise to the misnomer *T6*.

Back ashore, from the clues we had gathered, Jim was soon able to identify the wreck as the World War I casualty *Gelsina* – a 227-ton, 118-foot long Grimsby steam trawler which had sunk off Girdleness south of Aberdeen, after striking a mine on 25 June 1917. On the bright side, at least we now knew one place where the *T6* was not.

Two weeks later and we were back launching at Stonehaven very early on a Sunday morning for another 15-mile journey up the coast to check out the second of the five positions Jim had got for the fabled *T6*.

After a bash up the coast in relatively benign conditions, our two RIBs closed in on the position and very quickly our echo sounder was showing a big bottom trace of what looked like a substantial shipwreck. We had two full boatloads of some six divers, all eager and keen to get wet. Would this be the *T6*?

Everyone started getting dressed in and ready to dive. Away to the north there was the usual bustle of oil supply and service vessels entering and leaving Aberdeen harbour for the North Sea oil platforms. Further out to sea, large vessels were moving up and down the coast. Not far away a fishing boat seemed to be lumbering slowly along as it trawled. It was busy out on the water this day.

All the divers were going to be diving in one wave today. I was diving with Tony and Mike Wilcox. In the other RIB we had Jim, Mike Rosie and Phil Hodson. They were ready before us and rolled in off their boat first. Once they had started heading down the shot-line, Tony, Mike and I rolled off my RIB and started down the line a few minutes after them.

Although we had had pretty good visibility on the *Gelsina* a few weeks before, it was soon clear that today's dive was going to be totally different, for as we went down the line, very quickly the visibility became extremely poor and all ambient light from the surface was filtered out. Poor visibility and total darkness enshrouded us.

We arrived on the seabed clumsily at about 55 metres. Mike Rosie's big commercial strobe was flashing away on the shot-line, its pulses momentarily transforming the pitch darkness into a cloudy opaque haze. We were standing on a silty seabed and there was no sign of the wreck anywhere. We had missed it. As I stood at the bottom of the shot-line with 200+ feet of water above me, I could see here and there a faint glow from the torches of other divers who were searching around the line looking for the wreck.

One diver – I didn't know who – had clipped a reel around the downline and was obviously searching at the end of the reel-line. As I looked around for some clue on the seabed – some wreckage to show we were in the right area – a torch appeared with the silhouette of one of our divers behind it reeling back in. In the poor visibility I couldn't tell who it was to begin with – but I got a signal that he was giving up looking for the wreck and going to head up to the surface.

Just then – as the ghostly silhouette of that diver started ascending above me – I thought I momentarily saw a flash of light in the distance and higher up. But it was so brief I could have been mistaken. 'Should I go for it?' I wondered – it might be nothing and time was ticking by. I didn't want to get separated from the line and the other divers in these poor conditions.

Tony must have got a better view of the flash than I did and bravely decided to go have a look. So he headed off into the darkness and rose up towards where the light had been seen. I decided to follow the other diver back up the line and give up on a finding a new wreck that day. There wasn't much of our bottom-time left and even if there were a wreck there, then there would be little time to explore it. I didn't want to venture off into the darkness so late in the dive.

On the surface we had four divers back, all of whom had done a bit of a seabed survey of HMS *Inthevicinityof* – but Mike Rosie and Tony Ray were still down. The two of them eventually appeared some 40 minutes later having had an epic big dive. It turned out that it was the flash of Mike Rosie's torch Tony and I had seen. He had been doing a circular search around the downline – keeping the flash of the strobe in eyeshot – and had managed to run slap bang into the hull of a big steamship sitting on its keel. He made his way up the hull and onto the deck and from there could see the dim flash of his own strobe in the distance, as well as the glow of our torches. He had been signalling to us with his torch from up on the wreck's deck.

Tony had swum across, moved up the hull and joined Mike on the deck. The two of them were then able in their remaining bottom-time, to explore what looked like a World War II merchant vessel sitting on its keel. In the short time that they had left down on the wreck they had skilfully managed to get a good look around a large part of it. The *T6* it was not.

We suspect that this was the wreck that our tech instructor Dave Gordon of Aberdeen Watersports had dived on air ten years earlier – a wreck which local fishermen refer to as the 'Grass Boat' because it was reputed to be carrying a cargo of esparto grass. If that had been her cargo, it would long ago have disappeared, and neither Dave (ten years earlier) nor Tony and Mike would have seen any evidence of that.

There was a known ship – the 1,137 ton SS *Tasmania* which had grounded ¾ mile north of the River Don, Aberdeen on 10 February 1883 whilst carrying esparto grass. But she was clearly not the wreck we had dived and I suspected this wreck's local name might just be a case of the histories and names of ships getting jumbled up over time. The *Tasmania* was a far older wooden vessel, which had run ashore a good few miles further to the north.

We have never been back to dive this steamship wreck again, and have never established its identity conclusively. This we will leave as another gem for the next generation of tech divers to work out. But for our purposes, this was another possible location of the *T6* ruled out. We've got three more positions here to check out in the coming seasons and hopefully one of these will yield the *T6*.

To be continued…

CHAPTER FOURTEEN

OVER THE HORIZON

In the summer of 2005, my fisherman friend Ian Balgowan got in touch with a position for a snag some 15 miles directly out into the North Sea, which looked very close to the approximate charted position for the tanker *Desabla*. She was a 420 feet long, 6047 grt tanker torpedoed 15 miles east of Todhead Lighthouse on 12 June 1915 by *U-17* whilst en route from Port Arthur, Texas to the UK with a cargo of oil. I had considered trying to find her for a number of years.

When we plotted his position for the wreck on our chart, it seemed to lie in an area where the depth varied from 69–75 metres. Such a large vessel would easily rise up 10 metres or so off the seabed and this would put her in a very diveable range for us of 60–70 metres. But as the position was so far offshore, it would require a full expedition to get out and dive it. So, Tony and I decided that rather than getting everyone's expectations up by setting up a big offshore dive where there might not in fact be a wreck – or where the wreck might be just too deep – that we would do a non-diving dry recce. If we got nice calm seas, then we could quickly nip out with *Stonehaven Diver* lightly laden. If we could find and mark the wreck on our GPS, we would check out the depth and then set up a full-blown expedition thereafter when we could guarantee success for the team.

As Tony and I studied the Admiralty Chart in the run up to the trip we saw that our route out would take us over two large trenches in the seafloor – each about 1 mile wide – which run southwest/northeast. The inshore trench, known locally as the Dog Hole, runs for some 20 miles or so. The outer trench is also a mile wide but is shorter, running for some 8 miles. The seabed drops off almost vertically from around 60–70 metres all the way down to more than 120 metres at the bottom of both trenches.

The Highland Boundary Fault runs all the way across Scotland from Arran and Helensburgh on the west coast and reaches the North Sea on the east coast, just at the north side of Stonehaven. It was here that the world's oldest air-breathing fossil was recently found – a 420 million year old fossilised millipede (20 million years older than the previous record holder). The two great sea trenches that we would pass over must be linked to that fault line – we would look out for them.

On a bright, shimmery calm early morning, Tony and I launched *Stonehaven Diver*, punched in the GPS coordinates and pressed the 'GO TO' button. The GPS quickly gave us a highway route 15 miles out to the possible position for the wreck of the *Desabla*.

Although *Stonehaven Diver* was basically empty, instead of being laden with heavy dive kit as normal, we still took along a couple spare Jerry cans of fuel lashed to the console. I made sure that my back-up handheld GPS was fully charged and took along my back-up handheld VHF radio, in case the main fixed console-mounted VHF radio should fail. But it worried me that we would be over the horizon and that our VHF radios – which work on line of sight – would be rendered largely useless.

My Yamaha 90 hp engine roared into life and as soon as we were out of the 3-knot speed limit of the harbour and after a safety radio call to the coastguard to report what we were doing, I throttled the boat up onto the plane. She quickly pushed over the bow wave and our speed leapt up to 25 knots. Once on the plane, to conserve fuel, I throttled back until we were skipping over the sea at about 20 knots.

The coastline started to recede into the distance behind us and as the miles started to clock up, so it started to disappear down below the horizon. Soon only the inland hilltops to the west were visible. From time to time as we skipped along I glanced down at the echo sounder. The depth to the seabed scrolled out a steady reading of 60–70 metres. Once we were about 10 miles offshore, I glanced at the echo sounder just as the depth reading suddenly fell away almost instantaneously down to about 125 metres. We had arrived at the first rip in the seabed – the Dog Hole. I imagined what it must be like down there at the drop off. Near vertical cliffs, that plunged down for hundreds of feet. What mysteries lay at the bottom?

The Dog Hole proved to be about one mile wide as shown on the chart – for just as suddenly as it had dropped off, we passed over the other side of the trench and the depth leapt up again to the standard 60–70 metres. We knew the second trench was yet to come.

About two miles further out and we hit the unmistakeable signature of this second trench. The seabed dropped away vertically from 70 metres down to 115 metres again. We screamed across this second underwater chasm, a mile later hitting the other side where the depth reading again leapt up instantaneously to about 70 metres. We now had about 3 miles to run to our target.

We closed at a steady speed of 20 knots – and the depth stayed at a uniform 70 metres. With the constant depth we were seeing, the wreck looked as though it would be in a very diveable depth – if it were as big as we expected then this would be extremely interesting.

By now the land had disappeared completely beneath the horizon to the west of us. Out here, there was only Tony and myself and our lifeline, *Stonehaven Diver*. We peered at our GPS and echo sounder as we approached what was perhaps going to be the fabled wreck of the *Desabla*.

Two miles from the target and the depth was still 70 metres. Excellent. One mile from the target – the depth was still 70 metres. Fantastic. Half a mile from the target – depth still 70 metres. Top diving on a large steamship from World War I in a reasonable depth beckoned. But then, as we got within half a mile, the seemingly constant depth readings ominously started to change. Suddenly it was 75 metres, then 80 metres – and it just continued getting deeper and deeper. The closer we got the greater the speed of depth increment.

85 metres…

90 metres…

And then in a depth of 95 metres came the unmistakeable outline on the echo sounder of a wreck far below on the seabed. Although the nearest depression on the charts was shown a few miles away from our location, it was clear that the charts were inaccurate and that we were motoring over the start of an uncharted depression. If it was the *Desabla*, she was sitting on a fairly severe slope – which perhaps led down to the charted depression a few miles away. But as I looked at the wreck outline on the sounder it became clear that this was the wreck of a smaller vessel and not the 420-foot long wreck of a 6,000-ton tanker.

Whatever the wreck, at the huge depth of 95 metres and 15 miles offshore, this was too serious, too deep and too risky an expedition to stage out here in RIBs. It would be possible on a hard boat, but if anything were to go wrong we would be a long way from help or assistance. A bend or embolism would be bad; engine failure, bad; a fire … the consequences did not bear thinking about. This far out – out of sight of land – would our VHF radio transmissions be picked up ashore? Like the steamship off Aberdeen we had located whilst trying to find the *T6*, this particular wreck also awaits exploration by the next generation of technical divers.

By way of a post-script to this story, in 2010 divers from Eyemouth managed to successfully locate and identify the real *Desabla* lying on her side in about 70 metres of water. What the wreck we were looking at was, I suspect I will never know.

CHAPTER FIFTEEN

SS *KILDALE* AND SS *BRETAGNE*

In October 2005 Jim Burke arranged a 'mixed gas weekend' for our group diving off the well-equipped Lossiemouth-based dive boat, *Top Cat*. We would work out of our favourite harbour at the northeast tip of Scotland – Sandhaven, just a few miles to the west of Fraserburgh. The local harbour trustees had just gone to a lot of trouble building a new quality slip from which you can launch and retrieve RIBs at all states of the tide. The deeper section of the harbour would also easily allow *Top Cat* in and out at most tide states.

Top Cat skipper Bill Ruck took her along from Lossiemouth (which lies well to the west) on the Friday night and we arranged to meet early at the harbour the following morning to get out and make the most of the day. Jim had a connection with a sub-sea survey specialist who was going to come along to trial some very expensive commercial side-scan sonar kit for the day. Jim had also worked out a list of about ten possible wreck sites from just a few miles offshore to more than 10 miles out and we would spend the whole of Saturday and Sunday out on the water looking for these wrecks and diving where we could.

Phil Hodson – a well-known technical diver who started off with Aberdeen Watersports in the 1990s – joined our usual group of Jim Burke, Tony Ray, Mike Rosie, and Mike Wilcox. Phil had moved down to Deep Blue in Plymouth for a number of years but eventually missed the Northern Lights so much he moved back up to Aberdeen. I'd like to think that was because of the quality of the diving – but it was most likely the lure of the opportunities offered here in the subsea oil world.

We ran out for 8 miles or so from Sandhaven to the wreck of our old friend the liner *Remuera*, which Ewan and I had first found in 2000 and which (as mentioned earlier) our group had gone on to purchase a few years later. We knew exactly where it lay, having dived it many times, and intended to pass up and down it a few times to give the side-scan sonar chap a chance to play with his shiny piece of very sexy kit.

We had always wondered why the *Remuera* appears not to show any sign of any of her vast deckhouse superstructures. She lies on her port side and she is not far off being upside down. Afloat, she was almost heavy with a large midships superstructure lined with portholes, but down on the wreck there was little sign of this. On one of the passes we seemed to see the outline of a man-made structure on the seabed away from the main wreck itself. Could it be that part of it had come off during the attack or as she sunk? Another target for a future dive presented itself there and then.

After an hour or so honing our skills on the *Remuera* we moved about 3 miles to the west and started sweeping in the vicinity of one of Jim's possible positions. Very soon we had picked up the outline of what looked like a small wreck on the sonar and echo sounder. Bill Ruck started running over the site, punching in marks in his GPS for each end and what seemed to be a high point amidships. Could that be the bridge?

We got ready to dive as Bill dropped a shot-line right on the high midships point.

We all entered the water as one group – about six divers in total, all following each other one after the other into languid, oily calm water. Slack water had been calculated spot on – there was absolutely no current. The depth to the seabed was 75 metres. We were 10 miles offshore.

Slowly we dumped gas from our suits and buoyancy wings and started to drop down the line, in pleasant good offshore visibility of about 20 metres. As usual, once we got down to about 35 metres all the ambient light disappeared and we were plunged into pitch darkness.

We pressed on down and it just got blacker and blacker as we dropped through 40 metres, 50 metres, 60 metres and then down to 70 metres – when at last, heavily rotted steel beams and spars started to appear in our torch beams. We landed on the seabed amidst the skeleton of a very rotted and disintegrating small steamship, which although sitting on her keel, was slowly being engulfed by sand. Bill Ruck had been spot on dropping the shot-line, as just a few yards away I could make out the rotted framework of the bridge superstructure.

I started to explore the wreck and very quickly got to the other side of the silt-filled hull. The beam of this ship was only about 35 feet. Behind the bridge superstructure I came across a single boiler and a small triple-expansion engine. Not wanting to venture too far away from the relative safety of the shot-line in these pitch-black conditions, I retraced my steps forward passing the bridge and the shot-line. I hope I'm not the only tech diver who likes to get back to the shot-line to ascend in poor visibility. I always have a nagging fear of carrying out a free ascent away from the shot-line – and rising up in the darkness into billowing trawl nets snagged on the wreck.

In the remnants of the foredeck hold I came across a cargo of coal. So we had a small steamship, which from the state of hull disintegration seemed probably World War I era. We knew she had a beam of about 35 feet and was carrying a cargo of coal. I reckoned by a rough rule of thumb that she would have been about 1,000 grt. That should be enough to identify her.

Our bottom time of 20 minutes had by now elapsed and we all rendezvoused at the shot-line and started the long slow ascent, pausing at the required stages for our decompression stops. An hour later we were on the surface and Bill was expertly coming in to pick us up.

Like all good diving hard boats, Bill had a few good reference books aboard and we went straight away to look and see what casualties there had been around these parts that fitted what we had just explored. Very quickly, one shipping loss was jumping out of the pages at me: the SS *Bretagne*.

The Danish steamship *Bretagne* was listed as 224 feet long with a beam of 39 feet. She was 1,110 grt and was listed as sunk 8–9 miles northeast of Rattray Head by *UC-45* on 17 April 1917. The dimensions were right – as was the age of the vessel. That a U-boat had sunk her would explain the poor condition she was in – a torpedo would make a real mess of a small steamship such as this. But on the other hand, being a smaller vessel, the U-boat might not have used a torpedo but may have boarded her and sunk her by grenade.

The location of her sinking was well out – by almost 10 miles. But in the days of dead-reckoning it was not uncommon for vessels to be several miles out. A crewman's evidence of what he thought his position was in the heat of a sinking might be well off – what if the position was a guess given by a survivor perhaps not involved in the ship's navigation? It was completely understandable for the position to be well out. I read on.

The *Bretagne* had been en route from Newcastle to Copenhagen when she was sunk by *UC-45* and guess what? She had been carrying a cargo of 1,503 tons of coal. There it was – a cargo of coal just as I had seen in the foredeck hold.

There wasn't any other ship of these dimensions and age with a cargo of coal listed around here. Everything about this fitted and we felt confident that we had got a good identification for this particular wreck.

We headed back to Sandhaven and Bill tied up *Top Cat* for the night. We had all taken rooms in a small hotel in Fraserburgh for the night, so after a full meal it was an early night for us. We would be back at Sandhaven early on Sunday morning to get out for some more wreck hunting in advance of slack water.

The next morning we were joined on *Top Cat* by Paul Haynes, who I hadn't seen since I did a couple of dives with him in 1998 during the development of the Divex Stealth Clearance Diver Life Support System Rebreather. It was this chance meeting that would introduce Paul to our group and he would become an ever-present Stonehaven Snorkellers Deep Cave Rescue Team stalwart for many years subsequently.

Top Cat left Sandhaven harbour once again, blessed with smooth oily calm waters. We settled down onto a northeast heading as we motored the 10 miles out to where we were going to search around two wreck positions marked within a few hundred metres of each other (at approximate position 57 45N, 01 46W). One chart position had the numbers '(56)' inside the wreck symbol – showing that it was known to be clear down to a depth of 56 metres over the obstruction. The other wreck symbol had clearance numbers of '(45)' inside it and had the letters 'PD' beside it – the Admiralty Chart abbreviation for 'position doubtful'. I suspected that these two vague wreck symbols marked as lying only a few hundred metres away from each other were probably both inaccurate positions for the same wreck. Importantly however the '(45)' wreck symbol had a straight line above it showing that it had been found during a survey, so there was definitely something in the approximate vicinity.

Once on site in between the two wreck symbols, we started a tow with the side scan sonar. Very quickly we picked up a wreck on the seabed a few hundred metres to the west of the west-most of the two wreck symbols. There was nothing else lying around on the seabed so it seemed to be the case that they were both slightly inaccurate marks for the same wreck.

Bill Ruck passed over the site a few times to work out the orientation of the wreck and then dropped a big shot-weight down onto the highest point. The depth was showing 86 metres. We got rigged up and ready to dive.

Whereas yesterday we had had a dark gloomy dive, as soon as we were in the water this time it was clear that conditions were much different the 8 or so miles further out to the east here. As we descended there was clarity to the water and ambient light flooded down. The visibility was much, much better.

We spotted the wreck beneath us from about 65 metres as we dropped down, finally landing on flattened metal amidst huge boilers that were sticking up through the wreckage. The vessel sat on its keel but its whole structure seemed to have collapsed, perhaps pounded flat by the shock of the wave action transmitted through the water – even at this great depth. I tried to visualise how the ship would have towered around me if its structure had still been intact.

I was diving with Tony Ray and we had taken our underwater Aquazepp scooters so we could get a good tour of what topside had looked like – a big vessel from the side scan images. Surrounded and dwarfed by massive boilers, we clipped our strobes to the downline and set them flashing. Tony had rigged his video camera to the top of his scooter and filmed as we gunned our Zepps and randomly set off into the darkness in one direction. Almost 300 feet of water towered above us.

We passed beyond the huge boilers and the absence of an engine room told me we were heading forward towards the bow. I don't remember seeing much in the way of bridge superstructure – everything seemed flattened and confused. We passed over the tangled mass of flattened plating and leaving it behind, soon came upon the hatch for a huge hold with a large expanse of deck either side of it. The ship seemed to regain its shape here, but when I looked into the hold there was no depth to it because of the general collapse of the wreck. The hold also held absolutely no cargo. I was already starting to think she was a war loss in ballast.

Tony and I pressed on side-by-side on our scooters and soon came upon the hatch for a second big hold. The size of the holds, hatches and the beam of about 50 feet indicated a big steamer of 400 feet in length or more. We made it up to the very bow and swept round the stem at full speed before scooting as fast as we could, straight back down the ship aft towards the boiler room where we hoped we would catch sight of the flashing strobes. At the bow in such a great depth I felt very isolated and alone. If anything happened to Tony or I there, the others would never know about it or be able to assist. There would be safety in numbers back at the shot-line if anything went wrong.

As we reached the line and detached our strobes, the headlamps and din of Jim and Mike Rosie's Zepps came towards us from the opposite direction. Aquazepps are great scooters, but it's safe to say they are not quiet. We sometimes home-in on each other if separated, just from the noise of the motor, which transmits through water from some distance. Hearing the din of a scooter in the depths is strangely reassuring – it's always comforting to know that there are other divers alive and around you, somewhere. If Jim and Mike had gone astern and Tony and I had circumnavigated the bow, between both our two groups it looked like we had explored the whole wreck. I looked forward to the topside debrief.

We started our ascent – we had been at 86 metres for just over 20 minutes and so decompression would be long and slow. Our first decompression stop would be at 47 metres – in itself a deep dive. However at that depth, because of the massive volumes of gas in our tissues and the pressure change from the seabed, our tissues would actually start off-gassing, strange though it seems.

The ascent was long, tedious and boring – and it was well over an hour later before we could surface for Bill to come in to pick us up. Once de-kitted we immediately exploded into animated chatter as we swapped stories of what we had seen: how many boilers, how many holds, the beam of the ship etc.

Soon, between us all, we had built up a fairly good picture. She was a large vessel of World War II era. We agreed that she was 350–400 feet long with a beam of around 50 feet. It was straight to the reference books for us and as with the *Bretagne*, a likely candidate was soon jumping off the pages at us. The SS *Kildale* was a large steamship reported as being attacked and bombed on 3 November 1940 by German aircraft 7 miles off Fraserburgh. This was extremely close to the position we were diving. We looked further.

The 3,877 grt *Kildale* was built by W. Pickersgill of Sunderland in 1924. Her dimensions were 363.5 feet long with a beam of 51.4 feet – very close. At the time of her bombing she had been en route in convoy WN45 from Barahona in the Dominican Republic, bound for London with a cargo of sugar – a perishable cargo of which all trace would by now be gone. The wreck's holds had been empty.

She had been bombed amidships. On the dive I had wondered where the bridge superstructure had gone – perhaps this explained its absence. Her entire crew of 36 and one gunner had abandoned ship as she quickly sank, and were picked up by the convoy escort-vessels *HMT Pentland Firth* and *HMT Northern Wave*. A search by aircraft the next day failed to locate the ship afloat. Everything about the *Kildale* fitted what we had seen down on the seabed. We were confident we knew her identity.

Bill Ruck had prepared lunch for us whilst we were underwater. His legendary speciality is curried roast potatoes and beans – just fantastic after a couple of hours in the water. But as I finished off my grub I noticed a slight numbness in my right elbow. At first I put it down to a sore arm from hanging onto the shot-line during the hour or more of the ascent – but it soon became clear that I was having a minor elbow bend. My grip was a little weakened but thankfully the numbness soon passed. It was an unwelcome reminder of the reality of the bend I had had in the North Channel two years before. This was the deepest, longest dive I had carried out since my bend and here I was getting a niggle again. Tony and I still remained the only open-circuit divers of our group – the others were all diving their closed-circuit rebreathers successfully, repeatedly and without incident. It was noticeable that for the same bottom time, the CCR (closed-circuit rebreather) divers had been able to get out of the water well ahead of Tony and I – and none of them were having any decompression symptoms like I'd just had. The memory of my bad bend in the North Channel still haunted my diving. After every dive I would be wondering if the slightest ache or pain was a bend coming on again. So far there had been nothing, but this was different. It was clearly a minor elbow bend.

Having clung to my old established ideas of open-circuit Trimix diving, the North Channel bend had got me thinking about a move to rebreather diving, but I had been slow to get a move on. Now here I had had a niggle in my elbow on the *Kildale*. The pressing need to change to a rebreather was right back in my face again with a vengeance.

CHAPTER SIXTEEN

THE DARK SIDE BECKONS

Ewan and I qualified as open-circuit Trimix divers in 1995. In 1997 after many years of research and development, Ambient Pressure Diving Ltd launched the world's first production closed-circuit rebreather to the sport diving community, called the Inspiration.

Rebreathers however aren't a recent development – they have been around for a long time and were heavily used by the military. In World War II, early oxygen rebreathers were used by many of the navies to allow frogmen to clandestinely attack enemy shipping – often with great success.

Open-circuit scuba diving allows a diver's exhaled breath to bubble up to the surface. These bubbles increase in size as they near the surface and water pressure decreases. Often large bubbles make a 'blooping' sound as they break a calm surface. Sitting in a boat on a calm day above divers you can hear bubbles of different sizes breaking the surface. Whereas large bubbles bloop, hundreds of smaller bubbles produce a hissing or fizzing sound as they break the surface. It is possible to follow where OC (open-circuit) divers are just from their bubble streams. Their bubble trails can easily be seen on the surface and are visible even in rougher water. In wartime it was a deadly tell tale giveaway for an attacking frogman.

In the military realm, rebreathers allowed a clandestine attack at a target with no tell-tale bubble stream to alert anyone looking down into the water. 'No bubbles, no troubles' went the old navy diver's adage.

The military rebreathers of World War II were rudimentary pure oxygen rebreathers, and because pure oxygen becomes toxic deeper than 9 metres, they were very limited in depth. However, by carrying just a small cylinder of oxygen as opposed to the usual bulky scuba tanks, the fact that a diver was rebreathing his expired oxygen allowed a far longer duration of dive, in addition to the stealth aspect. A human being doesn't metabolise a great amount of oxygen as he breathes, so a small supply can last quite a long time.

Modern open-circuit Trimix diving is very expensive – the main constituent, helium, naturally occurs in only two places in the world. Due to the strong presence of the oil industry in Aberdeen with its need for helium for commercial diving, we had some of the lowest prices for helium in the world. To fill a set of twin 12 litre back-tanks with reasonably strong helium Trimix used to cost me around £40 – I believe it cost far more elsewhere in the UK.

But even so, on just one dive it was possible to breathe through all your Trimix – the breathed out mix just bubbling to the surface and being lost. The offshore oil industry used a very expensive helium reclaim system, but there was nothing like that for us poor open-circuit Trimix divers. Tech diving was expensive diving. That is, until the advent of closed-circuit rebreathers – called CCRs for short.

Ewan had waited for the first production unit of the AP Inspiration rebreather with bated breath. Having been involved to a degree in the trialling of early versions, he could see its advantages in opening up deeper, longer, shorter deco dives. I had no experience or great knowledge of rebreathers and until my bend in 2003 had remained comfortable with my open-circuit Trimix set up.

After the first Inspiration units hit the market, Ewan was one of the first to get one. Before I knew what was going on, he turned up at my house unannounced, walking in with a great big yellow box on his back and making out he'd forgotten he had it on. He managed to take a big chip out of my doorframe with it as he went through. After that, Ewan turned up with it on his back wherever he could – he famously walked into our local dive shop wearing it and claiming to have forgotten he had it on. Swanking around the local dive shops with it on was one thing, but the time would come when he had to dive the unit in earnest.

The beauty of the closed-circuit rebreather is that when you breathe out, the expired air or gas doesn't vent to your surroundings but is carried from the mouthpiece along a corrugated rubber tube and fed into the bottom of a scrubber canister set in the middle of the unit on the diver's back. The scrubber canister is filled with a material that looks remarkably like cat litter – called 'sofnalime' and sometimes 'slime' for short. This ingenious material absorbs and removes the carbon dioxide (CO_2) in the exhaled air passing through the scrubber canister and clean air (devoid of CO_2) comes out the top.

Your body naturally produces CO_2, which is exhaled and got rid of as you breathe out. That carbon dioxide is extremely dangerous if rebreathed. If you breathe it in again, CO_2 levels in your body start to increase. Continue breathing in your expired CO_2 and you are in for trouble. For example, if you breathe in and out of a polythene bag for a time, this will lead to a CO_2 build-up. The astronauts in Apollo 13 suffered badly from a huge CO_2 build-up during their round the moon trip after the explosion, and famously had to construct their own CO_2 scrubbers from rudimentary materials they had aboard. Similarly, a young child using a larger adult snorkel doesn't have the lung capacity to fully blow out all the air from it. As a consequence the child's expired CO_2 doesn't get blown away but sits in the lungs and snorkel and is rebreathed. The snorkel never gets cleared out of CO_2 and the child can black out.

A CO_2 build-up can have terrifying consequences such as dizziness, nausea, tunnel vision, apprehension, mental confusion, headaches and can in extreme circumstances lead to unconsciousness or death. For rebreather divers the possibility of a CO_2 build-up is far more real than open-circuit, where it's difficult but not impossible to get a CO_2 build-up. I wrote in *Into the Abyss* about Ewan's black out at 45 metres, 3 miles offshore on the wreck of the SS *Fram*. We believe that was caused by a CO_2 build-up. It almost killed Ewan – it has killed many others.

One of the problems with rebreathers is that the air spaces in the equipment are many and large and there exists a larger potential for a CO_2 build-up. The mouthpiece is larger than an open-circuit mouthpiece. A 1½ inch thick corrugated hose carries expired air from the mouthpiece to the scrubber canister and a rubber O-ring seals around the canister inside its case. If the O-ring is worn, doesn't seal properly or (heaven forbid) a diver forgets to put it in during set up, then CO_2 can bypass the scrubber material and go straight back into the breathing mixture for inhalation. My good friend Jim Burke – a veteran open-circuit and closed-circuit rebreather diver with 1,000 technical dives under his belt (500 on rebreathers) – did just that. One day he made a simple mistake that could have killed him. He built up his rebreather for a 60-metre dive in something of a hurry. Once in the boat at the dive site, he got dressed into his unit and jumped over the side. He felt things were different on the surface swim to the shot-line, but just thought he was feeling light-headed because he was exerting himself. Once he got to the shot-line and started descending, the increasing depth and pressure magnified the problems. His symptoms started to get worse – mental confusion and anxiety overwhelmed his senses. He got down to about 15 metres and realising something was wrong – but not knowing what – he followed his training and flushed his rebreather breathing loop with Trimix diluent gas. This so-called 'dil flush' cures a whole host of rebreather problems by flushing clean fresh breathing gas through the system.

Jim's dil flush improved the position temporarily and perversely, thinking all was now well, it allowed him to continue the descent. By the time he got to 25 metres his CO_2 symptoms were back – and a lot worse. His training would have taught him at this point to bail out off his CCR onto his emergency scuba tank under his arm, but the intoxicating mental effects of the CO_2 build-up made him misinterpret what was happening. He flushed again with diluent – again making things temporarily better and again allowing him to continue further down the line. At 35 metres the CO_2 effects came back on like a train, magnified this time because of the depth, and he almost passed out there and then. He managed to signal to his buddy that he was in trouble and that he had to go up. He was assisted to the surface, but once safely back on the boat he still didn't realise he was suffering a CO_2 hit. It was only when he got home and went to prep his unit for the next day's dive that he saw the missing O-ring and circular black plastic spacer sitting and staring back at him on his work bench where he had built up his unit in a hurry that morning. The penny dropped.

Ewan – as part of his self-styled crash test dummy status – took his rebreather to a local pool, which is used for dive training. He had decided to deliberately flood the breathing loop of his rebreather to see what happened in a controlled environment (the loop being the mouthpiece, the corrugated hoses, the counter lungs and the scrubber stack). He unscrewed the manual gas injector that bleeds breathing gas into the CCR counterlungs. These are the two clever artificial lungs at the front of the diver's chest which are open with the diver's own lungs. When a CCR diver breathes out, his expired gas goes into the right-hand-side exhale counterlung, which inflates. From here it passes via a corrugated hose over his right shoulder, into the bottom of the scrubber unit on his back. Here the CO_2 is removed as the expired gas passes through the stack. The cleansed breathing gas then circulates from the top of the stack (via another corrugated hose) over the diver's left hand shoulder into the left hand side inhale counterlung. This provides clean breathing gas via another corrugated hose to the diver's mouthpiece as he breathes in. By unscrewing the manual gas injector, this allowed water to flood into the counterlungs. He then started swimming about in the pool until the water reached and started to react with the sofnalime in the scrubber stack on his back. This produced a fiercely painful mixture. Military oxygen rebreather divers of the past dreaded this effect and called it a 'caustic cocktail'. Ewan describes the effect of what happened next as like being hit in the face with a baseball bat. He shot out of the water like a penguin and was extremely unwell.

On another occasion Ewan decided to try and give himself a CO_2 hit, so that he would recognise the symptoms if it happened for real on a dive. I don't know of anyone else who has adopted this particular practice, but I would caution against it. He used some old sofnalime that had been breathed for about 10 hours – well beyond the recommended 3 hours maximum duration. He swam and swam around the training pool, trying to watch how much oxygen he metabolised and working hard to push the scrubber unit as much as he could. Suddenly a CO_2 hit swept over him. The first anyone knew anything was wrong was when he shot his head out of the water spitting out his mouthpiece with a blinding headache. Surprisingly, he has never tried that drill again either. We were going to get a crash test dummy sticker for the back of his CCR unit.

After spending time getting acquainted with his new rebreather in quarries and shallow sea dives, the time came for his first deep Trimix sea dive.

We decided to dive the wreck of the SS *Cushendall*, 5 miles out of Stonehaven harbour. This small yet lovely 185-foot steamship sits on her keel in 58 metres. I had foolishly tried diving this on air five years before and had bottled it and bailed out. I hadn't been back.

For some reason – involving switching hoses on the CCR at depth – the counter lungs of the rebreather compressed as we descended and he couldn't breathe so we had to ascend. I can still see the look on his face when he found he was sucking on a vacuum. It was after this – and a few other mishaps – that I started to see parallels between Ewan and his rebreather and Peter Sellers as Inspector Clouseau and his manservant Kato, who always leapt out and tried to kill him when he was least expecting it. So I christened Ewan's rebreather 'Kato' and the name has stuck ever since.

As we continued to dive, Ewan became more proficient with his rebreather – and its fair to say that with all he had been through, not many people understood the CCR's workings as well as he did. I stuck to open-circuit Trimix diving – not least because the price tag back then for the rebreather was a cool £4,500.

We soon found that an open-circuit diver diving with a closed-circuit rebreather diver was not the best pairing. When I was diving with Ewan he would be on a very strong helium mix, which allowed him to dive deeper without worrying about narcosis levels. The pre-mixed bottom-gas in my twin 12-litre tanks might not be as strong or suitable for the same depth.

On the ascent, at about 20 metres, I would physically swap over from breathing from my bottom-mix by spitting out my breathing regulator and sticking the regulator for one of my deco-mix tanks into my mouth. These, for a number of good reasons, we always pre-mixed with a nitrox mix; EAN 50 (50% nitrogen and 50% oxygen). Once I was on EAN50 that was it until the surface. The rebreather however, cleverly feeds a diver increasing percentages of oxygen as you get shallower, so by the time you are on your final 6-metre deco stop, a rebreather diver is breathing almost pure oxygen – hugely beneficial in warding off the bends.

Because of the increasing percentage of oxygen being breathed (compared to the poor open-circuit diver stuck rigidly on 50%), the length of decompression time required for a

CCR diver was dramatically shortened. I started to find that when I was diving open-circuit paired with a rebreather diver, the CCR diver would be cleared from decompression stops when I had some 15–20 minutes more of deco stops left to do. Sometimes I was left in the water alone on my final stops, hanging there miles offshore whilst the CCR divers got a flask of coffee cracked open topside.

As our diving got more adventurous and we were diving deeper and longer, the more rebreathers seemed to come into their own. My North Channel bend had got me thinking seriously about moving to a rebreather for the first time after years of saying I never would. My elbow niggle on the *Kildale* a couple of years later had refocused the issue. Our local dives highlighted the shortcomings of open-circuit every week clearly enough and now it wasn't so much if I would change, but when.

CHAPTER SEVENTEEN

HMS *PRINCE OF WALES* AND HMS *REPULSE*

The turning point finally came in late 2005 when Ewan and I went on a trip aboard the *MV Mata Ikan* from Singapore to dive two legendary British warships – HMS *Repulse* and HMS *Prince of Wales* in the South China Sea. The two ships were sunk on 10 December 1941 in an attack by 85 Japanese torpedo bomber aircraft, just three days after the stunning raid by Japanese forces on Pearl Harbour ushered in America's involvement to World War II. The brand new state-of-the-art British battleship HMS *Prince of Wales* and the mighty World War I vintage Renown class battlecruiser HMS *Repulse* were overcome by the scale of the attack and sent to the bottom with great loss of life 200 miles north of Singapore.

Until this moment, the battleship had ruled the waves – it was the supreme embodiment of a nation's sea power and majesty. The sight of a heavily-armoured enemy battleship with guns that could strike at targets more than 20 miles away had until then struck fear into the hearts of merchant and naval seamen alike. Throughout the first half of the 20th century they had been considered almost invincible.

The loss of HMS *Prince of Wales* was the first time that a battleship had been sunk by air attack in modern warfare. Her destruction is now regarded as marking and defining the end of the era of the battleship and the beginning of the era of the aircraft carrier, which projects immense air power over vast distances.

HMS Repulse, *sunk by Japanese aircraft along with HMS* Prince of Wales *in 1941, 200 miles north of Singapore.*

HMS Prince of Wales, *sunk by Japanese aircraft in 1941, 200 miles north of Singapore.*

Lt. Col. Guy Wallis of the Parachute Regiment had been with me on our 1997 trip to Scapa Flow to dive and survey HMS *Hampshire*. A tall, strong and immensely capable deep technical diver, his military knowledge and his ability to pick his way through the corridors of power at the Ministry of Defence had been hugely helpful. We had kept in touch, dived and shared a beer together on a few occasions since then.

A few years before in 2001, he had been in touch with a proposition. The British Armed Forces are very keen to encourage their service personnel to embark on adventure or 'on the edge' type expeditions in the belief that it develops mind and body. Guy was by now assistant chairman of the Army Sub Aqua Diving Association (ASADA), which had yet to embrace and accept the new technical diving revolution. Air diving was OK, but the gas mixes that crazy civilian technical divers were breathing had been off limits. But the Association however, was now looking at possibly accepting the use of 'mixed gas' and Guy had the idea of a two-week mixed-gas expedition to dive and survey the wrecks HMS *Prince of Wales* and *Repulse*. This would demonstrate the benefits of mixed-gas diving, as these wrecks were beyond the standard air diving depth limit of 50 metres. A TV documentary crew would also join us to film the expedition for a BBC *Timewatch* programme to be entitled *The Death of the Battleship*. Would I be interested? I thought about it for all of two seconds before leaping at the chance of getting out to dive these two fabled deep wrecks. Guy told me that part of my role would be to survey the ships as best I could and have artist's impressions created of the wrecks lying on the seabed.

We flew out from London two days after the 9/11 outrage – Heathrow seemingly clogged with grounded American planes. After landing at Singapore and making the 200-mile voyage up the east coast of Malaysia we spent one week tied into HMS *Prince of Wales*. Underwater cameraman Dan Burton shot dramatic underwater footage for the *Timewatch* team whilst we surveyed the wreck. The scale of this wreck is awesome – an immense battleship some 745 feet long and displacing 43,786 tons. She lies completely upside down in 70 metres with her superstructure deeply embedded in the seabed underneath the hull. Her hull is in such good condition that she looks as though she would still float today.

The dimensions of the *Prince of Wales* were staggering. I had dived and surveyed the German World War I battleships at the bottom of Scapa Flow many, many times for my first book, *Dive Scapa Flow*. These giant wrecks are all about 575 feet in length and displaced about 26,000 tons. If you haven't swum round a sunken battleship from that era it is hard to convey the scale of them. As divers, we see the whole ship including the huge part of the hull normally submerged and out of view topside. These battleships are the length of two football pitches, with their hulls rising up for some 25 metres – a wall of steel, 75 feet high. Whilst afloat, their upper superstructures and top hamper extend upwards for more than a hundred feet, and their masts even higher up. If the German World War I High Seas Fleet battleships at Scapa Flow are impressive, *Prince of Wales* at 745 feet in length was a quantum leap ahead from the 575 feet of the German battleships. With a massive 43,786-ton displacement, she dwarfed the 26,000-ton Scapa Flow leviathans.

Prince of Wales was a brand new battleship and was still being fitted out at the beginning of World War II when *Bismarck* broke out into the North Atlantic to start terrorising Allied shipping. The order went out from Churchill to 'Sink the *Bismarck*'. *Prince of Wales* – Britain's newest and most formidable battleship, with its massive 14-inch guns – was assigned to take part in the search for and subsequent destruction of *Bismarck*. She immediately set off on her task, even though there were still around 100 civilian contractors aboard completing her fitting out. They were taken to sea and continued their work as she sped to intercept *Bismarck*.

Prince of Wales and Britain's most famous warship – the massive battlecruiser HMS *Hood* – engaged *Bismarck* in a legendary battle. Shells from *Bismarck* struck HMS *Hood*, completely destroying her in a single cataclysmic explosion that instantaneously killed all bar three of her ship's complement of around 1,000 men. *Prince of Wales* went on to land three crucial shots on *Bismarck*, even though one-by-one her guns (which had not yet been made fully operational) went out of action. At one point she only had five functioning guns left.

In May 1941, *Prince of Wales*, along with the battle cruiser HMS *Repulse*, was assigned to Singapore as part of 'Force Z' – intended as a deterrent to a threatened Japanese invasion of Malaya. Two weeks earlier Japanese forces had advanced into Indo-China and were now just 300 miles away from Malaya and Singapore. The Royal Navy was already stretched to the full by the war against Germany but Churchill feared for Singapore, which protected vital trade routes from the Empire. To try and deter Japanese aggression, Churchill had demanded a battleship fleet be sent to Singapore.

Churchill insisted that his much-beloved and newest battleship *Prince of Wales* be sent, and chose Admiral Sir Tom Phillips to command. An aircraft carrier was also despatched to provide air-cover for the two British warships, but it ran aground en route. *Prince of Wales* and *Repulse* were ordered to go on alone and without air-cover they had suddenly become very vulnerable. As they reached and entered Singapore amid great fanfare, the two capital ships were in fact already exposed and almost indefensible.

On 7 December 1941 the Japanese carried out a daring air attack against Singapore. Suddenly British command woke up to the fact that the Japanese would not be deterred from an invasion campaign by the presence of the two British ships – no matter how powerful they were. At the same time the Japanese fleet crept up on the American base at Pearl Harbour in Hawaii and delivered their savage early morning attack. This devastatingly successful surprise attack was a preventative attack designed to keep the U.S. Pacific Fleet from interfering with Japan's military actions in Southeast Asia against the overseas territories of Great Britain, the Netherlands and the U.S. itself. Five of the seven battleships and one ex-battleship berthed in Battleship Row were badly damaged as well as three cruisers, three destroyers, an anti-aircraft training ship and a minelayer. There were also 188 U.S. aircraft destroyed, along with 2,402 servicemen killed and 1,282 wounded. Churchill realised how exposed his two ships were to a similar attack, even within the confines of Singapore harbour.

Three days after the daring Japanese strike at Pearl Harbour, British intelligence learned that Japanese forces were rumoured to have started a land invasion 200 miles further north up the Malayan peninsula at Kota Baru. Accordingly, at 5pm on 8 December 1941, *Prince of Wales* and *Repulse*, escorted by 4 destroyers, set out to locate the invasion forces (if any) and repulse them. They headed out into the South China Sea, hoping to surprise the Japanese forces at dawn. The series of events that would lead to the death of the battleship, now started to unfold.

En route to the possible invasion site, a signal was received advising that shore-based air-cover – on which the naval commanders had depended – could not be provided, as a result of a large force of enemy bombers further north. It also transpired that the invasion intelligence was inaccurate – there was in fact no land invasion occurring at Kota Baru.

The poor visibility, which had cloaked the British warships as they sped northwards to investigate, ominously cleared and a Japanese reconnaissance plane and a submarine spotted the British force and reported their location. Japanese torpedo bombers were scrambled for an attack. Without air-cover and now lacking the element of surprise, the British force turned and headed south, back towards Singapore, unaware of the forthcoming attack.

The fleet of 85 Japanese torpedo bombers soon located the British force. Wave after wave of bombers swooped down on the exposed British warships, dropping their bombs and aerial torpedoes. The commanders of the two British warships threw their charges about as though they were nimble destroyers, twisting and turning the ships to face bow towards the torpedoes streaking towards them. If they could 'comb the tracks' of the torpedoes, the torpedoes would miss and pass harmlessly down the side of the ship. The sheer number of torpedoes in the water and the inability of the ships' anti-aircraft defences to knock the Japanese planes out of the sky finally overwhelmed them. A single torpedo hit the *Prince of Wales* right at her most exposed point, near the propellers and rudder. It was her 'Achilles' heel'.

The most vital parts of the ship were protected inside the armoured 'citadel' and were almost invulnerable. But like any ship, the propellers and rudder have to be free and exposed to the sea to function. The single torpedo strike blew a hole in the hull right beside the unarmoured outboard port-side propeller and destroyed the A-bracket, which held the free section of the shaft in position to the hull. The propeller and shaft (no longer fixed to the hull) corkscrewed and thrashed around until the propeller came clean off.

The thrashing of the shaft also caused massive damage inside the ship. The forward engine drove the outboard propeller and the propeller shaft ran for more than 250 feet inside the ship, all the way up to the forward engine room. The hull plates around where the shaft entered the hull were buckled and torn open by the thrashing shaft. Tons of water started flooding into her and ominously her rudder jammed.

Slowly, the water rushing into her port side caused the great ship to start to list to that side. To try and trim the vessel, the crew started flooding compartments on the opposite starboard side, but this couldn't be done quickly enough. She listed more to port and as she did, so the starboard side of her hull started to rise up out of the water.

The next wave of torpedo bombers now swarmed towards the higher starboard side of the *Prince of Wales*. With her rudder jammed, *Prince of Wales* could no longer manoeuvre – she

The wreck of HMS Prince of Wales, *South China Sea.*

was a sitting duck. Three torpedoes struck her starboard side. One of the torpedoes hit near her bow about 20 feet back from the stem, blowing a hole clean through the ship from one side to the other. This explosion alone would not have been fatal to *Prince of Wales*, as bows are designed to survive collisions and serious damage whilst leaving the main structure of the ship further aft, watertight. The second torpedo hit slightly forward of amidships beneath the raised armour belt. The third torpedo hit the aft section of hull, just at the end of the armour belt. *Prince of Wales* now had four massive holes in her, each about 25 feet across. Together this meant some 100 feet of her hull had been opened up to the sea. The end was inevitable. She slowly turned turtle and sank with huge loss of life.

On my first dive on this sunken leviathan I was initially struck by how good condition the hull seemed to be in. Battleships are very heavily armoured and extremely strongly constructed. Of all the types of ships that end their lives as wrecks, battleships stand up to the test of time the best. The hull of the *Prince of Wales* seemed almost intact and just covered in a carpet of marine growth. But then, as we explored further we started seeing evidence of the battle and the wounds that sank her.

As we scootered along the starboard side we saw the three large torpedo explosion holes – each one about 25 feet across and large enough to drive a bus through. The explosion near the very bow (and forward of the collision bulkhead and armoured citadel) had blown right through from the starboard side to the port side, leaving a passageway through the hull from one side to the other some 25 feet across.

The second and third torpedo impact sites were just under (and now above) the armour belt. The torpedoes had struck the soft underbelly of the vessel in the space between the armour belt and her bilge keels – the two large thin strips of steel that project a few feet downwards at either side of the hull and run nearly the complete length of the flat bottom to give the hull a cutting surface for manoeuvring.

The second hole back from the bow was at the very start of the starboard bilge keel and right beneath the bottom of the armour belt. The bottom sections of armour plating (which were now higher as the ship is upside down) were unmarked but angled into the hull where they had been knocked backwards by the force of the blast. It appeared that the armour belt had taken the blow easily but deflected the blast downwards into the softer unarmoured

150

underbelly. Had she not been listing, the torpedoes would have struck her armour belt and, from the apparent lack of damage at the second strike site, would have withstood them with ease.

We remained on-site above the *Prince of Wales* for a full week, diving her each day and surveying her remains. On one dive I decided to go under the upturned foredeck to see if I could glimpse A-turret with its four massive 14-inch guns.

As I moved under the foredeck I found that there was a gap of about 8 feet between the seabed and the main deck above. The visibility down here on the seabed wasn't good and when I moved under the hull it was pitch black. 'Ah, just like a British wreck dive' I thought.

As I tentatively made my way further under the upturned hull, in the distance it seemed there was a horizontal sliver of light green at the other side of her 100-foot wide deck. It dawned on me that this was open water at the other side of the foredeck, and then it clicked that the whole foredeck from A-turret forward to the bow, was being held up off the seabed. The whole bow section for almost 100 feet forward was held aloft – suspended and defying gravity – by the crumpled superstructure and foredeck gun turrets that had been driven down into the seabed. What strength the construction of this ship had to stand like that despite the ravages of more than 60 years on the bottom. I hoped that she would hold up for a few minutes more.

I retreated and got hold of our cameraman Dan Burton and Guy, and together we retraced my path and went under the main deck. The four 14-inch barrels of A-turret must have been 45 feet long at least and were seemingly lying on top of the seabed.

We filmed in the darkness of this man-made cavern as we scootered past this famous and very recognisable quad turret. This time we kept on going and passed right across to the clear water at the other side of the foredeck. It was extremely disconcerting having the complete bow section of a 43,000-ton battleship suspended above me. If the bow section were to fracture and collapse right then we would be squashed like flies. No one would ever find us. I was hugely relieved once we had completed the filming and could leave this dark, silty, cavern.

At the end of the week we filmed as Guy flew a Royal Navy ensign from the wreck's starboard side propeller shaft in memory of those who were lost. As the ensign unfurled, it hung on its buoys and the flag waved gently in the 2-knot underwater current, just as it would topside. It was a visually haunting and atmospheric moment and we knew immediately that that dramatic footage was how the documentary would close.

After our week diving *Prince of Wales* we moved over to HMS *Repulse*, which lies some 8 miles away. The *Repulse* lies on her port side and is well heeled over – almost but not quite, turned turtle like the *Prince of Wales*.

Although the upmost starboard side of *Repulse* overhangs her main deck, her bridge superstructure lies flat on the seabed and is open for exploration. She too is largely intact and as she is not completely upside down like the *Prince of Wales*, there is a lot to see on her. Her jackstay at the very tip of the bow, from which her ensign would have flown, still stands in situ and her massive anchors are still snug in their hawse pipes. The twin 15-inch gun barrels of the partially buried B-turret project out of the sand and are perhaps one of the most moving and powerful images on this wreck.

Before leaving this wreck we also flew a Royal Navy ensign from the bridge superstructure. It was extremely moving to be hanging motionless in the beautiful blue South China Seas

The wreck of HMS Repulse, *200 miles north of Singapore, South China Sea.*

watching service personnel flying an ensign above the grave of fallen comrades. Even in this far off part of the world, 50 miles offshore, the fallen were still remembered.

Having had such a momentous time surveying these two wrecks in 2001, I had always been keen to return to them, and Ewan was keen to see what I had been going on about for the last few years. So in 2005 we joined one of Jack Ingle's very well run South China Seas trips, coincidentally in the same vessel (the *Mata Ikan*) that I had been on during the 2001 military trip.

Leaving Singapore aboard the *Mata Ikan* we threaded our way for many miles in between anchored ships of all shapes and sizes and started the long 200-mile run up to the *Repulse* and *Prince of Wales*.

Unlike the last military trip when we had just made a 200-mile beeline straight for the British wrecks, on this occasion we would be fitting in a number of other wreck dives along the way to break up the journey.

On the way up we dived a massive modern 262m long, 90,000-ton super tanker, the *Seven Skies*, which was struck by lightning in 1969 and sank on her maiden voyage. The huge multi-level bridge superstructure was like an island rising out of the depths. When not diving, Jack kept us entertained with lots of classic diving stories. The one I remember the most was the tale of another wreck that had been carrying a cargo of liquid fertiliser – a cargo that is heavier than water. The liquid still sat safely in the cargo holds. Jack told how he had gone into one of the holds and put the tip of a fin into the liquid. His fin disappeared. He was then able to sink slowly down into it so that his legs and body seemingly started to disappear.

We arrived above the wreck of HMS *Prince of Wales* and anchored beside it. Jack went into the water first to make sure the downline was tied in properly, and Ewan and I started into the water about half an hour later. We met Jack as he was coming back up the downline and he gave me a signal I didn't understand – his hand making a motion like a snake slithering over land. 'What does he mean?' I wondered.

Ewan and I pressed on down the line and the wreck came into view in rather poor cloudy visibility. The line led us right to the stern propellers and there I was surprised to see that the ensign that Guy had flown four years earlier was still there – well faded, but still hanging on her buoys. We also found that the Ensign on the *Repulse* was still there and I learned that successive parties of divers over the years have been looking after the ensigns and replacing the buoys or lifting bags as they failed, to keep the ensigns flying above the wrecks.

As the days passed I was given a clear example of the strengths of rebreathers in this sort of deep Trimix diving expedition. My twin 12-litre bottom tanks had to be laboriously filled and gases mixed each day after our one deep dive. It was a lengthy process. Ewan had one fill of his small 3-litre diluent tank in his rebreather and that would last him for three to four dives without needing to be re-filled.

My bottom tanks, although designed to take 232 bar, were being filled to around 200 bar at the most. We were diving at a depth of 50–70 metres each day and often swimming into the steady 2-knot monsoon current. Working hard in a current raises your breathing rate and you use up your gas faster. On some dives I felt I was running perilously short of bottom-gas whilst I tried to keep up with Ewan who had a seemingly endless supply in his rebreather. As if that wasn't bad enough, when it came to the hour-long decompression stops I was finding that Ewan was getting out of the water after clearing his decompression stops 15 minutes before me. I also knew that his decompression was far more beneficial to his body than my open-circuit decompression.

But what really did it and forced me to consider getting a rebreather was the day we moved from the wreck of the *Prince of Wales* to the wreck of the *Repulse*, 8 miles away.

That day we were up early and had a dive at 8.00 a.m. on the *Prince of Wales*, coming out of the water 1½ hours later. Some of the party had decided not to dive the *Prince of Wales* in the morning, but to wait for an afternoon dive on the *Repulse*.

My one dive on the *Prince of Wales* put me out of action for the rest of that day. After my North Channel bend there was no way I was going to risk two deep Trimix dives in one day, particularly given where we were – 200 miles north of Singapore and 50 miles offshore. I suspected Malaysian recompression facilities might not be quite as good as back home.

After surfacing from the early dive, the *Mata Ikan* was moved and was on site above the *Repulse* two hours later. Ewan was then able to dive straight away on the *Repulse*, with a surface interval of just 2 hours. There was no way I could compete with that on open-circuit. I had finally seen the light and after much gnashing of teeth, I decided that on my return to the UK I would finally turn to the 'Dark Side' and become a rebreather diver.

The *Prince of Wales* and *Repulse* trip to the South China Seas had shown me the undoubted benefits of the closed-circuit rebreather, which excelled on mixed-gas technical expeditions such as that. I had clung to open-circuit mixed-gas diving for a long time – too long. This time I would change just as soon as I got back home.

Ewan had qualified as a rebreather instructor a few years earlier, so on the 13-hour flight back from Singapore, I arranged with him that he would put me through a course. Back home, one of our group – Richard Colliar – was already a qualified CCR diver and he kindly offered up his Classic Inspiration rebreather for me to train with.

Ewan and I started off at a quarry near Peterhead as he took me through the workings of the CCR and gave me a glimmer of understanding. Diving open-circuit scuba is relatively simple. You strap a tank of compressed air on your back and off you go. A rebreather is a far more complicated piece of kit, which requires extremely carefully preparation before each dive. A single simple mistake can be fatal. If open-circuit diving is like riding a bike, diving a rebreather is akin in complexity to flying a plane.

After training in a local quarry for several weeks we booked ourselves on a five-day trip up to Scapa Flow aboard the *Radiant Queen*. I was in the process of finishing off amendments to *Dive Scapa Flow*, which was badly in need of being updated and a 4th edition was planned to take into account the increasingly rapid deterioration of the German wrecks. I wanted to produce new artist's impressions of the wrecks on the seabed, as the old impressions had been made up for the first edition of the book in 1989 and were well out of date. I also wanted to refresh the book by adding in some new photography.

We hatched a plan to dive open-circuit on one of the German wrecks each morning to survey the changes, and then I would be free for a rebreather training dive in the afternoon. Scapa Flow is a great place for dive training.

On day one we did a big dive on the battleship *Kronprinz Wilhelm*, something like 45–55 minutes bottom-time at 35 metres with a big decompression hang. I was diving open-circuit and Ewan was diving on his beloved Inspiration rebreather 'Kato'. As a result, he was ready to come out of the water after only five minutes decompression. I had to carry out an additional 20 minutes of decompression, hanging on the line. The benefits of rebreathers were right in my face again.

In the afternoon we went to do a rebreather training dive on the light cruiser *Karlsruhe*, the shallowest of the German wrecks in 25 metres. Although I still found the rebreather cumbersome and buoyancy control with it a bit wild, the dive went flawlessly. The open spaces inside the scrubber and the counter lungs make buoyancy with the unit for a newbie like me a bit tricky.

On day two we dived the light cruiser *Cöln* open-circuit in the morning and then did another rebreather training dive in the afternoon on another light cruiser, the *Brummer*. This time Ewan wanted to do a few drills and he had some plastic cards with prompts on them for me. The one I remember the most is settling down on the forward turret's 5.9-inch gun barrel at about 35 metres. Ewan produced a card that instructed me to bail out from the rebreather onto the back up open-circuit regulator, which connected directly into the small 3-litre tank of breathing gas (diluent) in the rebreather. As I was getting ready to do this the resident seal which inhabits the bridge of the *Brummer* suddenly appeared right beside me, close enough to touch. It started buzzing around as I took hold of the rebreather mouthpiece and twisted the valve to seal it off for bail-out. Pushing the mouthpiece and corrugated hoses up over my head I stuck the open-circuit regulator in my mouth. Despite the attentions of the seal, there was nothing to it – well at least in that sort of controlled situation.

On the journey up to Orkney in the ferry from Aberdeen, Ewan had decided to go through his set of theory slides in a Power Point presentation on his laptop. I recall there were 134 slides in all to get through and we had a seven-hour voyage up in the ferry, five days in Orkney and another seven hours back in the ferry at the end of the trip. For some reason, in all that time we only managed to get to slide 37. OK there was a load of theory, but either Ewan was giving me a Rolls Royce performance or I was a slow learner. Then again, perhaps it was just the beer.

I left Orkney only part trained, but would go on to complete my training during a live-aboard trip to Norway where I was able to dive my rebreather twice a day. Although I had now amassed a lot of time on the rebreather, I still felt a complete novice. The guys who had trained before me all told me that you need to get a lot of hours under your belt on rebreathers – it was very true. You need to dive them as much as you can, to practice drills and just learn how they behave. Even now, five years later, I still learn something about the unit on every dive.

CHAPTER EIGHTEEN

NORWAY

The traditional week's hard boat diving along the west coast of Scotland was seriously challenged during the early 1990s. For the same cost as a week's diving in cold, rainy and often rough conditions, divers found they could get a week's diving in the sunny, crystal-clear waters of the Red Sea. Hard boat dive skippers in Scotland started to notice a fall off in bookings.

In the mid 90s a few dive boat skippers started to eye the crystal-clear waters and scenic diving of the Norwegian fjords as a new and adventurous diving location – and one which rugged Scottish dive boats and tough UK divers would be ideally suited to. New horizons might attract divers looking for a change from British waters.

The first skipper to give it a go was the indomitable Gordon Wadsworth and his fine 75-foot dive boat, *Jane R* – a well-kent sight along all of Scotland's dive sites and beloved of many British divers. If ever you were out in RIBs diving somewhere remote, the *Jane R* always seemed to be on the horizon busily going somewhere. Oban on the west coast was her main playground and she was often seen in the Sound of Mull, sometimes overnighting in the small, gaily painted harbour of Tobermory.

Gordon is a tall, immensely strong chap with a tough but fair character. He is great company, enjoys a lot of fun and is respected by all who know him. Gordon started out working in the Yorkshire mines and started diving initially as a means to get at valuable scrap metal. The diving side of things took over his life and soon he had bought the 53-foot Scottish ring netter *Maise Graham*, a legendary sight along Scottish coasts before she sank in 1997. She was the first Scottish dive boat to start working in Norway in 1993 and the *Jane R* was purchased as her successor. After many years taking trips around the traditional Scottish dive sites and further afield, Gordon blazed the Norwegian trail for Scottish dive boats with the *Maise Graham*, researching, tracking and finding wrecks from Bergen all the way north to Narvick, into the Arctic Circle and all the way up round the North Cape into the Barents Sea to Russia. Soon he had amassed over a hundred wreck sites, with a rich variety to cater for all diver abilities and tastes.

For many years I had heard tales about the quality of Norwegian diving and so, as a complete contrast to the previous year's trip to HMS *Repulse* and HMS *Prince of Wales* in the warm South China Seas, Ewan and I booked on an Aberdeen Watersports (AWL) week-long dive trip out of Bergen aboard the *Jane R.*

After a 13-hour flight to Singapore last year followed by a 20-hour steam north to the British warships, this journey was strikingly simple. A hardy AWL employee, Lea Cobley, would take a transit loaded with the whole group's tanks, rebreathers, scooters and the like from Aberdeen up to Lerwick in Shetland and from there across to Bergen. Ewan and I booked the cheapest seats money could buy on Scandinavian Airlines – just over £100 return to Bergen. The regular oil traffic between Aberdeen and Bergen made this a well-travelled route and kept ticket fares down.

The flight itself over the North Sea, with its scattered oil platforms, took just over an hour. Soon we were banking over the most picturesque rugged coastline of creeks and inlets, where every single wooden house was brightly painted red, green, brown or yellow and had its own boat slip. We touched down shortly after and soon had ourselves a taxi to our hotel on the waterfront in the heart of Bergen.

First impressions of Bergen were that it was extremely clean and well presented. Some of the old, crookedly slanting, medieval waterfront wooden buildings had survived – now set amongst more modern buildings. Their ancient walls seemed at awkward angles and little alleys meandered amongst them. Directly opposite, the waters of the port itself held endless hours of interest for the ship enthusiast – ships of every type and vintage were tied up all over the place. Bergen seemed a brilliant place to visit, but for us it was just the starting point of our journey.

We met up with the rest of our shipmates that night in a Norwegian restaurant and soon found the price of beer shockingly expensive at a sterling equivalent of about £8 a pint. Luckily, the beer was a poor, fizzy belly wash that put you off drinking too much. After not too heavy a night, we retired to our hotel ready for the off the next morning.

After breakfast we got a taxi to the other side of the port where the *Jane R* was sitting, silently waiting for us. This was her first trip of the season and she was still being loaded up with all sorts of stores. I had never been aboard this legendary dive vessel before, although I had seen it and heard a lot about it. She turned out to be a well kept, clean and comfortable dive boat with a fine array of maker's plates from various wrecks screwed around the saloon walls.

Our sleeping accommodation was a row of eight comfortable cabins, four either side of the central corridor below decks. I stashed my dry kit and got back on deck to help ferry the mountain of gear that had just arrived with Lea in the transit van after a long solo sea journey from Aberdeen. Well done, Lea.

Once the *Jane R* was loaded up we cast off and she turned her bow to the north and started steaming up the main fjord that led towards the open North Sea. The western coastline here is a mass of islands and fjords that made exposing the *Jane R* to the open sea to the west unnecessary. The towering stone cliffs of the fjords would almost always shelter us.

By mid afternoon we had made quite some distance from Bergen and Gordon was taking the *Jane R* close in towards a shore lined with small cliffs, and aiming almost directly for a small house on the rocky shoreline. Almost directly below this would be our first shake down dive – the wreck of the SS *Spring*. This would be a chance for us all to get our kit put together and dive an easy wreck in sheltered, safe conditions, only 50 feet or so way from the shoreline.

By this time I had bought myself the next-generation Inspiration CCR – called a 'Vision' – and this would be the first time I would use it in earnest. Ewan and I got dressed into our kit and very soon were striding off the *Jane R*. Popping my head under the surface, the famous clarity of Norwegian water was immediately evident – a change from the murky darkness of my part of Scotland. We did a simple duck-dive down to the wreck, which started at about 10 metres and ran down a slope to a depth of 20–30 metres at the most. The dive was unremarkable but good for getting everything sorted out.

Forty-five minutes later we were out and the *Jane R* was heading off further north. Although the water had proved to be extremely clear, it was immediately apparent that it was very cold at 6 degrees. That is winter North Sea, Scotland temperature and this was May. The water hadn't had a chance to warm up yet.

That night we made our way towards the location for the next day's diving – the wreck of the 5000 grt German cargo vessel SS *Frankenwald* lying at Gulen. Built in 1922 she was a sizeable 122 metres long by 17 metres wide – a tough functional workhorse of the sea. The *Frankenwald* was lost in January 1940 when she hit dangerous rocks in a narrow channel. Her bow sits in 40 metres and her stern in 35 metres, lying up the slope towards nearby rocks. We anchored up in a sheltered location not far from the wreck.

The next morning we made the short passage over to the wreck site and very soon the *Jane R* was tied in to the wreck. Ewan and I got kitted up, and with our scooters jumped in to descend down the line, which it transpired had been tied off to the auxiliary steering helm at the very stern of the vessel. The visibility was a clear 25 metres, although we soon noticed the cold again once we got down on the wreck. The water seemed warmer in the shallows but once at depth seemed to be a uniform 6 degrees or so. We kicked our scooters into life and started a circumnavigation.

The main deck was at about 30–32 metres and peering over the gunwales we could easily see the clean white sandy seabed 5–10 metres below. We passed over cavernous open cargo holds, before passing through and under the midships bridge superstructure, then more open holds led us up to the fo'c'stle and the very bow itself. With our scooters we had easily circumnavigated this 400-foot long vessel in a very short time, and as we headed back towards the stern we were able to spend some time having a look at particular areas of interest. We returned to the downline, still tied to the helm, and made a slow easy ascent. The dark hull of the *Jane R* was visible far above us, silhouetted against the ripples of surrounding lighter water.

After lunch we remained tied in and had a second dive on the wreck at about 5.00 p.m. As we had circumnavigated the wreck in the earlier dive, we left the scooters behind this time and took cameras in, spending more time around the bridge and engine room.

We remained tied into the wreck overnight and the next morning were able to get up early and get a pre-breakfast dive in on the wreck at 8.00 a.m. before Gordon untied the *Jane R* and we headed off to our next location in a nearby fjord called Krakhellasund, where we would dive the *M/S Ferndale* and *B/D Parat*. These two vessels lie within touching distance of each other in much the same way as the *F2* and *YC21* lie close to each other in Scapa Flow – except that these two are much, much closer.

On the 15 December 1944 a German convoy of six ships crossed the Sognefjorden in darkness led by the *Ferndale*. The German Luftwaffe had no planes available to provide air-cover for convoys, so convoys sailed only at night. At Krakhellesundet, strong currents caused the *Ferndale* to strike the Seglsteinen rock. The remainder of the convoy managed to manoeuvre away from the reef and continued their voyage to Ålesund. The *V5305* and the tugboat *Fairplay X* stayed behind with the *Ferndale* until the salvage tug *Parat* could arrive.

The small group of ships was still there at noon the following day, when 19 Allied Mosquitoes swooped down to attack with cannons and rockets. Both *Ferndale* and *Parat* were set on fire at the cost of one aircraft shot down. The crews on *Ferndale* and *Parat* fought to put out the fires, but exploding ammunition cargo thwarted them.

One hour later, eight more Mosquitoes arrived and attacked the ships once again. *V5305* hit one of the planes, which subsequently crashed straight into the mountain near Seglsteinen. Both *Ferndale* and *Parat* were hit and sunk during this second attack.

The wreck of the *Ferndale* now sits on a steeply sloping seabed with her bows in towards shore in about 10 metres. Her hull runs down the slope to about 40 metres and there at the starboard side of her stern, the *Parat* can be found, sitting upright in deeper water that goes down to about 60 metres. When both ships sank the *Parat* settled upright alongside an underwater cliff with her bows behind *Ferndale*.

The salvage tug Parat was attempting to save the SS Ferndale when both vessels were sunk by RAF Mosquito aircraft © Ewan Rowell

The salvage tug Parat lies in deep water at the stern of the SS Ferndale © *Ewan Rowell*

The next morning we had another pre-breakfast early dive on the *Ferndale* and *Parat*, before moving over to dive the wreck of the Fleetwood steam trawler *MFV Macbeth*. We found the stern section lying on its port side in 39 metres, but despite a good swim around were not able to find the bow section.

Steaming further north, the *Jane R* took us next to the resting site of the massive 7,000-ton SS *Wilheim* in Brufjorden. She was a supply vessel for German forces during World War II and was loaded with coal when she was torpedoed by the Norwegian *MTB 717*. As soon as she was hit she started to sink quickly. The crew steered her for Tansoy but the speed of water rushing into her was too great and she rolled onto her port side and sank. Her bows now sit in about 22 metres and her stern in 70 metres. This is a massive, eerie ship in a gloomy location. I felt dwarfed by her scale and bleak, foreboding presence.

Lying in a fairly sheltered location in deep water, the *Wilheim* is structurally intact other than the torpedo blast hole. Huge cargo cranes still jut out and overhang you as you pass under them and descend. It is possible to get very deep on this wreck and it is difficult at times to keep track of your depth. The wreck just draws you down into the depths as you pass by anti-aircraft gun positions on the bridge and stern. On the seabed far below are piles of her wartime cargo of coal.

After we surfaced from the dive, the *Jane R* moved further north to the island of Fedje where we were going to dive the wreck of the SS *Optima*, otherwise known as the 'cheese and brandy wreck'. The *Jane R* moved into Floro harbour and manoeuvred alongside working quays, along which were all sorts of present-day industrial units, all being used. This historic wreck lies hidden from modern eyes just a stone's throw from the quayside in 42 metres.

The *Optima* was built in 1926 and after a long life at sea, the voyage that would be her last would be to supply German High Command in northern Norway with provisions for celebrations to follow the capture of Murmansk. Amongst general provisions would be vast amounts of wine, cognac and round cheeses.

Whilst being loaded in Floro harbour she was attacked in a daring torpedo raid on 14 March 1943 by the Norwegian *MTB 619*. She sank at her mooring against the quay, rolling over onto her port side on the steeply shelving seabed. It is hard to imagine how bold the MTB's attack was. Often these small craft were hidden amongst the innumerable outlying islands and would risk a daring exposure to make an attack. Here *619* had come right into the heart of a German controlled and defended harbour. What courage.

Because this wreck lay against a working quay in a busy harbour she was not buoyed, so our intrepid guide Lea was given one end of a long thin blue line and told by Gordon to hop over the side, swim directly to the bottom and then swim down the slope until he hit the large wreck that lay broadside to the quayside. Minutes later, job done, we were tied into the wreck.

Ewan and I jumped into the water and started heading down the line. The water here was dark, gloomy and silty – reminiscent of British waters and in complete contrast to the crystal-clear Norwegian water we had become used to. We arrived near the stern and were immediately confronted with the auxiliary helm – a large spoked steering wheel, still sitting in its correct position. It would be used if control of the rudder from the bridge was lost or disrupted. The auxiliary helm allowed direct steering of the rudder directly below.

Moving forward we moved into one of the rear holds and inside on the seabed below, saw large heaps of slender-necked blue cognac bottles, still with their contents held in by their corks. Looking up at the starboard side of the ship (which now formed a roof over our heads) there were hundreds of large circular white cheeses, each about 1–2 feet across and still in their waterproof wrappings. All were welded firmly to the roof to where they had floated and become trapped after the sinking.

The next day we moved over to Luta Island to dive the 265 feet long SS *Havda*. Built in 1881, she was an old lady of the seas and had served as a passenger/cargo mail boat, latterly

The bow of SS Havda © *Ewan Rowell*

The atmospheric wreck of the SS Havda © *Ewan Rowell*

running from Trondheim to Stavanger in the run up to World War II. She was sunk by British airplanes outside Luta Island on 9 December 1944 while en route from Måløy to Bergen, and now lies relatively intact in 16–30 metres on her port side. The seabed around her is strewn with glass bottles and crockery, and apparently part of her cargo was a number of dead German soldiers being brought back for burial.

The following day saw diving on the *Solvang III* – a small intact fishing vessel in 25 metres, which sank in 1991. She sits perfectly upright on her keel with her masts and rigging still intact and rising to 4 metres short of the surface. Being such a recent wreck, her paintwork is still visible on some of her steelwork. This was the furthest north we would be on this trip and soon the *Jane R* had turned her bows to start running back south. On the way back we would break the journey to dive the *Frankenwald* once more.

Gordon was a brilliant skipper. His knowledge of the sea and Norway was immense – he understood diving and divers, and kept us entertained with tales of days past. The one that sticks out in my mind is how with a party of divers he had anchored the *Maise Graham* in Lunan Bay on the east coast of Scotland overnight. The divers were keen to go ashore to visit the local pub, but Gordon wasn't for moving. Not to be put off getting a drink, his divers got dressed into their dry suits and put a dry change of clothes into black bin bags. They then dropped over the side and swam a mile or more to the shore, towing their black bin bags. Once ashore they got changed into their dry clothes and then marched to the pub – except that it had sometime previously been converted into an old folk's home. No beer = sad divers. I bet the swim back out to the *Maise Graham* seemed a lot longer.

The food on the *Jane R* on our trip was full and excellent. As a diver himself, Gordon knew how many calories a grown man or woman had to get down his or her neck to keep him dive-fit for the week and made sure that we had a full intake. If calories were missing then we topped up with his fine home-brewed ale that he kept aboard.

The bow of the Solvang III. *© Ewan Rowell*

Gordon also believed that it aided decompression – and body and soul generally – for his divers to go ashore frequently for a stiff walk up an imposing hill or mountain. It would be harsh to call them forced marches, but divers were (how can I put it?) encouraged to take part. The one that sticks out in my mind was Den Norsk Herse – the Norwegian Horse – a small island with a massive single mountain on it. It was quite a walk from where the boat tied up against a pier in a small bay just to get to the foot of this imposing mountain – a mountain which got even more imposing the nearer you got to it.

A steep 1½ hour walk up through boulder fields and gorse brought you to the summit where, in common with a lot of Norwegian mountains, there was an old tin box with a signing book and some iron rations in case walkers were caught out by conditions. From there we were able to approach with much trepidation, the top of 1,000-foot high cliffs that towered directly over the bay where the *Jane R* was tied up. The cliff was so steep that we went down on our stomachs and crawled gingerly to the edge to peer over and look straight down to the speck of a boat that was the *Jane R*, sitting far below in the crystal waters of the bay. I am good with depths but not heights and had a distinctly queer feeling in my stomach as I got to the edge.

The Norwegian people proved to be extremely polite, friendly and welcoming. Gordon was known wherever he went and universally received a warm welcome. On one occasion he decided we would overnight at a small island called Flora. When we arrived there we found a small cluster of delicate houses surrounding a working harbour. There was one restaurant on the island, which was closed normally at this time of year. But a party of businessmen on another boat had wanted to eat there and the owner had decided that as we had arrived as well, he would lay on a karaoke. The bar was a large bare room filled with rustic wooden benches and tables.

We sat down en masse and someone got a stack of tinned beer from the bar. I'm not a great fan of karaoke but we were already a tad oiled from wine with the meal and the beer soon had the desired medicinal effect. The owner, speaking in lilting English through a mike, indicated that he would pass round pieces of paper and we could all write down what songs we wanted and put our names down for which ones we wanted to sing. At this stage, Ewan foolishly decided that he wanted to go to the toilet – perhaps not wanting to be involved. Bad move. As soon as he disappeared into the toilet, as if with one accord we all decided to write Ewan's name down alongside Tammy Wynette's old classic *Stand By Your Man*, which starts with the immortal line 'Sometimes it's hard to be a woman'. 'Perfect' we thought. The slips of paper were duly put into the hat and passed back up to the MC on the stage. Like little children we all sat there at our table trying to stop smirking as Ewan innocently walked back from the toilet.

A wee while later the MC kicked off the karaoke and dipped his hand into the hat holding the slips of songs and names. We felt he could hardly go wrong, as all 12 of us had written Ewan's name and the Tammy Wynette song. There could only be 30 to 40 slips in the hat – and 12 were for the unsuspecting Ewan. In stilted English the MC announced: "And now for the first song, from Scotland we have Ewan singing *Stand by Your Man*." The look on Ewan's face was priceless: jaw to floor. But to his great credit he got up and went on the stage and gave it lalldee. He was completely uninhibited and if the Eurovision Song Contest was going out live from Flora then there's no doubt that Royaume Uni would have won. He was brilliant and because he went for it in such great style, everyone picked up on the mood and soon the whole bar was rocking. I hazily recollect singing Tom Jones' *Delilah* solo, then singing it as a duet with Ewan, and then with someone else. I think I sang about five songs, which is something for someone who has never sung at a karaoke before. It was a great night.

When we closed at about 2.00 a.m. we went back to the *Jane R*, where more drinking followed. I dimly remember having written in felt tip pen on a large white dive briefing board the words to the chorus of a sea shanty Ewan sings:

> Wrap me up in me oil skins and jumper:
> No more by the docks I'll be seen.
> Just tell me old shipmates,
> I'm taking a trip mate
> And I'll see you down on Fiddler's Green.

Ewan would sing the verse and then I'd bring in the whole dive crew with the chorus.

That night the *Jane R* was a warm oasis of noise and light in a dark cold Norwegian night, and we sang and laughed until 4.00 a.m. The next day it was time for the long steam back to Bergen. There were a lot of sore heads that day and a few people had to very quickly get themselves outside into the cold and the rain for some fresh air as we laboured back.

◆　◆　◆

In amongst all the heavy-duty tech diving I was doing, there were a lot of lighter moments. Jim Burke is legendary for his diving ability and stamina. He does enjoy his diving and gets quite a kick out of it. On one occasion Jim was getting all excited about heading off on a dive. He lives in an old farmhouse, which is accessed up a half-mile private roadway, and it's a bit of a pain for him because the refuse collection lorry won't come up the private driveway, so he has to get his wheelie bin down to the public road. Jim has developed the trick of hitching his wheelie bin to the tow ball on his Land Rover and driving it down to the public road. Except on one occasion, in his excitement about the forthcoming dive he got distracted as he drove down the private road and forgot to stop and dump his wheelie bin. He drove for several miles until he reached the town of Ellon where he noticed that several members of the public seemed to be gesticulating wildly towards him about something. 'Wonder what that's all about' he thought as he drove on through the centre of Ellon. And then he looked in his rear view mirror and saw a trail of bin bags, litter and general rubbish seemingly emanating from the rear of his Land Rover. He pulled over and found that the bottom of his wheelie bin had been completely rubbed away. The two black wheels had melted and disintegrated, leaving only a knot of melted black compound on the red-hot spindle.

On another occasion I was on holiday in Mallorca with my wife Claire and my two daughters Nicola and Catriona. We were staying in the northern town of Puerto Pollensa that fringes a large shallow bay – a favourite anchoring spot for yachts. One windy day we had gone down for a bit of fun in the section of beach to the west that is fringed by overhanging trees. I like that part as it gives nice shade from the sun's heat. The kids wanted to hire a pedalo complete with slide. I was less than enthusiastic as there was a strong offshore wind and I knew who would have to do all the pedalling back to the beach at the end of the hire. It would be windy but I thought we could handle it. Sometimes it's impossible to say no. One pedalo duly hired, the four of us pedalled out to sea, and though there were two pedal seat positions I'm sure I was the only one pedalling.

We got out so far and then started diving and jumping off it and using the slide. I even had a go at the slide but skinned my hips – it clearly wasn't wide enough for a 6'2" Scotsman's backside. As we larked around, fighting from time to time to pedal back towards the shore against the wind, I spotted a small, grey tender, like a zodiac, with a sun bleached, shaggy haired older gent in Speedos. He was rowing for all his might back towards the shore but the wind was so strong that almost comically, he was still being blown offshore.

As we watched, we saw him collide with a moored yacht. 'Ah', I thought; 'he owns that yacht and is purposely heading for it'. But then he was standing up, his fingers frantically and fruitlessly grabbing for something on the yacht's smooth hull to hold onto, as the wind swept him along the side of the yacht and carried him away. He then started rowing back to shore again for all his worth, but was still being blown in the opposite direction. In fact, he was rowing so hard that his oars popped out of their oarlocks and splashed into the sea. He managed to retrieve them quickly before they could float away. Next he had a small anchor out and lobbed it as far back to the shore as he could. He then started trying to pull himself, or kedge himself, back towards the shore. He did that several times before the effort got too much for him and he started rowing to shore again – all the time being blown further out to sea. He seemed to be starting to panic – as again both his oars simultaneously popped out of their oarlocks again and splashed into the sea. This time he couldn't grab them in time and his tender floated away from them. He threw in his anchor again, but it didn't hold him. The rope wasn't long enough for the depth. We were perhaps 300–400 yards away from his tender and it was clear that he had no options left. He continued to drift out to sea.

"Kids – we're on a rescue," I said with my lifeboat crewman's head on. We turned the pedalo (with feature slide) towards him and started pedalling as hard as we could up to our top speed ... of about 2 knots. Slowly we started to gain on him and began to close. As we got near him I realised that, although he would have been a rugged shaggy-haired blonde beach god in the 1970s, he was now a bit past his sell-by-date. He got excited and animated as we approached and stood up balancing precariously in the small tender to wave to us. He was a large man now but his Speedo's would have been too small for him when he bought them in the 1970s. As we closed for some reason the words, 'Ca va?' came out of my mouth – why I don't know. He clearly wasn't British – but why was I talking French and not English?

"Fatigué – fatigue" he replied in French with a German accent – obviously thinking we were French.

"Assiez vous, s'il vous plait", I said in a Scottish accent – fearful that he was going to fall into the sea. Then realising I was in fact British – not French, I asked him to throw me his bow rope in English. He must have been very confused. Nicola, a sea cadet for seven years grabbed it and tied off a skilful round turn and two half hitches to the rear of the pedalo. Our 1970s beach god sat down and seemed to calm down.

I could see his oars floating about 50 yards away so we towed him over and picked those up. After that we turned and headed back to the pedalo hire area, which was by now a long way away. We didn't want to run over our hour rental and have to pay for another hour. Fifteen minutes later and the Royal Navy pedalo (with slide) – and attached tender with

German beach god – arrived back to a small crowd. I think I sensed my chest puffing out as I beached the pedalo and jumped out to untie the tender's bow rope. After a few words, our sailor departed rowing very carefully a few feet away from the shore.

I had a word with the pedalo rental chap and mentioned that we'd been on a rescue – in the hope of getting a free hour, but he wasn't for budging. You win some you lose some.

CHAPTER NINETEEN

THE FLEETWOOD STEAM TRAWLER LOWDOCK REVEALED?

Very early in my wreck-hunting career I had bought a wreck print-out from the Hydrographic Office covering the whole northeast coast of Scotland from Montrose to Fraserburgh. This official print out lists all the vessels known to the Hydrographic Office as being lost within any defined parameters you provide – along with their recorded positions. Some positions are quite accurate – others are very inaccurate. I asked for a print-out of all wrecks recorded as lying up to 5 miles offshore.

When it arrived, as I started going through the wreck information and plotting the latitudinal and longitudinal positions onto my Admiralty Chart, I noticed that some of these positions were shown to have been surveyed or wire swept. Others were clearly inaccurate, being listed as 'position approximate' ('PA'), or 'position doubtful' ('PD') on the chart, and their position was only given to the nearest nautical mile. Most of the wrecks were from the days of dead-reckoning and these could be several miles away from the actual position of the wreck.

Once we started diving the positions, we discovered just how jumbled up the wrecks and their identities were. Around Stonehaven itself (as mentioned earlier), the wreck charted as the SS *Cushendall* turned out to be the SS *Gowrie*. The wreck charted as the *Matador* and listed by one author as a 3,400-ton steamship turned out to be the SS *Cushendall*. The wreck charted as the SS *Gowrie* turned out to be the small steam trawler *Matador* – it wasn't a 3,400-ton steamship at all. Pity – that would have kept me happy for a very long time. Divers trying to dive the wreck charted as the *Cushendall* (but in fact the *Gowrie*) stumbled on the wreck of a fourth uncharted vessel, the SS *Fernside*. So, just here in Stonehaven Bay alone, there was quite a confused picture and I could understand why people who could not personally go and dive these wrecks would perpetuate the misinformation about wreck identities and locations. But this confusion did not just reign in Stonehaven Bay – it was the same position round the whole of Scotland and there are almost 20,000 recorded shipwrecks in Scotland alone.

In the early 1990s the hot-spot cluster of wrecks 3–6 miles offshore from Inverbervie (10 miles south of Stonehaven) was the first area to catch my eye. Several of the wrecks appeared to be very close to the 50-metre depth contour on the charts so I thought they may well be just in air-diveable range. This was in the era of 'Deep Air', before mixed diving gases became commercially available to the sport-diving community.

We decided to try and find the shallowest of these wrecks as a starter, recorded as being situated at 56 48 30.00N, 002 12 45.00W. The wreck symbol on the chart showed that this wreck lay some 2–3 miles offshore and it was listed as being a World War I tanker the *Baku Standard*. When we eventually found the wreck, dived and identified it, it turned out to be the MS *Taurus*, sitting almost 3 miles away from its reported sinking position in World War II of 56 49 25.00N, 002 09 25.00W.

Three miles further out from that at 56 47 10.0N, 002 11 45.0W was another wreck symbol that was shown as having been wire swept – so we reckoned that that position would be fairly accurate. The Hydrographic Office print-out recorded this mark as a '(Probable) U Boat'. George Mair spent some time out on the water in his RIB searching around the position and eventually located the wreck. When we subsequently dived it, we found it to be the wreck of the World War I loss, the 1893 tanker *Baku Standard* (itself charted where the *Taurus* lay), sitting in 60 metres about one mile away from its officially recorded position. A pattern of confusion was emerging.

The wrecks of the *Taurus* and *Baku Standard* at depths of 50–60 metres were right at the very edge of safe deep-air diving. We would go on to carry out 20–30 air dives on them, exploring them fully.

Once Trimix became readily available to UK sport diving in the mid 1990s, the old 50-metre air-diving depth limitation was stripped away and we were able to dive deeper, more safely and venture far further offshore to a seemingly endless series of undived, virgin wrecks. The years that followed heralded the start of an exciting new wave of wreck exploration. It was and still is, a time of great discovery in which the sea has revealed many of her secrets. Our ten-strong band of technical divers has been able to roam far offshore, finding and diving an average of five virgin wrecks a year from Fraserburgh down to Montrose. The wrecks of the liner *Remuera*, the steamships *Trsat*, *Anvers*, *Simonburn*, *Muriel*, *Norwood*, *St Glen* and many others filled our diving days with wonder and excitement.

We located and dived a small wreck about 3 miles offshore southeast of the dramatic Todhead Lighthouse at Catterline, just 5 miles to the south of Stonehaven. When Tony and I made the descent in glorious visibility, we found a small steam trawler sitting on an even keel with its entire superstructure rotted away and nothing particularly identifiable on it. Records of the loss of the Fleetwood trawler *Lowdock* had it as having been rammed and sunk 3 miles southeast of Todhead – although the Hydrographic print-out recorded it as sitting 5 miles east of Todhead at 56 53 06.0N, 002 03 08.0W. The wreck we had dived had the right dimensions for the *Lowdock* and fitted the bill size-wise. So we started calling the wreck the *Lowdock* – but as it was so small and uninteresting, we mentally filed it away as not worthy of another dive.

In 2006 we decided to make a determined effort to find the rumoured U-boat that the Admiralty had charted in this area, the wreck position for which we had already dived and found to be the World War I tanker loss *Baku Standard*. We had managed to acquire a position known locally by the fishermen as 'the sub', right in the middle of the hot spot of several

The Fleetwood steam trawler Lowdock, rammed and sunk in 1941 and discovered by the Stonehaven Snorkellers in 2009 off Inverbervie.Courtesy of Fleetwood Maritime Heritage Trust.

charted wrecks off Inverbervie, although there was no wreck actually shown on the charts at the position we had been given. Late September came, weather conditions looked favourable and the underwater visibility looked good, so we set up a dive to see what was down there.

On a flat calm early morning we launched *Stonehaven Diver* at our local slip and filled it with all the paraphernalia for a modern technical dive – we knew this dive would be around the 60-metre mark. Rebreathers filled the dive boat – all crammed full with a strong 17/70 helium mix (17% oxygen and 70% helium). Even at that depth our heads would be clear from narcosis and the inevitable long ascent shortened as much as possible.

With Dave Hadden boat handling and Paul, Tony and myself ready to dive, we powered up *Stonehaven Diver* and flashed southwards down the rugged east coast at a steady 20 knots. Majestic Dunnotar Castle – once besieged by William Wallace – moved slowly astern: dark and brooding, high on craggy sheer cliffs. When Wallace eventually took the castle the whole English garrison were locked in a nearby church and then burnt to death. Brutal times and brutal deeds are very much part of the history of the castle, which was made internationally famous when it was used as a film location for the Mel Gibson version of *Hamlet*.

Soon we were passing by the towering cliffs of the Fowlsheugh Nature Reserve, its vertical cliffs home to countless thousands of gulls, guillemots and puffins, and stained pure white from generations of birds leaving their mark. Brilliant white gannets with black heads and yellow tipped wings swooped past us, whilst seals eyed us warily from their rocky haul-out sites. A pod of dolphins could be seen forming up into a feeding circle, raising their tails to beat the water and herd their fish prey into a bait ball. The seas were busy this day.

Within about half an hour we had covered the 10 miles or so down the coast and the GPS was telling us that we were only a few hundred yards from the target. I slowed the RIB and it dropped off the plane until we were right down to just a few knots. Motoring slowly right up to the position, our eyes eagerly watching the seabed trace on the echo sounder as it scrolled out a uniform 60 metres to the bottom. Then suddenly, the bottom line leapt up by 5 metres in the unmistakeable electronic signature of a shipwreck. We had arrived.

Tony made ready the shot-line as we motored around above the wreck, marking several other 'high' positions on the GPS and building up an image of the length and orientation of the wreck below us. From the outline developing on the GPS screen, it seemed that we had a small wreck between 100–200 feet in length, rising up 5 metres from the seabed. It was the right size for a U-boat. Could we really have found a lost U-boat that easily?

Once we were over the middle of the wreck, Tony dropped the shot and the weighted line plunged down through the depths towards our target. All the hassle of getting the boat and kit ready for a technical dive was instantly a forgotten irritation, as I rolled backwards over the side tubes of the boat into the sea in an explosion of white bubbles. Tony and Paul soon followed and we all made our way along the side of the boat to the downline at the bow. Once we were all there and after a round of 'OK' hand signals, we started down the line hand over hand.

Rule number one on east coast diving is never to let go of the downline on a descent. Our coasts are very tidal and although we had timed the dive to start just before the Holy Grail of slack water arrived, in the poor dark underwater visibility and even in the gentlest of currents it is all too easy to momentarily lose sight of the downline and in a flash get disorientated. Once it is drifted away out of eyeshot then it can be impossible to find again.

On this dive the visibility here in the shallows seemed greenish but reasonably clear – hopefully the visibility down on the wreck would be half decent. As usual, the deeper we went the darker it got and by the time we got to a depth of about 35 metres there was no ambient light penetrating down at all – it was pitch black. The beams from our powerful dive torches cut through the darkness, the downline fluorescing as they swept over it.

At 45 metres down I knew the wreck was just 10–15 metres below me in the inky void. My eyes strained into the darkness for the ever-present threat of trawl nets suspended like a curtain, still floating on buoys. At 50 metres down I started to make out the faint outline of straight man-made lines to my side and below me. Was it a U-boat? I couldn't tell. At 55 metres down, suddenly I could see the shot-weight sitting just off the wreck on a flat sandy seabed 5 metres below me. I swept my torch round and to my side and there was the unmistakeable outline of a small but intact bow, the fo'c'stle of a small steamship.

Keeping the downline in my hand, I swam over to the wreck and tied the line off on a rusted and encrusted mooring cleat on the wreck – the first time that cleat had been used in a very long time. I clipped a spare torch to the downline and switched it on. The powerful beam swept around slowly like an underwater lighthouse, lighting the downline for a later return to the surface.

Once all the practicalities of tying into the wreck were sorted out I felt a brief wave of frustration overcome me – the target was not the fabled U-boat but a small steamship, perhaps even a trawler. The vertical stem showed this was a ship built in the early 1900s, but there was no steamship of this size listed as being lost in this area. So now we had a new challenge – to identify this unknown wreck. What was it and why was it sitting uncharted here in the depths?

I swam over the port gunwale of the bow and moved up and over the fo'c'stle deck itself. Here, delicate anchor chains ran out to anchor hawses on either side and in between was a small copper or brass raised skylight structure a couple of feet high and some 3 feet square. Small portholes were set around its base to allow light down into the fo'c'stle rooms below, where some of the crew would have had their quarters.

Moving aft, on the port side of the fo'c'stle deck there was a small toilet deckhouse, conveniently set backing out over the side of the ship. From here there was a drop down to a collapsed area, which looked like the remains of the fish hold of an old steam trawler. At the port side of this fish hold was a large single-curved steel beam like a slender upturned 'U' – a gallows housing for a trawl door. We now knew we were diving an early 1900s steam trawler – but which one and how did it end up lying here?

Moving aft we left the fish hold, passed a large deck winch with its trawl wire still wound around it and moved up to where the wheel house had once stood. It looked as though this had been accidentally trawled into aeons ago by an unknowing fisherman, as the whole wheelhouse (bar a few inches at the bottom) was gone, along with everything that had once been in it. Moving further aft I came across a dark circular opening some 5 feet across, where the smokestack had once stood. Further aft and I arrived at the engine room – its deckhouse walls and small roof were completely gone, leaving the top of its triple-expansion engine completely exposed below decks. Aft of that and we came to an intact deckhouse near the very stern of the ship, complete with some small portholes still in situ. We started to move around a delicate rounded stern and here we found the cause of the ship's sinking (and thus the first major clue as to her identity).

The seemingly delicate schooner-type stern had clearly been rammed from behind – it was crumpled up and folded completely back over on top of the deck. And there in the very middle of the mess of mangled steel was a big V-shaped groove where the bows of another ship had hit her from behind and ridden right up and over the stern rail, pushing the deck down and underwater. She had been rammed in the stern – it was unmistakeable.

By now our allotted time on the bottom was fast running out and it was time to return to the downline at the bow for the ascent. As we neared the bow, the beacon beam of our fixed torch on the line brought us back to safety. For our 25 minutes of time on the bottom we would spend about an hour on a slow ascent to decompress.

Once we were all safely back on the boat and heading back up north to Stonehaven, we started talking through the dive. It was clear that we had a small early 1900s steam trawler, about 125 feet in length I guessed. I was already familiar with the circumstances of the loss of each of the wrecks around this neck of the woods – and there was one I remembered that had been rammed in the stern in World War II – the steam trawler *Lowdock*.

Once back ashore I pulled out my reference books to check the *Lowdock*'s details. She was a 276 gross tonnage Admiralty 'Castle'-class steam trawler built by Smiths Dock Co. Ltd at South Bank on Tees and launched on 9 March 1917. She was 125.5 feet long with a beam of 23.4 feet and a draught of 12.8 feet. Her Official Number was 143965. Originally known as the *Peter Lovitt*, she saw service during World War I between 1917 and 1919 as a minesweeper, before re-entering civilian life after the Armistice.

In 1934 the *Peter Lovitt* was sold to South Shields Engineering & Dry Dock Co Ltd and renamed *Lowdock*. As the skies of Europe clouded with the dark clouds of the second great conflict of the 20th century, dangerous days were again fast approaching for the *Lowdock*. On 5 February 1940, under the charge of skipper J.E. Moore, she sailed from Methil in Fife for the Longstone fishing grounds far offshore. At 11.15 a.m. four days later on 9 February, 21 miles east of Scarborough en route to Hull, she was attacked by two German aircraft that strafed her with machine-guns and bombed her for good measure. One aircraft was skilfully hit by one of the *Lowdock*'s crew with a Ross rifle and retired from the contact. The Ross rifle was a single-shot, straight-pull, bolt-action .303 rifle, of some antiquity in World War II. They were produced in Canada from 1903 until the middle of the World War I when the rifle was withdrawn because of its apparent unreliability. However, by then it had proved itself to be a superior marksman's rifle for many people. And here, almost 30 years after it had ceased being manufactured, the Ross rifle was in action on the *Lowdock* – a poor defence against the machine-guns and bombs of a modern state-of-the-art German aircraft, intent on using all its weapons to sink her. A single-shot rifle in skilled hands had disabled a fast German aircraft.

The other aircraft – a Dornier 17E – dropped over 20 bombs at the *Lowdock*, the final one exploding in the water so close to the ship that it lifted the stern out of the water and damaged telegraphs, steering gear and the wireless. Miraculously there were no casualties.

The *Lowdock* managed to limp to Hull, where the next day (10 February), she was slipped for survey. On her subsequent un-slipping, water was spotted getting into the stokehold and further repairs were required before she returned to service. Just over a month later on 19 March 1940, on a passage from Methil to Aberdeen under the charge of 31-year-old skipper Frank Brunton at about 11.00 p.m., she was rammed by *HMT Lady Philomena* (H230/P. No.FY148). According to the records, this happened some 3 miles east of Todhead Lighthouse, 5 miles south of Stonehaven. She was noted as having sunk quickly with the loss of all but one of her crew of twelve – the mate Thurston Atkinson, who was also well-known locally in South Shields as a skipper.

The mate would later give evidence to a Board of Enquiry of how the tragedy came about and in the run up to that hearing, a statement (called a 'precognition') was taken by lawyers, in which he outlined the evidence he would give. He told how at 4.00 p.m. on the afternoon of Tuesday 19 March the *Lowdock* had left Methil for Aberdeen with a big swell running in from the east. Visibility was good and no other boats left with them. The Admiralty had ordered *Lowdock* to set a course north-by-east from 1½ miles east of May Island in the Firth of Forth until they reached a black buoy 15 miles along on that northeast bearing. Thurston Atkinson (the mate) came on watch at 6.10 p.m. and took over from the third hand, at which time the ship's log was set from abreast of May Island. He was told to keep a look out for the black buoy, which was north near the Bell Rock – a dangerous outcrop of rocks some 12 miles offshore from Arbroath. The Bell Rock is awash at high water and was such a danger to shipping that in 1811 Robert Stevenson had built a now-famous lighthouse on it to try and stop the catalogue of shipping losses there. Notwithstanding the lighthouse, HMS *Argyll*, sister ship to HMS *Hampshire* (on which Lord Kitchener perished off Orkney in 1916) famously ran aground on the Rock in 1915 and was totally wrecked.

The black buoy was sighted at 7.30 p.m. when *Lowdock* was 5 miles inside the Bell Rock. The mate altered course to northeast for Aberdeen and in terms of their Admiralty orders continued on this course at full speed making 9 knots. When it came to lighting up time at 8.00 p.m., the only lights lit were the smoked glass sidelights and stern lights. Admiralty orders were that masthead lights were not to be shown. Throughout the voyage the mate was taking soundings by echo meter. There was a fresh wind from west-northwest but it was a clear night with intermittent rain. Several Admiralty trawlers were passed coming down from the north on the starboard side – identifiable by the gun on their bows. They did not show their sidelights until they were approaching – and then only for a short time again following orders for naval vessels.

The skipper had left orders for him to be called when 25 miles on the log had been recorded. By 9.45 p.m. that distance had been covered and the mate left two deckhands on the bridge and went down to the skipper's bunk to tell him that there was a flashing light on the port bow. The skipper told him that the light was Todhead Lighthouse. The mate recorded that the skipper told him to keep on the northeast course, which was right for Aberdeen.

At 10.30 p.m. the mate went off watch and handed over to the third hand and two deckhands. On his way astern to his cabin, he told the skipper that they were now approaching Todhead Lighthouse. The only light from other vessels he could see was a white light away on the starboard side about a point abaft the beam. The mate retired to his cabin in the stern deckhouse and turned in fully dressed. He recounted that the skipper was awake when he had spoken last to him, lying in his bunk just below the wheelhouse and that he had got his clothes on. That would be the last time he saw the skipper and he could not say whether the skipper had gone up on the bridge or not. The mate recorded that at about 11.00 p.m. on his cabin clock, whilst he was lying in his bunk in the stern deckhouse, he heard the *Lowdock* give one short blast on the steam whistle and at practically the same time the engine telegraph rang.

He jumped out of his bunk and almost immediately there was a loud crash. He then stated that he saw another ship's stem (bow) come into his berth, which was on the port side of the stern deckhouse just beside the port after gallows (where the aft-most trawl door would be suspended). After this lucky escape, the mate rushed out of the stern deckhouse onto the deck and saw the other vessel, which proved to be *HMT Lady Philomena*, backing away from the *Lowdock*. The mate called to the other vessel, asking the crew not to back away as the *Lowdock* was now sinking. He could see the port, starboard and masthead lights of the other vessel, which was by now some 10–15 yards away going astern. The mate pulled some board casing off a grating and put that on deck and sent two young lads of the crew over with a raft. By now the *Lowdock's* stern was under water and she was sinking fast. He pulled another piece of board off and found himself suddenly in the water, clinging to it. He started to shout for help and saw the raft he had cut adrift coming towards him. He hoped he could get on it and expected to see the two young lads in it, but when he reached it the raft was empty. By now the *Lowdock* had vanished from sight beneath the waves and there was nothing but rigging floating about. Crew onboard the *Lady Philomena* saw the mate's raft and he was picked up. He was the only survivor.

The mate's evidence was that before the collision, the *Lowdock* would have been making 9½ knots and he placed the scene of the collision about three miles directly abeam of Todhead. The mate spoke to the lieutenant in charge of the *Lady Philomena*, who told him that both he and the sub-lieutenant were on watch. The mate recounted how the lieutenant had said: "I saw your green light on my starboard bow and said to the sub-lieutenant that it would be alright to pass green to green and he altered course a bit to open his green light a little more." He had then left the sub-lieutenant in charge and went to look at the chart. Whilst he was doing that, the sub-lieutenant called him and told him that a vessel had its red light open. The lieutenant had at once gone on the bridge and put his engines "slow astern", then "half astern", then "full astern". By the time of the collision he had been going astern for almost three minutes. The Lieutenant had told the mate that if the *Lowdock* had kept on a straight course when crossing his bow, they would have had a narrow escape. The *Lowdock's* stern however had kept coming towards him.

◆　◆　◆

Clearly there was a very good chance that the steam trawler we had found and dived was the *Lowdock*. The collision damage in the stern was unmistakeable and there was no other steam-trawler charted or listed as rammed in the stern for tens of miles. But we needed something more definite to conclusively identify her – she was after all sitting more than 2 miles away from the sinking position given in the mate's precognition and almost 5 miles away from the Hydrographic Office print-out position. But we were a bit thrown as we had already dived the wreck 3 miles southeast of Todhead (the mate's approximate position for the *Lowdock*) the year before – and had always assumed that one *was* the *Lowdock*.

That night I did a Google search on the Internet for the *Lowdock*, not really expecting to find very much. Much to my surprise there was a discussion thread about this very vessel on a marine website, where a relative of one of the deceased crew members (now living in Australia) was looking for information about the loss of the ship. I emailed her to say that we had just dived a wreck that we tentatively thought might be the *Lowdock* and that we were planning to dive it again soon. If we confirmed it to be the *Lowdock* we would let her know.

Another contributor to the website, Pete Harris, was then in touch with me and kindly forwarded on photos of the *Lowdock* and copies of newspaper articles from *The Fleetwood Chronicle* which carried the banner headline:

FLEETWOOD SEA TRAGEDY

11 LOST WHEN TRAWLER SINKS IN COLLISION

Mate The Only Survivor.

The photo of the ship itself was very helpful in letting us understand what we should be looking for. The curator of a local maritime museum at Fleetwood suggested that if we could measure the three cylinder tops of the triple-expansion engine, then we could compare those measurements with the measurements that were recorded along with basic ship details by Lloyds Register of Shipping for every new ship built. We resolved to dive the wreck again as soon as possible to do this. Tony Ray would try to video the whole wreck whilst I would attempt to measure the exact beam of the ship and the engine cylinder tops.

Two weeks later we were sitting in *Stonehaven Diver* 60 metres above the wreck, having shotted it in the hour before slack water arrived. Paul Haynes again would be diving with Tony and myself.

We splashed backwards from our boat into the water and pressed on downwards, pausing for a bubble check at 6 metres on each of our rebreathers. Satisfied that all was well, I led the way down into the darkness. At 55 metres down, the sandy seabed appeared out of the darkness and there was the anchor and chain sitting in exactly the same spot on the seabed as last time, right beside the delicate bow with which we were now becoming familiar.

I pulled the downline across to the wreck and tied it off on the same mooring cleat I had used on the previous dive and fixed a powerful strobe on the line – its pulses of brilliant white light could be seen from a very long way off. As Tony opened up his video lights and started to meticulously video the whole wreck from the bow to stern, I quickly made my way over the fish hold, past the remnants of the bridge and the black circular funnel opening and reached the engine room – all within the first couple of minutes down on the wreck. The deckhouse around and above the engine room was completely missing, leaving the large rectangular opening in the deck through which the engine would have been lowered or removed when necessary. The tops of the three cylinders of the triple-expansion steam engine stood open, just under weather deck level.

I pulled out my metal tape measure and measured the beam of the wreck in three sections. Firstly I measured from the starboard gunwale of the wreck to the side of the engine room. Then I measured across the engine room itself. Lastly, I measured from the other side of the engine room to the port gunwale. Adding the three measurements together gave the total beam of the wreck at approximately 23 feet. The *Lowdock* had a recorded beam of 23.4 feet. We were getting close.

A triple-expansion engine nearly always sits fore and aft on the centre line of a ship in the engine room, just aft of the boiler room. The three engine cylinders start with the smallest high-pressure cylinder nearest the boiler and each of the successive two cylinders is bigger than the preceding one. High-pressure steam exits from the boiler and enters the first cylinder of the engine. This is the smallest cylinder – the high-pressure cylinder. As the steam enters the high-pressure cylinder it expands, and this expansion pushes the piston to move producing torque, which moves the connecting rod (the 'con rod'). The con rod turns the crankshaft and transmits power to turn the propeller shaft. Once the steam has expanded in the small high-pressure cylinder and the piston has completed its stroke, the steam then passes into a second larger cylinder. Here it expands further but at a lower pressure, but again moving the piston, con rod, crank shaft and in turn the prop shaft. This combination of a larger cylinder but lower pressure produces exactly the same power and stroke as the smaller, higher-pressure cylinder. From this second cylinder, the expanded steam then passes to the third low-pressure cylinder – the largest. In the low-pressure cylinder the steam expands again and produces exactly the same torque and power as the two smaller cylinders. The result is that all three different sized cylinders deal with different volumes of steam at different pressures and are set up so that they each produce exactly the same stroke for each of the three pistons. Each cylinder develops exactly the same turning force, giving a smooth delivery of power through the con rods and crankshaft to the prop shaft. It is a very, very clever piece of engineering. The expanded steam is then fed into a condenser where it is returned into a liquid state, ready to go through the whole process again. The cylinder measurements are fairly specific to each individual engine and are recorded at the time of construction by Lloyd's Register of London – they are a great clue to identifying a ship.

I dropped down into the engine room and landed on top of the 15-foot long engine top and measured the high-pressure cylinder top, noting its dimensions on my wrist slate. I then went on to measure cylinder number two and then the third low-pressure large cylinder. The measurements turned out to be exactly the same as the *Lowdock*'s. This wreck was the same beam, had the same cylinder-head sizes and was rammed in the stern. I became almost certain that our wreck was the *Lowdock* – even though it was sitting 3 miles away from where it should be. Job done I thought.

As I was finishing measuring the cylinder tops, Tony came into view beside me and filmed for a short period. Then together we finned aft and arrived at the stern deckhouse, which we found to be structurally intact with small portholes still set in its walls. The port after gallows (mentioned by the mate) was still in position on the port side of the ship immediately adjacent. We moved over the after deck to the rounded stern itself, where part of the stern had been thrust up and the metal folded over on top of itself like cardboard. And there on top of the crumpled heap was the big 'V' cut into the crumpled metal by the bows of the ship that sank her. Paul, Tony and I then turned the dive at this point and headed back towards the flashing strobe – well out-of-sight some 125 feet in the distance ahead of us at the bow.

Even though I had convinced myself that this wreck was the *Lowdock*, I still felt a lingering doubt, for on top of the fo'c'stle on the port side was a small one-person WC deckhouse – the sort with a direct flush over the side of the boat. That deckhouse wasn't shown in the topside photograph we had of the *Lowdock* in her fishing heyday. But it was possible that the deckhouse was added after the photo was taken, perhaps at the start of World War II. The other thing that bothered me immensely was the mate's precognition – where he stated that he had been in his berth under the aft gallows when the bows of the *Lady Philomena* crashed right through the steel deckhouse wall beside him. From our dives we knew that the stern deckhouse was intact – there was no damage to it at all. The deckhouse seemed a long way from the V-shaped damage at the stern – some 20–30 feet. The deck itself, from the actual V-shaped gouge at the stern right up to the deckhouse, was also intact and didn't show any evidence of the *Lady Philomena* slicing her way up to and into the deckhouse. It looked more as though the offending vessel had ridden up on top of the stern, pushing the whole stern under and allowing it to flood.

Yes there were a lot of things that fitted this being the *Lowdock* – but equally, the WC deckhouse that shouldn't be there, as well as the mate's evidence, was at odds with what we found down on the wreck. Could it be that the mate's evidence was wrong or worse still, false? Was it possible that his story was a concoction, fabricated perhaps to absolve him of blame? Was it possible that he had been on watch; that perhaps it was his error that led to the collision? Was he – the only survivor – covering his tracks? I thought about the possibilities long and hard and didn't like where they led. I decided that I wouldn't risk opening old wounds by even suggesting publicly that there was a question mark over his evidence. There will still be relatives of the mate and the crew around. Best let sleeping dogs lie I thought.

Tony was able to produce a full 20-minute video survey of the *Lowdock* and as we reviewed it and compared it to the photo of the ship afloat, the more we saw of her the more we understood her. We became convinced that she was the *Lowdock* despite the apparent conflicts.

STV picked up on the story and wanted to run a news feature on the find. So on a bright but cold November Monday morning we met an STV outside-broadcast unit down at Stonehaven harbour and let them take shots of us launching the RIB and zipping about at speed in the bay. After doing interviews with Tony and myself, it was all cut together with some of the underwater footage and aired several times. Tony made a DVD with the full 20-minute survey and the STV news feature and sent this to the relative in Australia.

And that, I thought, was the end of the story. However, a couple of days after the STV news feature went out, the receptionist in my law practice Raeburn Christie, Clark & Wallace, rang through to say that an elderly gentleman had called into the office asking to see me. As a lawyer, I didn't usually see people without appointments – my day would very quickly have descended into chaos if I did. So I asked the receptionist to ask what the enquiry was about and see if she could help. She rang through again a second later to say it was about the *Lowdock*. I asked her to show the gentleman right through.

As he came into my room I guessed he must be well into his 70s or 80s and I recognised him as a Stonehaven local. As we shook hands he said: "Mr Macdonald, I am right pleased to meet you. I fished on the *Lowdock* out of South Shields in the 1930s." You could have knocked me down with a feather.

We sat down and he told me how his uncle had been skipper of the *Lowdock* in the 1930s when he lived in South Shields, and how as a young man he had gone out as a deckhand on many an occasion to the fishing grounds aboard her. He told me that he had been aware that she had sunk, but never dreamt that she lay so close to where he now lived – or that he would ever see her again or indeed meet someone who had seen her just in the last few weeks.

So, the two of us sat in my office talking – both from first-hand knowledge of a ship that had been sunk 66 years earlier. We each had seen a different aspect of the *Lowdock*, our memories of her separated by 66 years. He was able to talk me around the ship and answer all my questions about its layout, the way it worked and was able to describe how the mate – the only survivor – had occupied his cabin on the port side of the stern deckhouse (which corroborated that part of the mate's evidence that I had seen). The second engineer had his cabin on the starboard side of the same deckhouse and there had been a small mess table in the middle around which they would eat and drink.

After half an hour or so, he got up to leave. I asked him if he would like to see the video footage of his old ship. He said no – he would prefer to remember her the way she was in her prime. It is hard for us who have never experienced war and the great losses and tragedies that go with it to truly understand the emotions stirred by what we see and find in the depths.

Subsequently the grandson of the skipper of the *Lowdock* (who had been lost that night in 1940) contacted me. His mother had only been five years old at the time of the sinking. We directed him to the STV news feature and gave him all the information we had about the sinking. He kindly replied to me, thanking me and indicated that his mum and dad were now clearer about what went on.

Sometimes when you dive shipwrecks they seem remote, rusted pieces of steel and it's often hard to think that anyone could be interested in what we do. But when from a single wreck like this humble steam trawler you get such human interest, perhaps we can on occasion help those with unanswered questions from long ago. As I look into the histories of particular ships I often find that there are people out there searching for answers. When you browse Internet maritime websites and see how many people are looking for information about lost ships and relatives, the true scale of the human loss at sea becomes evident and somehow overbearing. The human consequences of hundreds of thousands of lives lost at sea still encircle and haunt the globe today.

The Chapter on the *Lowdock* was closed – or so I thought.

CHAPTER TWENTY

A SURPRISING FIND

O ur quest to find the '(probable)' U-boat listed as sunk off the Gourdon area continued throughout 2007 and 2008 and we dived all sorts of new positions and marks in an effort to work out what everything was. Thinking that the *Lowdock* was identified 6 miles southeast of Todhead we had moved on to explore other wrecks and didn't return to dive it or the smaller trawler sitting in the *Lowdock*'s recorded sinking position 3 miles south east of Todhead.

We were given the latitudinal and longitudinal coordinates for three snags from a local fisherman and took time out on the water to go and carry out searches around each position. Sadly one of the positions turned out to be an area of rocky hard ground in an otherwise featureless expanse of sandy seabed and we couldn't find anything at all in the vicinity of the remaining two positions. These were a translation to GPS coordinates of old Decca positions. The two systems have never sat well together and transposed positions are often at variance.

Then one day in October 2009, Ian Balgowan phoned to say that in his fishing boat on the way to check one of the positions, he had been lucky enough to run right over a wreck one fifth of a nautical mile away from one of the three positions we had been given. He was able to give me the precise GPS coordinates. We were in business again. Would this turn out to be the U-boat?

The following weekend, although the tides were favourable with weak neap tides due, the weather was looking marginal. Strong 20–25 mph winds were predicted which would stir up the sea, making it very bumpy and uncomfortable in our open RIBs. Nevertheless we could see even in Stonehaven harbour that the water clarity was exceptional – the clear 'October waters' were upon us and we were conscious of the end of the diving season in late November being only four weeks or so away. We determined to try getting a dive in on the new wreck if we possibly could.

Because of the predicted high winds we decided to launch at Gourdon, the small harbour about 10 miles south of Stonehaven. From here it would be 5 miles straight out to sea to the wreck site. We wouldn't have to endure bashing our way 10 miles down from Stonehaven to the north.

When I woke up on the morning of the dive, the wind was whistling through the tree branches in my garden with some vigour. Slack water was due later in the day at 2.00 p.m. so I had a lot of time to prepare the boat and cram as much food down me as I could. At about 11.00 a.m., I hitched up *Stonehaven Diver* to my jeep and headed down to Gourdon harbour. As you drive down the steep brae road into Gourdon there is a magnificent panorama over the harbour and out to sea and from this high vantage point I could see that the sea was speckled with white crested waves. Already I could tell conditions were marginal.

As I pulled up at the slip I found another dive group from the Deeside branch of the British Sub Aqua Club (BSAC) assembled with a RIB to similar to mine. Jumping out of my jeep I had a quick word with them and found that they were calling off their planned dive for safety reasons because of sea conditions. The rest of our team – Paul Haynes, Tony Ray and Richard Colliar as coxswain – then arrived en masse and after talking about it we decided to tough it out and at least head out to the site. If it was too rough we could turn and come back. Richard Colliar – who was going to boat handle for us this day – was an extremely competent sailor, fellow Trimix rebreather diver and lifeboatman: I felt safe with him at the helm of my RIB in these conditions. There would not be many other people who I'd have trusted to the job this day.

We motored slowly out of the harbour and immediately were in a sizeable swell with large masses of water moving towards the shore swiftly. It's always lumpy in the shallows outside Gourdon harbour so we weren't too put off by it – we thought it would settle down a bit further out. Once we were out in deeper water we would make a call on whether we would dive or not.

We moved along quite swiftly considering the conditions – at about 16–18 knots. Fortunately we were riding across the path of the waves instead of directly into them, riding obliquely up the face of the waves, careering along the crest before motoring back down into the trough. It really wasn't too uncomfortable – suddenly a dive had become a possibility.

Twenty-five minutes later and as we approached the wreck site I was conscious of Tony, Paul and Richard straining over my shoulders to watch the LCD readout of my echo sounder. Would this be our long lost U-boat? As we moved up to the wreck symbol, suddenly the bottom trace on the echo sounder leapt up from 58 msw (metres of seawater) to about 53 msw. There was something on the bottom rising up by 5 metres from the surrounding seabed. That would be fairly consistent with the size of a U-boat. I even thought I detected a small higher midships area on the echo sounder – a conning tower perhaps?

I pushed the GPS 'Mark' button to plot the actual position and then started moving back and forth across the wreck taking other marks. This started giving a picture of the way the wreck was sitting on the bottom. I worked my way to both extremities of the echo sounding trace and measuring this distance gave me an approximate length for the vessel of 100–150 feet, which still didn't rule it out from being a U-boat. Only a dive would tell us what it was.

The four of us looked at each other and at the white water on the crests of the waves rocking *Stonehaven Diver*. Richard stoically said he was happy enough to remain topside and let us dive, although he did draw to our attention a rather obvious frontal weather system visible to the south down towards the Firth of Forth, which seemed to be heading our way.

But nothing would stop Tony, Paul and I diving right by now. We were 55 metres above a virgin wreck.

Once we got orientated over the wreck, Tony dropped the shot-line and chain into the water and fed out the sea-steel rope we now used as a downline. We had found that the cheaper blue polypropylene rope was very buoyant and negated part of the weight of the shot and chain. As a consequence, in any sort of sea the buoyancy of the rope was contributing to the shot and chain being lifted up as a swell passed by and causing it on occasion to come off the wreck. Sea-steel was a robust rope, which had a thin steel filament or wire running through it. It had less buoyancy and also would not sever easily if rubbed up against a rotted sharp edge of metal on a wreck.

The wreck now shotted, we went through the familiar routine of getting rigged up – each diver alone in his own thoughts before a deep dive. Soon we had our rebreathers on our backs and were bringing the electronics to life to start going through the pre-dive preparation set up. All of our group dive using 17/70 diluent so, on the bottom at 60 metres, our equivalent narcotic depth for an air dive would be about 10 metres. There would be hardly any narcosis at all.

Once rigged, we pre-breathed our rebreathers whilst we sat on the tubes of the boat. If there is going to be a problem it is better that it happens during the pre-breathe on the boat, rather than once you are committed to the water. We clipped our bail-out tanks onto our harnesses, one under each arm. Finally we were ready.

Richard skilfully took the RIB close in to the shot and moved slightly up current. The gentle current was now dropping off towards slack water, but was still strong enough to drift us down to the shot. If we dropped into the water downstream of the buoy we may not be able to swim against the current to the buoy. One by one we rolled backwards into the water and collected at the Dhan buoy, leaving Richard alone in the RIB – a solitary figure sitting in our orange RIB in tumultuous seas under leaden grey skies.

The dive group started to move down the shot-line, stopping at 6 metres for a safety check. All was well so we turned and kicked to swim straight down the line into the darkness. The water had a noticeable clarity to it, despite being completely black beneath us for as far as the eye could see. We pressed on down feeling the crush from the surrounding water pressure and soon blackness enveloped us. I stopped at 40 metres and turned to look up at my companions. I could see their forms darkly silhouetted against the lighter water above.

On a deep dive like this you need to rely on your night vision, which takes 20 minutes or so to fully kick in. As a consequence, on the descent your vision is poor – still adjusted for topside daylight. You must rely on what you can see in your torch beam and by the time I was at 55 metres, neither the seabed nor wreck had yet put in an appearance. But then, quite suddenly, there was our shot-weight and chain just lying on a sandy desert.

I landed on the seabed and keeping one hand on the downline looked up the line. High up in the darkness I could see the occasional flash of Tony and Paul's torches as they descended towards me. I swept my powerful Halcyon torch around in the direction of where I assumed the wreck would be – and there about 5 metres away at the limit of my vision was the dark silhouette of a rounded section of hull. Could it really be a U-boat?

Kicking off the seabed I swam over to the hull, pulling the downline, Paul and Tony with me. As I reached it I swam up the side of the hull over a gunwale onto a flat deck. It clearly wasn't our U-boat – but it was still a virgin wreck.

Tony and Paul arrived down beside me as I was cleating the downline off to one of the wreck's convenient mooring cleats. I clipped my big 'Rosie Strobe' light to the line and set it flashing. One of our Peterhead divers, Mike Rosie, had made this for me from my old UK600 torch casing into which he had fitted a strobe of the type used for the tops of power station chimneys. You could hear this thing charging up for some distance and didn't want to be looking directly at it when it flashed in something akin to a mini supernova. That would be your night vision gone for sure.

Once we were all sorted out and comfortable, Tony started to deploy his video camera and lights whilst Paul and I swam over the deck. Immediately I noticed two or three small fish hatches leading down into a cavernous fish hold. We were on a large deep-sea trawler – one that seemed to be in good condition. Paul and I moved over the fish hold and then came to the fo'c'stle, which had a few small portholes with their glass still in them, set in the aft-facing deckhouse. Two aft-facing doorways led inside. I kicked my fins and moved up on top of the fo'c'stle where most of the deck had rotted away, but a sturdy anchor windlass with its chain running up through a single hawse pipe on the starboard side still dominated the area. I peered in through the rotted roof of the lamp room and saw two 2–3-foot high copper masthead lamps with their all-round glass still in place, half buried in silt. One had a corroded copper plate on it - which although difficult to read seemed to say 'St Andrew's Dock'.

Moving astern we passed over the fish hold again, the decking having rotted away to expose the steel framing beams running athwartships. Paul dropped down through the deck beams into the fish hold and as I kept an eye on him I noticed a large heap of coal on the port side. (Ian Balgowan later told me that as a young man he had fished on one of these deep-sea steam trawlers which used to run up as far as the Faeroes. The practice was to keep the vessel's coal in the empty fish hold on the outward journey). As the coal here all seemed to be lying in a heap on the port side I started to think that this meant the ship had gone down on her port side and the cargo of coal had shifted as she sank.

Passing the fish hold my night vision was by now kicking in and I began to be able to see around me for some 10 metres or so. I spotted the large main trawl winch, which still had its cable wound round it, sitting in front of the skeletal framework of a single-storey deckhouse, on top of which would have been the wooden wheelhouse itself. I paused in front of this bridge deckhouse and swept my torch around inside the lower level. The wall plating had all turned to dust and disappeared leaving the whole room open for inspection. The structure was only supported by the upright beams at the four corners and was a scene of utter confusion. Jumbled about on the floor were brass wall-mounted electrics boxes, portholes that had rotted and fallen out of bulkheads, and a toilet and hand-basin still gleaming white. Thick old-fashioned electric cables hung down in graceful loops. The roof of the lower level of this deckhouse had rotted through and sections of it had collapsed downwards, allowing fitments from the wheelhouse above to fall through.

I moved round to the starboard side of the bridge deckhouse and heard Tony calling out to me. I looked over and he was pointing out something large lying on the deck. As I swam over a heavily encrusted, intact telegraph – complete with an enamelled white face and brass pointer – came into focus. I pulled the encrusting sponges off the face to reveal the maker's name: 'Mechan's, Scotstoun, Glasgow'. The brass pointer was at 'Stop'.

I shouted to Tony through my mouthpiece (with the comically high-helium, Donald Duck voice you get on deep diving) the single word "*Gowrie*". He clicked straight away that this was exactly the same style of ferrous telegraph made by Mechan's as is on the wreck of the *Gowrie* off Stonehaven – the only difference being that its pointer is at 'Standby'. Mechan's made a huge range of ferrous and non-ferrous telegraphs for steamships for many years and this alone didn't give any clue to the wreck's identity. We left the telegraph visible for future divers and moved on with our exploration.

The wooden walls and roof of the deck level above – the wheelhouse – had all rotted away and disappeared, but still standing there in open water was the helm. The spoked wheel itself was gone but the telemotor and gearing column still stood proud, locked in position forever. All the parts of a disintegrated ship's compass lay collapsed in a heap beside the helm, along with yet more large brass boxes; green with verdigris – a radio and perhaps an early Decca. As the walls of the wheelhouse disintegrated, the screws holding the boxes had pulled out. The boxes had fallen to the bridge floor and lain there undisturbed for decades until we ventured upon the wreck.

Passing behind the deckhouse we came to the circular opening of the funnel and then to the small pitched roof of an engine room deckhouse. One of the skylights still had its glass in it – the other was open but unfortunately too small to accommodate a diver. I stuck my torch in and shone it around, lighting up on the centre line of the vessel, a completely intact and rather sizeable triple-expansion engine surrounded by catwalks.

Moving further aft we came to a stern deckhouse exactly the same as on the *Lowdock* with portholes in its sides. The deck aft of this, where the lifeboat would have hung, was clear and undamaged. We dropped over the stern guardrail and moving under the sweep of the stern we caught sight of the rudder and propeller, still in situ.

We moved back up and onto the deck and started to move from the stern up the port-side gunwale towards the stern deckhouse. Rotted openings in the port-side deckhouse wall allowed a glimpse inside. On the starboard side, a large range or stove sat amidst scattered crockery lying on the floor, which gleamed white in our torches – the galley. Chest-high in the remnants of a wall-cupboard, I spotted a white mug lying on its side against the aft wall of the deckhouse.

As I started to move further forward up the port side of the deckhouse, quite suddenly and unexpectedly I came across the reason she had sunk. A large V-shaped gash in her hull showed the unmistakeable outline of the bows of a substantial ship that had run straight into her side at nearly a perfect right angle. I swam up to the gap and stretched my arms out to either side – I could barely touch each side. The gash was perhaps 6 feet across at deck level, narrowing to a point near her keel. The torn metal work of the hull had been smoothly curved backwards into her innards at either side of the gash, which was right beside the aft gallows, about 40 feet forward from the very stern. The gash opened directly into the port side of the engine room below the deckhouse. With such a catastrophic wound, water rushing into the engine room would very quickly have put her engine out of action. No wonder her telegraph was at 'Stop'. The volume of water that would have flooded into her here was so huge that I felt sure that this ship had sunk within a few minutes.

With the huge gash in her port side she would have listed quickly to port, causing her coal stacked in the fish hold to shift to the port side. Like most trawler losses she had righted herself as she sank, landing on her keel on the seabed. But there was no deep-sea trawler such as this, other than the *Lowdock*, listed as lost in a collision around these parts. Perhaps, I thought, it's a war loss when, for security reasons, some sinkings were not published

By now our agreed bottom time of 25 minutes had elapsed and it was time to start the long ascent to the surface, to Richard and to safety. In all the excitement of the dive we had forgotten about the rough conditions he would be toughing out, sitting topside. We headed back to the strobe and after switching it off, I unclipped it from the line and clipped it off onto a D-ring on my harness. I untied the downline from the mooring cleat and once we were all ready we started up the rope. As we left the wreck, in the lovely visibility and now with our night vision well adjusted, we could easily see the wreck below us for some 15 metres as we ascended.

One hour later, all our decompression stops were finished and our heads broke the surface to find Richard looking very alone, cold and very exposed, riding large waves but keeping station not far from the buoy. He quickly came in beside us and we started passing up cameras, torches, bail-out tanks and the like, before with a hard kick of our fins we hauled ourselves up on the grab-lines and over the tubes into the RIB.

Soon we were heading for shore skipping over the waves and shouting euphorically to each other as we rehearsed the dive and tried to fill it in for Richard. Our pathetic attempts to drink coffee in these lumpy seas simply had it spilled over us in no time. Back ashore we reviewed Tony's video footage and talked it over with Ian Balgowan, our resident expert on all things to do with fishing boats and the sea. We estimated the vessel to be 40–50 metres in length. There was coal in her fish hold and she lay headed north on the seabed. She had a triple-expansion engine – construction of coal-burning steam trawlers like her stopped in the early 1950s. She was in very good condition, with (unlike the *Lowdock*) her bridge deckhouse still in situ. Because of her condition I started to feel that we were dealing with a ship that had been built in the 1920s to 1940s and by the look of it had been sunk in the 1940s or 1950s. The Mechan's, Glasgow telegraph didn't tell us much as they were so common. I thought there must surely be a record of such a traumatic collision and loss somewhere, but all my searches through official records drew a blank. Ian talked to local fishermen but initially no clues were forthcoming.

An old Hydrographic Office print-out of the area threw up two possible names, but no details. One was listed as *Our Merit LT 291*, lost whilst under tow. After checking the trawler archives I eventually located a photo of *Our Merit* and found that it was a wooden smack with a sail. Definitely not what we had dived.

Then another name jumped out of the Hydrographic Office records – the British steam trawler *Tarvartness*. She is listed as sunk on the same latitude, but about a mile away on a different longitude. Searching as I could, I have been unable to find any further reference so far to a steam trawler of that name. I wondered if it could have been a corruption of *Tarbert Ness* but have not been able to find anything solid on that name either.

Ian Balgowan talked to some of the older fishermen in Gourdon – the nearest fishing port to the location of our unknown steam trawler – and called me to say that one old fisherman remembered that a steam trawler had been rammed whilst minesweeping in 1944 and sunk offshore. He did not know the name of the vessel but recollected that after the trawler had sunk and was sitting on the bottom, the paravane float (an underwater glider, the wings for which force the body away from the tow ship and which suspends the mine-sweeping wire) had remained on the surface and had to be cut free. This was our first big lead – there was no other trawler recorded as sunk by ramming in this area other than the *Lowdock* – and we had already found and tentatively identified her a couple of miles to the south. This wreck was about 4 miles southeast of Todhead.

I trawled through other records for naval losses and then a name jumped out at me – the Strath Class trawler *Mirabelle* GY1336. The *Mirabelle* had been built in 1918 by the Aberdeen ship builders Hall, Russell & Co and was originally called *Edward Barker*. She was 203 gross tons with a length of 115 feet and a beam of 22 feet. She was bought in December 1921 by the Consolidated Steam Fishing & Ice Co and renamed *Mirabelle* in 1922. In September 1927 she was registered to Consolidated Fisheries Ltd and in October 1935 moved to Aberdeen owners Gorspen Steam Trawling Co Ltd and registered as A176. In 1937 she was sold to A.A. Davidson, Aberdeen and in 1944 she entered Admiralty service as an auxiliary patrol vessel and fuel-carrying trawler. She was engaged in minesweeping in the English Channel in the lead up to D-Day. In 1944 she was rammed and sunk 'in home waters'. But that was as much information as I could find on her. The *Mirabelle* was an Aberdeen trawler, but she could have been sunk anywhere – what did 'home waters' mean? Was that home waters for Aberdeen, or simply British home waters? One report suggested that the *Mirabelle* had been sunk in the English Channel so that perhaps put paid to her as an identity.

Alan Jones of Shipwrecks UK heard about our trouble identifying this wreck and after an exhaustive search helpfully came up with another possibility: the *Braconash*; a Strath Class trawler built by Alexander Hall in 1917 as the 223-ton *John Clay*. She was 115 feet long with a beam of almost 23 feet so fitted the bill size-wise. She was charted as sunk on 29 April 1932, following a collision with the Aberdeen trawler *Strathlethen* about 6 miles off Aberdeen in dense fog. The recorded collision site was some way away to the north but the fog could have confused matters. I felt that the wreck however was in perhaps too good condition to be as old as an early 1930s loss.

It was by now October, late in the 2009 season, and we would only manage to return and dive this mystery wreck once more before the weather closed in for the winter. The dive itself on that occasion did not reveal any other clues to the ship's identity. I remember this dive more for what happened once we were safely back and topside in the RIB. In stormy conditions, we set about rigging up our Jim Burke-patented system for quick and easy (well, usually) recovery of anchor, chain and line. We put a one-way rock-climbing ascender on the downline and clip a large Dhan Buoy to it. The line is tied off to a towing eye on the transom of the RIB before the RIB motors ahead. The wash of water pushes the ascender and buoy along the downline until the buoy lifts the anchor off the seabed. Motoring ahead drives the ascender and buoy (on the surface) all the way along the downline until the ascender hits the anchor chain. As it's a one-way ascender, the anchor and chain are then held suspended at the surface by the buoy. The RIB turns and goes back to the buoy, anchor and chain, which then get taken aboard and the 100 metres of rope can then be hauled in.

That is the theory, and it generally works well enough – except that on this occasion, the crewman (who shall not be named) put the ascender on the wrong way round. As we throttled ahead the ascender didn't move and we came to a sudden wallowing halt as the anchor dragged then snagged on the wreck below. The buoy was stuck right at our transom and as soon as I throttled down after realising what had happened, the tension on the rope pulled our RIB backwards driving the transom under water momentarily. We were now at the end of the line – literally. It was held taught and we were driven round downwind with the wind and waves coming at us from astern. The waves started washing over the transom and the boat then started to fill with water. As the line was rigid, and with wind and waves from astern, I couldn't get enough leeway to turn the bow into the waves and motor forward to gain some slack. We were getting well and truly pooped. I tried motoring astern a wee bit to try and free up some line to allow me to turn the bow, but that just resulted in even more water coming over the stern.

"Rod – we're sinking. The rebreathers are starting to float." Paul shouted to me. There was a lot of money in rebreathers sitting in the back of my boat – probably about £40,000 worth. I couldn't risk losing that or indeed endangering everyone by sinking the boat. We took the buoy and ascender off, cut the line and let the anchor, chain and 100 metres of line go. It disappeared instantly. If you ever dive this wreck and find anchor, chain and 100 metres of green sea-steel rope, you'll know its mine.

As the 2010 season started we began diving our local wrecks once again. One by one the wrecks of these fantastic ships drifted before our eyes: *Taurus*; *Baku Standard*; *Gowrie*; *Fernside*; *Cushendall*; *Greenawn*; *Matador*; and *Queensbury*. In between, we made our annual pilgrimages to the great centres of Scottish wreck diving at Scapa Flow and the Sound of Mull. But at the back of my mind niggled the fact that we had not been able to identify our mystery steam trawler. I tried every research avenue I knew but there was just no record of a second steam trawler being rammed and sunk in this area. I determined to have a good go at finding the bell – as that would have the ship's name on it.

A chance to dive the wreck came about midsummer and I set up a dive on it with a new diver to our group, Greg Booth. I had met Greg a couple of years earlier when he was a club scuba diver on a BSAC trip to Ullapool where, whilst trying to assist him back into the dive boat, I had managed to drop his fin into the sea and it promptly had sunk. Greg had not taken the mick too much and had been very gracious about it all, but I was delighted when he told me that another diver had found the fin a few months later. Greg had moved on to qualify for open-circuit Trimix diving and we had invited him along on a few Stonehaven Snorkellers dives. He had proved to be an immensely capable diver who picked up first time everything he was shown. He fitted in easily and I had grown to trust him.

I reckoned that the bell would have been fixed to the front of the wheelhouse and that if it hadn't been snagged and trawled off the wreck, its mounts would simply have rotted away, allowing it to drop down into the space between the trawl winch and the deckhouse. If there was a maker's plate it was likely that it was screwed to the front of the lower section of the deckhouse and may have ended up in the same place.

On an overcast May morning, despite strong Spring tides, Greg and I, with Simon Chalmers boat-handling, went out to dive the 'Mystery Trawler' – or *Mirabelle* as we were now calling it, for want of any other name.

After shotting the wreck in a fairly big sea, Greg and I left Simon alone topside and plunged down through the darkness – only to be met with a flat sandy seabed at 56 metres. The shot had been lifted off the wreck by the current. There was a noticeable scoured trench where the current had dragged the shot and chain with it, so I attached a reel to the downline, kicked my fins and headed off along the scour. Very quickly I saw the sweep of the trawler's stern appear out of the gloom ahead of me. We rose up onto the weather deck and I tied off the reel to a cleat so we knew we could get back to the downline to ascend.

I took Greg up the port side – pointing out the mug still in situ in the stern deckhouse – and then took him round the front of the wheelhouse to show him the telegraph. That done, I then spent the rest of the dive looking for the bell or maker's plate – all without success. The deck between the winch and bridge deckhouse had rotted away leaving a dark hole – into which I suspected the bell and maker's plate had fallen aeons before. A good dive, yes; but no identifying artefact to show for it.

Greg and I returned again for a final attempt on finding something to identify the wreck two weeks later and this time I went down into the fish hold and swam aft underneath the trawl winch to directly below the small gap between the winch and the wheelhouse. Sheets of rotted metal plating had fallen off the wheelhouse into this gap and it had been filled in to a depth of several feet with silt. If the bell or maker's plate is indeed down there, it won't be found until the whole wreck has rusted away and the silt has been cleared by the current – then some lucky diver in the right place at the right time will find the bell sitting free on the seabed. But for me, the mystery would not be solved, and having devoted so much time to this one small wreck I moved on with the season's diving and did not return. I posted the story of our attempts on my Random House Blog under the heading 'Mystery wreck remains a mystery'. This wreck's identity would be left for the next generation of divers to reveal.

And that, I thought, was the end of our attempts to identify the 'Mystery Trawler'. But life never works out that simply – particularly in the underwater domain. I had been asked to open the Scottish Sub Aqua Club Annual Scottish Dive Conference in Eyemouth on 13 November 2010. I was to give an hour-long talk about diving – so naturally it would be about shipwrecks. The year before, for the 2009 SSAC Annual Conference, I had given a Power Point stills presentation about shipwrecks in Scapa Flow, Norway, England and the South China Seas. This year I thought I would do something different and show some video footage of three of our local wrecks. I determined to show footage of the *Lowdock*, as well as of another wreck we had discovered – the SS *Greenawn* – and also our mystery trawler that we were calling the *Mirabelle*.

As I started preparing for the conference I got the footage Tony Ray had shot of the *Lowdock* set up first and aimed to show the footage where I measure the cylinder tops and the beam of the ship before moving on to the collision damage at the stern. Once I had set that footage into Windows Movie Maker I added the spellbinding footage Paul Haynes shot on our first dive on SS *Greenawn*. I thought that I would then close with the footage of the 'Mystery Trawler' showing the telegraph and helm – very photogenic and guaranteed to make the audience's eyes light up. The footage of the Galley and the poignant collision damage on the port side 40 feet or so forward from the stern would round off the human-interest side of the story. I also determined to open my presentation by reading over the precognition of the *Lowdock*'s mate, Thurston Atkinson, as it was a first hand account of what happened from the only survivor. Sometimes when divers dive a wreck they just see the rusted steel and perhaps don't know or appreciate the story behind what they are diving.

As I re-read the mate's precognition in preparation (for the first time in a few years) the conflict of his evidence with what we had found down on the wreck started to trouble me again. He was absolutely clear in what he said – the *Lady Philomena* had rammed the *Lowdock* beside the port after gallows, which were at the side of the stern deckhouse. He had told how the bows of the *Lady Philomena* had sliced into his berth. Could I – indeed should I – mention this?

Trying to add some flesh to the bones as to how the collision actually came about, I dug out my copy of the decision in the Admiralty Division court case 'The *LOWDOCK* v EDWARDS (THE *LADY PHILOMENA*)' that I had obtained many years before and which had been languishing in my file on the *Lowdock* (I keep a separate file on each of the ships I research). The owners of the *Lowdock* together with relatives of her master and crew had raised a damages action against Lieutenant David Malcolm Edwards, R.N.R. – the sub-lieutenant in command of the *Lady Philomena* – blaming him for the collision, which they alleged came about as a result of his negligent navigation. Edwards denied the allegation and contended that the *Lowdock* was solely to blame.

I sat down and started reading the case in detail. I had spent 15 years doing court work in my early days as a lawyer, so it tweaked my professional curiosity to immerse myself in the case. A single judge (Mr Justice Hodson) had presided, sitting with two expert seamen – Captain W.E. Crumplin and Captain R.L.F. Hubbard. The court would be required to determine who was to blame for the collision. In his judgment given on 19 June 1941, Mr Justice Hodson found that the *Lady Philomena* was the larger of the two ships – some 417 tons gross and 155 feet long. The *Lowdock* was 275 tons gross and 125ft length. The collision had taken place just after 11.00 p.m. in darkness off Todhead in the North Sea. He determined that the *Lowdock* had been travelling in a roughly northeast direction on a bearing of N.33.E true and was showing her sidelights and a fixed stern light. The *Lady Philomena* had been travelling roughly southwest on a bearing of S.24W true. Therefore he concluded that there was a difference in their courses of about nine degrees and that the two ships were not on a collision course bow to bow. She was showing a regulation masthead light (which was dimmed due to war time restrictions) as well as her sidelights and a fixed stern light. Both vessels were travelling at about 9 knots, so their closing speed was approximately 18 knots. The wind was northwesterly Force 6–7. In these circumstances, where the ships were steaming towards each other almost (but not quite) bow to bow, what had happened to cause the bow of the *Lady Philomena* to end up striking the port side of the *Lowdock* near her stern?

The *Lowdock*'s case was hampered by the fact that all of her crew had perished save for the mate Thurston Atkinson – who knew little of what happened as he was in his bunk. The *Lowdock*'s owners thus relied on interrogatories of the *Lady Philomena*'s crew made earlier at preliminary hearings. Interrogatories are answers given by witnesses to a series of formal questions (agreed by both sides in advance). Potential witnesses for an opponent may be hostile, uncooperative and unwilling to tell the other side in advance what their evidence would be. Accordingly, in the interests of fairness and getting at the truth, witnesses can be examined under oath in advance of a final hearing to see what their evidence would be. It would hardly be fair for a litigant, such as the *Lowdock*, not to be able to find out what the evidence of the *Lady Philomena*'s crew would be and thus be prevented from seeking redress through the courts. The crew's sworn interrogatory evidence thus formed the basis of the *Lowdock*'s case – they'd have been in trouble otherwise, as they had no first-hand witnesses of their own other than the mate.

The *Lowdock*'s case was that both ships were closing each other bow to bow on a collision course and that under the Regulations for Preventing Collisions at Sea (which still apply to this day albeit in an amended form), she was right in altering course to starboard in order to pass the *Lady Philomena* port to port – and that the *Lady Philomena*'s duty was to do the same – i.e., to move to starboard and pass port to port.

The *Lady Philomena* alleged a different position. Her case was that the two vessels approached one another in a position of safety, green to green – that is, starboard to starboard – and that the collision occurred because of the *Lowdock*'s attempt to cross ahead of the *Lady Philomena*.

After hearing all the facts Justice Hodson determined that Article 18 of the Prevention of Collisions at Sea Regulations (which deals with vessels approaching bow to bow on a collision course) did not have any application in this case. He held that the two ships were never on a collision course bow to bow – and before the *Lowdock* altered her position the two ships were in a position of safety, green to green. However, he also found that the *Lady Philomena* had contributed to the collision by the action that she took when she had seen the *Lowdock*'s red sidelight appear as it made its turn to starboard across her path. The danger had become apparent at that time, but rather than turn to starboard, the *Lady Philomena* went hard-a-port to try and turn into a parallel course to the *Lowdock*. The bow of the *Lady Philomena* was slow to come round and the commanding officer ordered her engines to "stop" followed by "slow astern" followed by "full astern" in quick succession. She had been going astern for 1½ minutes before the collision occurred and was almost stopped as she hit *Lowdock*. Indeed immediately after the collision she was observed by the *Lowdock*'s mate to be backing away. She had obviously lost almost all of her forward momentum. Justice Hodson commented in is judgement: 'Having regard to all the circumstances of the case, I find both ships guilty of negligence; that the responsibility for the collision must be primarily attributed to the *Lowdock*, and that she was three quarters to blame and the *Lady Philomena* a quarter to blame, so that the degree of liability must be apportioned accordingly.'

But it was the Justice's comment about the actual collision itself that jumped out at me: 'In these circumstances the vessels came into collision at right angles, the stem of *the Lady Philomena* coming into contact with the port side of the *Lowdock* about abreast the after gallows, that is to say about 40 feet from her stern.' There it was staring at me in the face. I had made the mistake of accepting as gospel a couple of brief second-hand historical reports that the *Lowdock* was rammed in the stern and not gone back and checked primary sources. I had tried to make our steam trawler six miles southeast of Todhead fit the bill – after all, it had all the same dimensions as the *Lowdock* and had been rammed in the stern. I had forced a round peg into a square hole and failed to give enough weight to the mate's evidence, which clearly conflicted with the damage we saw down on the wreck. Here was proof that the steam trawler rammed in the stern – that we had called *Lowdock* for several years – was not in fact the *Lowdock*. What vessel it was I still don't know. But the real *Lowdock* had now been revealed and the damage visible down on the wreck tied in exactly with the mate's evidence. The large V-shaped gash was exactly where he said it would be – beside the port after gallows 40 feet forward from the stern. The 'V' gash went straight into the port side of the stern deckhouse where he had had his berth – and indeed where the old crewman (who had come in to see me in my office after the STV News feature) had confirmed he had his bunk. The V gash was so large and deep that this ship would have gone down very quickly – as the *Lowdock*'s mate had said. The ramming damage on the other wreck we had called *Lowdock* was relatively slight and she would have taken some considerable time to sink. In his precognition, the mate had said that the *Lowdock* was running with her sidelights only and had not lit her all round masthead light. We had seen the masthead lamps still snug in the fo'c'stle lamp room. The 'Mystery Wreck' was headed bows to the north – as had been the direction of the *Lowdock*'s voyage. It all fitted. What's more, poignantly, the white mug that had gleamed in our dive lights sitting waist high on a shelf in the remnants of a port wall locker would have been the mate's mug.

The *Lowdock* had given up her secret at last – at the third attempt we now had identified it. As for the two previous vessels we had called *Lowdock*, *mea culpa* I still don't know the correct identity of those ships.

CHAPTER TWENTY-ONE

THE SILENT TRAGEDY OF THE SS *GREENAWN*

In October 2006, just a month after our epic two dives on the second wreck we had mistakenly identified as the *Lowdock,* we decided to have a look at another GPS position we had for an uncharted obstruction. We had by now dived most of the obstructions in the Inverbervie hot spot and if there was a U-boat in the vicinity we should be finding it soon. Would this be it?

We chose a weekend with weak neap tides and launched *Stonehaven Diver* with myself, Tony Ray and Paul Haynes diving and Dave Hadden boat handling. The *Buchan Diver* RIB from Peterhead was driven down and launched at Stonehaven with Jim Burke and Mike Rosie diving from it. In good calm conditions both fast RIBs powered the 10 miles down the coast and 5 miles out from the land in less than half an hour.

Very soon after arriving at the GPS position we had a wreck trace on our sounders – but we could immediately tell that it was too big a trace to be a delicate U-boat. This was the trace of a big steamship with a substantial hull rising 5 metres or more from the seabed with a decent beam.

Kitted up, Tony, Paul and I rolled over the side of *Stonehaven Diver* and started the descent. As ever at the end of the year, the underwater visibility looked startlingly good and I could see the downline disappearing off at least 15 metres beneath me into the darkness. I strained my eyes below as I gently sank down beside the shot-line, my first finger and thumb clasped loosely around the line. As I fell into the depths I eagerly awaited a first sight of our new wreck – what sort of vessel would it be? There were no other vessels this big listed as lost around these parts.

Disappointingly, as we neared the seabed, nothing materialised out of the gloom – we just kept going down and down until the seabed appeared at 62 metres with our anchor and chain lying on clean white sand. Bugger, I thought – the shot must have bounced or dragged off the wreck. At 62 metres this was no place for a circular search of the seabed.

I was first down the line and as I braked my fall and landed feet-first on the seabed I stood there, more than 200 feet beneath the surface looking up the line to where I could see the dim silhouettes of my companions, their powerful torch beams sweeping around. I turned around and swept my own torch about me. Suddenly a large rusty red steel rudder appeared in its beam less than 15 feet away. I was so close that when I traced my torch up the rudder and followed the curve of the hull I found that the stern was actually overhanging me. It was surprising that I hadn't seen it on the way down, but it was just a result of the darkness combined with the angle the gentle current had caused the downline to come into the wreck at. We had been right beside the wreck as we made our descent – but it had been tantalisingly just outside the range of our vision.

I kicked upwards off the seabed and swam up the side of the overhanging hull, holding the downline until I crested over the gunwale and landed on the main deck of a sleek steamship. We were at the very stern and of course here on the gunwale, very conveniently, were situated robust mooring cleats. I pulled some slack on the downline and cleated it off with a couple of locking turns onto the nearest mooring cleat I could find. I clipped my large powerful strobe to the line just above the wreck and set it flashing.

Tony and Paul arrived beside me on the main deck, both armed with underwater video cameras. Now that our night vision was kicking in I could see a large section of the wreck around me. The water was slack and crystal clear – perfect for the cameras. We started filming and set off on our exploration of this virgin wreck. What mysteries would it hold – what was this vessel?

At the very stern, just in front of the auxiliary steering gear was a large single-storey deckhouse, which stretched from almost from one side of the ship to the other. Its steel walls had rotted away in places, allowing a glimpse inside. I swam forward along the starboard side of this deckhouse at main deck level passing portholes with their glass still in them. Soon I came to an open doorway with a curved top (the door itself had long ago rotted from its hinges and fallen inside). Looking in here I could see right through the deckhouse to a mirror-image doorway leading out on the port side, some 30 feet away on the other side of the ship. On the floor, white crockery and glassware gleamed in the harsh beams of our underwater torches. The main central ceiling oil lamp lay fallen to one side of the deckhouse, welded to some pipework by encrustation but still with its delicate curved glass intact inside its protective cage.

We swam further forward along the starboard walkway outside the deckhouse and came across a second side door. Looking in here I could see catwalks leading off down to and around a large triple-expansion engine set low down, fore and aft on the centre line of the vessel. I kicked my fins and moved up on top of the deckhouse to see what was up there. The funnel itself was missing – no doubt rotted away or trawled off aeons ago, leaving now only a circular black hole some 15 feet across leading down to the boiler room. Some forced draft mushroom type ventilators had also been broken off leaving only the stumps beside the circular funnel hole. A small, pitched engine room roof still had its skylights and glass in place. I turned and gently dropped back down from the engine room roof to the starboard main deck, and a bit further forward came across the remains of the inner pipe of the funnel itself lying fore and aft along the side walkway.

As I reached the front of this large stern deckhouse I noticed that where the rest of the deckhouse was pretty much intact, here all the steel plating was completely gone, leaving only the structural beams and girders, some of which were twisted and torn. There seemed to have been some significant blast damage here to remove the plating and twist big steel beams so comprehensively.

Pushing on with our exploration we moved forward from the aft deckhouse and came to an open hold jam packed with bags of cement now set rock-hard. On the starboard side the otherwise neatly stacked bags were confused and jumbled. The large supporting 6–8 inch steel H-beams for the hatch cover (which originally ran across the hold) were bent, broken and scattered about amongst the bags of cement. Some bags of cement lay on top of the broken beams.

Only a few minutes had passed and yet already we were piecing together how this ship met its end. Here was direct evidence of something catastrophic – something strong enough to have stripped away the front of a deckhouse, thrown cement bags around effortlessly, blown the hatch cover off and caused such significant damage to its heavy-duty steel beams.

Moving through the mixed up bags of cement our team of three divers moved to the starboard side of the hull – and here was a rather neat blast hole. This was a high velocity projectile impact – an attack that had fatally wounded the ship by blowing a gaping hole 25 feet across in her hull, down under her water line almost to her double bottom. Her fate was sealed with this one strike and she would have gone down quickly.

Paul, with his military background was our very own expert in high-velocity projectile impacts and later would explain how the bomb had penetrated through the hull and exploded in the cargo of cement itself. The explosion had gone off inside the hold, blowing part of the section of hull outwards. The cement bags had deflected the main blast upwards and backwards blowing off the hatch cover and mangling the steel support beams. The deflected blast had removed the front of the large stern deckhouse that held the boiler room, engine room and the saloon. The ship's wooden lifeboats would normally be held in davits on top of this deckhouse, on the boat deck, and may well have been destroyed by the blast. This wreck was already looking like the site of an untold human tragedy.

Finning forward the length of the hold, we came to a slender midships bridge superstructure with steel steps leading up to it from astern on either side. A large modern trawl door and trawl cable were snagged on top of the bridge and trawl nets hung down into the first level of the bridge deckhouse, swaying slowly in the gentle underwater breeze. The top-deck level of the bridge – which most likely had been wooden – appeared to have rotted away or perhaps been dragged off by trawl nets and cables. We spotted the base mount for the ship's telegraph still bolted to what would have been the floor of the wheelhouse. Looking down into the rooms below I saw the telegraph head itself lying there in amongst a confused jumble of cables, spars, gauges and green brass bridge fitments.

Conscious of time ticking away and wanting to get round the whole wreck, we left the bridge and finned forward. Soon we had come across a second large hold, which still had its hatch cover cross beams in place. This hold was intact and undamaged and its hatch cover had still been on when it sunk. The hatch cover itself had long ago rotted away allowing easy access down into the cavernous hold. Dropping down into the hold between the cross beams we were confronted with a hold neatly stacked high with more rock-hard bags of cement. In amongst the bags of cement we came across the bridge helm with its brass rudder direction indicator seemingly welded on top of the cement bags and half buried in silt. It had either fallen or been trawled from its mount up beside the telegraph on the second bridge deck level and ended up here in the forward hold.

Leaving this hold we rose up to continue forward with our exploration. We approached the foc'stle, an elevated single-storey deckhouse with two aft facing doorways, black and ominous. Steel fixed stairways led up either side to its top, where anchor winches were situated. Looking into the starboard doorway, off a passage I could see into the lamp room where a number of large copper and brass navigation lamps were still neatly stacked but half buried in silt.

Standing just in front of the aft-facing deckhouse wall, I looked up and saw a large black mass overhanging us. It took a while for me to register what the ominous presence above us was – but it soon dawned on me that this was a large trawl net, still suspended on its buoys, towering some 10–15 metres above us and swaying slowly in the gentle current. I wouldn't like to have started a free ascent at the end of a dive here in poor visibility and get caught up under those nets. It might be hard to get disentangled and find a way out from them to the surface.

I swam out over the port gunwale of the wreck into free water and Paul videoed as we swam around the very bow itself, which was undamaged. Trawl cables for the nets swept down under some considerable tension to where they had snagged on the bow. The net itself, complete with cod end, was wrapped round the whole bow of the ship – a solid curtain of nets obscuring the bow and rising up for 15 metres. Some unfortunate large trawler must have come to a jarring halt long ago when she dragged her nets into this unmarked wreck with such force.

Passing round the bow, and conscious that it was time to be getting back to the downline for the ascent, we finned in a straight line back down the starboard side of the hull, heading for the line and our strobe which was flashing brightly at the other end of the ship. On our way we passed the forward hold, the midship's bridge superstructure and then the aft hold with the large bite out of its side. Within a couple of minutes we had arrived back at the stern deckhouse where we could eke out the last few minutes of our bottom time exploring. I spotted the 'T' shaped auxiliary steering column which had been pulled off with some force and dragged through the back of the stern deckhouse. It was now lying inside what we took to be the ship's lounge or saloon, amidst crockery and bottles strewn everywhere. Other than the single bomb hole, the ship was so intact that it looked as though it could quite easily float today.

We had now had a bottom time on the wreck of 25 minutes and it was time to unfasten the downline from the ship's mooring cleat and start our ascent to the surface 200 feet above. The ascent would take a full hour – but an hour that raced past as we busied ourselves with our slow incremental ascent steps. We took the time to reflect on what had been a monumental virgin wreck dive. There was so much to assess and discuss. Which ship was she – and why was she here?

Once back ashore I went straight back to the reference books to see if I could find any reference to a steamship of this size lying off our coast. I was aware of the names and histories of all the documented large vessels lost in this vicinity and had stalked and dived them by now – but the charts and books didn't reveal that there was any vessel of this size and style reported as sunk here. I estimated that the vessel was about 185 feet long with a beam of some 30 feet. I put her tonnage at about 800 tons (very approximately).

Tony managed to date a maker's mark on a crockery plate seen in the aft deckhouse lounge. The piece had been made in Bristol between 1932 and 1947. That dating allied with the obvious bomb damage to her made her a likely World War II casualty, and probably from the early part of the war when, from their Norwegian bases, German bombers wreaked havoc on shipping routes up and down Scotland. But the main clue must be her two holds filled with a cargo of cement.

I started doing a few Google searches for war losses with a cargo of cement and very quickly one name jumped out of a marine website: SS *Greenawn*. The *Greenawn* was listed as having left London on 25 March 1941, bound for Invergordon in the Cromarty Firth of northern Scotland with a cargo of cement. She had last been seen heading north past Montrose on 3 April 1941 and was never seen or heard of after that. She could be anywhere between Montrose and Invergordon. On 28 May 1941 the Joint Arbitration Committee had declared the ship a War Loss of 3 April 1941.

It became clear from the records that there had been no trace of her whatsoever after she was spotted off Montrose. She had gone down with all hands and without any distress call. There had been no survivors and no wreckage or debris from her passing was ever found. It was as if she had been spirited away without trace. How could such a large ship filled with fuel, cargo and human beings disappear so suddenly and without any trace?

The Missing Ship Committee determined that she had been lost at sea on 3 April; assuming that she had been bombed that day because German aircraft had attacked a local fishing boat from the nearby port of Johnshaven in that area. She was stamped as 'missing' in Lloyd's 1941 Register Book, and had remained missing until we stumbled upon her 65 years later.

I ordered a full Ship History Search from Lloyd's and soon had her details. She was a single-screw steamship of 778 gross tons built by A. Hall & Co Ltd in Aberdeen in 1924 – very close to my home. She had a length of 190.7 feet, a breadth of 29.1 feet and a draught of 11.9 feet. All this tied in very closely with our rough figures. The *Greenawn* was powered by a triple-expansion engine – the cylinder tops of being 16", 26½" and 44" and the stroke 30". Her engine developed 180 lb horsepower. She was registered in Goole and owned by E. Johnson & Co. Ltd of Goole.

To my shame, I had (until this point in my life) never heard of Goole or its rich maritime history. But as soon as I started to delve in, a flood of information started to come my way and very soon I had been sent from Goole a black & white photo of the *Greenawn* in her heyday – and this was exactly the ship we had dived and surveyed. The *Greenawn* had been found.

I located her crew list and found that a number of her crew were local to the northeast of Scotland. Her crew were:

1. VICTOR ABRAHAM ABEYSINGHE. Steward, age 42. Son of Don William Abeysinghe and Kachchohamy Ramasinghe, of Colombo, Ceylon.
2. HASSAN AHMED. Donkeyman, age 46. Husband of A. Ahmed of South Shields.
3. OLIVER JAMES EDWARDS. Mate, age 37. Son of Mr & Mrs D. Edwards of Newport, Pembrokeshire and husband of Edith Mary Edwards from Fishguard, Pembrokeshire.
4. HASSAN ALI. Fireman, age 40.
5. ROBERT INNES. Ship's Master, age 32. Son of William & Isabella Innes and husband of Meta Innes, Buckie.
6. WILLIAM INNES. Able Seaman, age 22. Son of Willie & Helen Innes.

SS Greenawn, *missing since 1941 and discovered by the Stonehaven Snorkellers off Inverbervie in 2006.*

7. JOHN JONES. Second Engineer Officer, age 67.
8. ALAN MARSHALL, Ordinary Seaman, age 17.
9. JAMES McAULAY, Boatswain, age 21. Son of James & Ann McAulay, Peterhead.
10. SALEH SAID, Fireman, age 50.
11. THOMAS SAMUEL. Able Seaman, age 21.
12. JOHN WILLIAM SLATER, Chief Engineer Officer, age 30. Son of William & Mabel Slater, husband of Edith Ellen Slater of Hull.

The *Greenawn* had a crew of 12 plus two DEMS gunners (Defensively Equipped Merchant Ship) when she set off on her fateful final voyage from London in March 1941. We had noted that the wreck was now lying on the seabed with her bows pointing south – as opposed to the northern route of her final voyage. When we plotted her course, her bows were pointing directly towards Montrose – the nearest large port that she had passed earlier on her final day afloat. It therefore appeared that after she was hit, she had had time to turn around and start trying to run for safety towards Montrose in a desperate race before the onrushing seas overcame her. It was a race that she lost. But why was there absolutely no trace of her after her sinking? There appeared not to have been any wreckage found: no oil slick, no distress call, no lifeboats recovered and no survivors. She had completely disappeared in an instant.

There is no doubt that most of the crew of 12 and the two gunners would have survived the fairly localised explosion in the cement bags of the aft hold. The foc'stle, the forward section, the midship's bridge and the majority of the stern deckhouse were all completely untouched by the blast. The young master, if on the midship's bridge, would have seen the blast well behind him in the aft hold. He would have seen the catastrophic damage to the starboard side of his ship, the rear deckhouse and the lifeboats above. The ship would have started to list to starboard very quickly and it would have been clear that she was rapidly sinking. He had wheeled the ship around to run for the land – perhaps he had hoped to get into shallow enough water to beach her.

We were starting to piece together a possible terrifying last few minutes for the crew. If the radio gear had been situated in the rear deckhouse and been destroyed in the blast then they couldn't communicate their distress. With such damage to the ship, she would have sunk fast beneath them. Had the lifeboats on the boat deck above the stern deckhouse been destroyed by the blast? If so, the crew may have known they were going into the water and that no one knew their plight. Perhaps they knew there would be no rescue. The North Sea in March is bitterly cold, an unforgiving 6 degrees Celsius. The crew would have lasted perhaps 30–50 minutes in the water before the cold overcame them.

It was possible however that one or more of the lifeboats or rafts did survive and that some of the crew had perhaps been able to board them. Although the wreck was some 5 miles offshore, that distance could be rowed if conditions were right. If the crew had abandoned ship into rafts and if there had been an offshore wind or gale that day, the rafts would have been blown further out to sea, away from safety, perhaps never to be seen again. I tried without success to delve back in time to see if I could find out what the North Sea weather was that day. I suspect that if that were the case, with the large number of ships travelling up and down the coast in the convoy route, they would have been spotted. We will never know the true story of the fate of the crew – but the last resting place of the *Greenawn* itself has now been found.

CHAPTER TWENTY-TWO

THE LOSS OF THE SS *CREEMUIR*

The 3992-ton British steamship SS *Creemuir* was attacked by German aircraft and torpedoed and sunk 14 miles northeast of Stonehaven on Armistice Day, 11 November 1940. She was a sizeable vessel, some 360 feet in length with a beam of 51 feet and had been leading the port column of convoy EN23. Made up of 31 merchant vessels, the convoy had left Methil in Fife northbound early that day at 5.00 a.m.

Convoy EN23 was scheduled to run up the east coast of Scotland, pass through the Pentland Firth (the channel between the north of mainland Scotland and the Orkney Islands) and then pass down the west coast to Oban. Here, in the deep-water convoy gathering point known as the Oban Roads, she would form up again in convoy for an Atlantic crossing in ballast to Yarmouth, Nova Scotia where the *Creemuir* was scheduled to pick up a cargo of pit props.

By the afternoon of Armistice Day, the *Creemuir* was leading her port column north just inside the Swept Channel some 10 miles offshore. The day was overcast and chilly and a beam wind blew steadily causing a moderate swell. At 3.00 p.m. the convoy was attacked by a German aircraft, whose bombs failed to score a direct hit but which exploded in the water

The SS Creemuir *off Johannesburg.*

close enough to one ship to stove in some plating and allow water in. That ship was forced to break off from the convoy and head to port for repairs. At 5.00 p.m., having just passed Stonehaven on her port beam, *Creemuir* was moving further north towards Aberdeen when the convoy was attacked again. This time it was a German seaplane, which came in beam-on and loosed an aerial torpedo when it was just 150 yards from the *Creemuir*. There was no time for *Creemuir* to manoeuvre out of the way and comb the track of the torpedo. It struck *Creemuir* in the engine room causing such catastrophic damage that the large ship sank in just 2–3 minutes. Sadly, there were only 13 survivors out of a crew of 42.

I had been aware of the name of the *Creemuir* and its charted location 14 miles northeast of Stonehaven for many years. In my early days when I got the Hydrographic Office wreck print-out and plotted all the wrecks, it lay too far offshore and was too deep to attempt. We considered it too far out for RIBs and for such a challenging technical dive. If anything went wrong we were a long way from safety and medical assistance. The North Sea can be very exposed and dangerous – I'd always felt that the *Creemuir* was more of an expedition, hard boat dive.

In April 2009 however I must have been taking brave pills and chomping at the bit to get the season going, for I set up a trip to check the site over. We would see if we could find the wreck, check out depths and gather all the other essential information we would need for an attempt to dive it. I wouldn't go out that far in just one boat so our lifeboat cox and good friend Andrew Buchanan agreed that he would come out too in his well-equipped sea angling boat, a Warrior 175.

On an overcast Saturday afternoon our two boats bumped and bashed the 14 miles out to the wreck site and sure enough we were soon picking up the unmistakeable trace of a large wreck on the echo sounders. Each of our boats ran along the top of the wreck to either extremity and we found that this wreck was indeed about 350 feet long and lay on the bottom in a broadly south/north direction. She lay in 70 metres of water about half a mile to the west (or inside) of the Dog Hole – the underwater canyon that runs NE/SW for about 20 miles. The Dog Hole is around one mile wide with almost sheer sides that drop down from an average seabed of 70 metres to depths of 125 metres or more. If she had sunk in there we would never have been able to visit her.

Having checked out her depth and orientation, we were all fired up to have a go diving her, so we agreed that if the weather was kind we would dive her the following weekend when weak neap tides were expected. Jim Burke would take his RIB *Buchan Diver* down from Peterhead, with a crew of divers. So again we would have two RIBs to give safety cover for each other.

Saturday came and with our two RIBs heavily laden and packed full of two teams of three divers, two boat handlers and all our technical dive equipment we made the 14-mile journey out to the site once again. Shotting such a big wreck was easy enough but for safety we decided to put two shots in – one from either RIB.

Each team of three divers rolled off the RIB tubes and splashed into the water, one by one. I was diving with Paul Haynes and Tony Ray – Jim was diving with Mike Rosie and Mike Wilcox from *Buchan Diver*. As soon as I was in the water and heading down the line I knew we had a deep, black and scary virgin wreck dive on our hands. It was early in the season and the water was black with run off and crud. Very quickly I was enveloped in an inky darkness.

As our group of three divers pressed on down the line, at about 30 metres I felt a tap on the back of my shoulder. I stopped my descent and turned round to see Paul's face close – he had his computer handset for his rebreather in his hand. He gave me a signal that his computer electrics – vital to keep him alive – had just crashed. In front of me, he slowly and carefully bailed out off his rebreather and stuck the breathing regulator into his mouth for his Trimix bail-out cylinder (slung under his arm for just this sort of scenario). Once that was done and the danger was over he signalled to me that he was fine but was breaking off the dive and would ascend. He indicated that Tony and I should continue the dive.

I watched him move up the line towards the surface for a moment and then after an exchange of 'OK' signals with Tony we agreed to press on down. We got to 50 metres and then continued on down to 60, and then 65 metres. As I did so, I got two red lights flashing in the 'Heads Up Display' (HUD) of my rebreather. This is a small piece of clever technology that is linked to the main electronic brain in the rebreather – it is your primary safety check and is independent from the information shown on your computer handset. The small unit clips onto the top of your mouthpiece so that it is just outside your normal vision – but still in your peripheral vision – at the bottom left of your mask. There are four little fibre optic lights set in the black plastic HUD unit. When diving you should have two green lights only – that means all is good. If you get two flashing red lights, it's a warning and time to check your main handset, which will tell you what the problem is. Fixed red lights means there's trouble. I pulled up my handset and saw that with the rapid descent down to depth I'd just had an oxygen spike where my PPO2 level had momentarily gone over the safe level – not that uncommon on deep rebreather diving. The red flashing lights soon stopped and went back to fixed green. I was good to continue down.

At about 68 metres, mangled spars and wreckage flared into my torch beam as I landed on what would have been the weather deck of a big ship sitting upright on her keel – but it was a scene of chaos with not much recognisable immediately. I clipped my big strobe to the downline, set it flashing, and moved over to the gunwale of the wreck to try and get myself orientated. The visibility was not good – probably 3–5 metres in our torches. The overriding impression was of blackness and devastation. It was also a chilly 6 degrees – I could already feel the water sucking the heat of my body out through my dry suit and I still had more than an hour due inwater.

As I reached the port gunwale it appeared that I was just aft of the midships bridge superstructure. I couldn't see the *Buchan Diver* strobe but guessed that as they had shotted the wreck about 100 feet north of us that they would be in and around the bridge itself. I shone my torch over the side of the wreck and could see the seabed about 5 metres beneath me. The *Creemuir* afloat was a big ship – her draught alone was almost 25 feet so with only 5 metres from the deck to the seabed it looked like the stern area here had collapsed down.

After about 5 minutes exploring the wreck around the aft holds I saw a dimly flashing torch beam moving slowly towards me. In the darkness I couldn't tell who it was until the diver was just a few feet away. It turned out to be Mike Wilcox who had become separated from his companion divers and got a bit lost in the darkness. He told me afterwards that he had unknowingly swum into the fo'c'stle anchor locker at the bow. He hadn't known that he had actually swum inside the deckhouse at first because the visibility was so bad. He had tried to return to the *Buchan Diver* downline to ascend but had missed it in the darkness, overshot and ended up seeing my strobe or torch in the distance. Far safer to ascend up a line where you'll meet other team divers on decompression stops than risk a free drifting solo ascent 14 miles offshore.

By now our allotted bottom time was up and it was time to ascend. For just 20 minutes on the bottom I had a total dive time of about 70 minutes inwater. As Mike had had a bottom time of more than 25 minutes, his inwater run time was some 90 minutes.

On the surface once all the divers were out of the water we tied our two boats together, chatted about the dive as we drifted, cracked open a thermos of hot coffee and scoffed some sandwiches. The *Buchan Diver* shot-line had landed right beside the bridge and Jim and Mike Rosie were able to have a good swim around the midships deckhouse. It was nearly completely intact although the walls and roof had rotted away to expose the structural beams. We had all been dwarfed by the size of the ship, which was largely in fine condition. We agreed to have a go at diving her again – but in better visibility when we would try to video her. And that was that – or so I thought.

My publishers Random House had been developing their own website and had given each of their authors an individual section – mine was at www.authorsplace.co.uk/rod-macdonald. Random House populated the site with the basic book details and blurb and each author was then able to go and tweak their section and pad it out. An online blog for the author was provided, which also allowed members of the public to post online comments. As the 2009 diving season came to a close for the winter I worked on the Random House site and made an initial blog posting about our northeast wreck projects for 2010. I mentioned the SS *Creemuir* in passing as one wreck we planned to re-visit and thought nothing more of it.

In early March 2010, I checked the site and was staggered to see a comment from one Noel Blacklock, who posted that he had been the radio officer on *Creemuir* when she was sunk and believed that he was the only member of the crew still to be alive. I managed to get Noel's email address from Random House and fired off an email to him. Noel was soon in touch and kindly provided me with his first-hand account written at the time. He has kindly allowed me to reproduce it here verbatim, as from his first-hand experience, he can describe far better than I what happened. This is Noel's account:

ARMISTICE DAY 1940

This is the account as written by 2nd radio officer
W.N. BLACKLOCK at the time. He was just 19 years old.

The afternoon of 11 November 1940 found SS *Creemuir* in latitude 57 degrees north about 75 miles north of the River Forth and just inside the swept channel which extends almost 10 miles out at this point. The day, although fine was overcast: there was a distinct nip in the air, and a beam wind was steadily blowing up causing a moderate swell.

SS *Creemuir* owned by Messrs Muir Young Ltd, of London – a ship of 3992 tons – was leading the port column of convoy EN23, consisting of 31 merchant vessels which left Methyl, north about, at 5.00 a.m. for Oban, and her final destination would have been Yarmouth, Nova Scotia, for a fresh cargo of pit props, had fate been kind to her.

She was moderately well armed with one four-inch gun, one Holman Projector, one Hotchkiss on the boat deck and two Lewis guns on the wings of the bridge. All

RN Radio Officer Noel Blacklock during World War II.

the automatic weapons were manned when at 3.00 p.m. a large twin-engined bomber appeared ahead of the convoy, travelling towards it at a low altitude; to myself it seemed to be an enemy plane (a fact which I mentioned to one of the gunners at the time, but he, and one of the escorting vessels, one sloop and two armed trawlers were of a different opinion, and they held their fire). Slowly and gracefully the large bomber sailed over the *Creemuir* and passed towards the rear of the convoy, making the typical thrumming noise of a German diesel-engined plane. While it was in view my eyes never left it; I was temporarily petrified, and by no means surprised to see a stick of bombs leave it in a row as it passed over the sternmost ships. Terrific splashes appeared in the water but no material damage was done except in the case of one ship where a few plates were loosened and she had to put into port.

Not being on duty until 5.00 p.m. I had watched this episode from the main deck; only two ships of the convoy had time to fire on the aircraft and their shots did not seem to affect it. An Avro Anson of Coastal Command then dived down to the attack from the north and chased the Bosch into the A.A. Fire of our escorting sloop, from which it swiftly turned away and made off with the slower Anson in pursuit.

The fun being over for the present, it was decided that the 4th Engineer and myself should have a game of chess which we had previously arranged, but it was not a success, our thoughts being far from the chess board. Just previous to going on watch I left the 4th's cabin and proceeded to tidy up my own, making the bunk etc. which took about half an hour and was invariably left until the afternoon as I slept from 6.00 a.m. till lunch time. (In the early days when there were only two radio officers per ship it was not possible to keep a continuous watch, as we did later in the war, so I would have been on watch from midnight to six every morning with two more hours in the afternoon).

Promptly at 5.00 p.m. I marched into the tiny wireless room on the starboard side of the bridge deck and my mate Mr Gawthorne went down to the saloon for tea. By the time Portishead (GKU) had completed his transmission, and his messages been decoded, my mate had reappeared to relieve me for tea. It was half past five.

As I went down the companionways the sun was settling down on the horizon, the wind was increasing and I could see we were in for a dirty night. My tea of egg and bacon pie was more than welcome, as the sea air had made me hungry.

The third officer Mr R. Gilchrist who had been relieving the chief officer was tucking away with great gusto when I walked into the saloon, and as was his wont, immediately started to comment on the lousy food in no uncertain terms. We had not been chatting more than 15 minutes when a dull resounding thud rent the air; the lights went out, and I was hurled from my seat towards the door. On picking myself up the stewards raucous voice came to my ears as the noise of the explosion passed away: "Lifebelts, get your lifebelts."

Without stopping to think, I ran along the corridor to the main deck and mounted the steps up to my cabin in record time; grabbed my lifejacket which had given excellent service as a bolster, and unfortunately put it on inside out, rendering it almost useless. For about two seconds I tried to think of something important that I could slip into my pocket, but it was in vain (£8 in cash was one of the many things only waiting to be picked up).

Out on the bridge once more, Captain Mankin was standing by the companionway, having just given his last order: "Take to the boats."

To me he seemed to be calmness personified; he made no effort to secure his own safety, and he went down as he would have wished in the execution of his duty.

I made my way aft without undue haste, thinking that the damage was only slight, but on climbing the vertical metal ladder to the boat deck, my mental perambulations were swiftly shattered. A loud hissing noise, which obliterated the hum of human voices, was coming up from the engine room. The after-well deck was completely submerged, hatch covers and wooden spars were being tossed about by the waves, and the gun on the poop was steadily sinking into the cold black water. Even at this early stage the ship had taken a heavy list to port.

Although a trifle dazed, I remembered I had been scheduled for the port lifeboat, but on reaching it my heart sank, for it was already floating at the top of the davits with none of the ropes severed. A veritable hive of men was standing in it and a few – notably the chief officer – were struggling to loosen the falls, but no knife could be found, and the axe that could have solved the problem was dropped into the sea.

I remember standing in the after end of the boat with water surging round my legs, and the davits gradually pushing it under, when a huge wave completely swamped the whole outfit and I passed into oblivion for a short period. My next recollection is of opening my eyes as I came up through the water and striking my head against a piece of floating debris. Trying desperately to reason with myself as to what was the best thing to do, I grasped a piece of timber and swam away from the ship, fearing that when it took the final plunge there would be a considerable suction.

By now it was almost dark and in the few glimpses I had of my old ship over the waves, she was silhouetted against the sunset in a truly magnificent manner. As the boilers blew up with a pronounced thud which could be heard over the din of falling wreckage, the funnel and the masts came adrift amid clouds of soot and black smoke and fell to starboard. The last mental picture I had of her was that of her bows, from the bridge forwards, standing vertically in the water, proudly defying the waves.

Having swum what must have been over a hundred yards through the waves, I sighted one of the ships rafts in the gloom rapidly drifting away, and leaving my companionable piece of wood I made for it post haste. Two pairs of willing hands pulled me out of the water and within a few minutes, when I had recovered my wind, I was shouting like a tipster for my comrades to swim to us; for although the craft was fitted with two paddles, these were useless in such a heavy swell.

Pathetic voices could be heard coming from the floating debris requesting assistance, but it would have been madness to leave the raft once we got hold of it for we should never have got back in the state we were in. Apart from that there were eight of us clinging on to it as we passed away from the scene of the action, and being only about five feet square it almost turned turtle several times.

There was the bosun, one gunner, two sailors, one fireman, one galley boy and myself the only officer. For almost two hours we drifted aimlessly, gripping on to each other and the raft, trying to keep warm and to prevent ourselves being carried away by the heavy seas. Other ships of the convoy seemed to approach us periodically only to fade away again into the darkness. To one side of us, another ship clothed in a cloak of flame from stem to stern and surrounded by black smoke was gradually settling down. She was the SS *Trebartha*, and a steady stream of tracer bullets continued to pour into her and into the surrounding water from above.

The intense cold combined with heavy rain proved to be agonising; my limbs and face were completely numbed, and I could only move them with difficulty. Up till then I had never known what it was to be really cold. At this stage, when we were all feeling very much under the weather, we happened to drift right across the bows of a ship, and shouting at the top of our voices it was soon obvious that we had been spotted.

A line was thrown to us but it fell short and we continued to drift further and further away from our goal, until she was almost out of sight. But they were coming to our assistance even though it meant endangering their own ship. No lights could be used for the enemy was still close at hand. A lifeboat had been launched and was even now racing towards us manned by a crew of brave Dutch lads. As it came alongside we stumbled into it and lay down amid pools of water, crouching to avoid the biting wind. The poor little galley boy was by this time in a very bad way and terribly sick. I put my arms round him and rubbed him to restore his circulation, but even I was close to being exhausted.

For what seemed like hours we remained nestled at the bottom of the boat, our shivering bodies entwined round the legs of the Dutch seamen, and on one occasion we heard the voices of our crew as they were taken on board. (Five of them had clung to an upturned lifeboat all that time, including the first Radio Officer, and were in a worse condition than ourselves, as I learned later). Eventually, with a feeling of intense relief, I felt the small craft bump against the ships side. Two rope ladders were lowered – it was the Dutchman SS *Oberon*.

At once it was evident that both my legs were paralysed with cramp and franticly I rubbed them before attempting the lofty ascent to her main deck, for she was light. The wind was now terrific; our small boat was being tossed up and down like a cork and it was a case of gripping the ladder whenever it came within reach. With my last ounce of energy I clambered up the slippery rungs with my arms alone and on reaching the top, three hefty lads lifted me over and carried me to the saloon.

There, amid some of my pals I was deposited on the deck by the radiator. Willing hands removed my wet clothing, took it to the engine room to dry, and came back with dry clothes and bedding etc. together with steaming hot coffee. Cigarettes and tobacco were next supplied out of the pockets of the Dutch seamen, who did without these luxuries for our benefit, and which proved to be a Godsend. From our vantage point on the deck we watched the remainder of our fellows being brought in, some much worse than others, and several of them out for the count. All of us were black as the ace of spades from head to foot, and looked more like trimmers than anything else. Naturally I thought I was different, for there seemed no reason for it, but to my disgust I was far and away the worst – my hair was absolutely matted with black grease and grime.

Shortly afterwards the 36 survivors of the *Trebartha* joined our miserable company. Although only four were missing, most of them were severely wounded by machine gun bullets and blast, and most of the newly acquired clothing was given to them, leaving us in our birthday suits.

The following details concerning the attack on our ship came to light after questioning the Chief Officer, shortly after he came round;

An unknown seaplane flying about six feet above the water had shown recognition lights, and those on the bridge thought it was going to land. Instead, when only about 150 yards from the ship and broadside on a torpedo left it and a white feather was seen coming towards us. The Chief Officer on the monkey island immediately shouted an order to the man at the wheel through the voice pipe: "Hard to starboard – there's a torpedo coming."

But it was of no avail: the wretched missile hit us plum in the engine room, and must have torn the bottom out of the ship, for she went down in approximately two minutes (being light hastened the inevitable).

Falling beams and concrete slabs had peppered the mate from all sides, and it was more by luck than judgement that he reached the boat deck comparatively unhurt. It had been his intention to prevent the boats being launched too soon, for even he did not think the damage was really serious.

The *Trebartha* had received a direct hit from an H.E. bomb, which penetrated the bridge and the saloon and set the bridge space bunkers on fire. The three radio officers were trapped in the wireless room and had no chance of escape, and one of the gunners was killed instantly by the blast.

In our ship as far as I know, only 13 were saved out of 42. These included the chief officer (who wrote a report that we saw and copied at the Public Records Office at Kew), the Canadian gunner and another fireman who were picked up from the upturned lifeboat, plus three who were on the raft with myself. Mr Gilchrist, the third officer and a good swimmer, was seen to dive in, but nothing more has been heard of him. The steward and cook are known to have lost their lives. It is just possible that others of the crew were rescued by another ship in the convoy, but unfortunately no vessels were actually detailed for such work.

At about 3.00 a.m. the Dutchman SS *Oberon* put into Aberdeen, piloted by the cox of the Aberdeen lifeboat, which was launched on seeing the fire in SS *Trebartha*. Stretcher cases were first removed to hospital by men of the First Aid Post, then we were taken in a large ambulance to the Seaman's Mission and given tea and cigarettes before turning in. Right from the start, Aberdeen treated us in a truly magnificent manner, and I have nothing but the highest praise for those kind Scots who did so much for us. The spotlessly white sheets we were given must have been practically ruined by our filthy anatomies, for not one of us was able to get as much as a wash until the following day – the bathing facilities being on the top floor, we should have disturbed the other residents.

Later it was learned with much joy from a radio report that two Junkers 87 Dive Bombers had been shot down in the vicinity of our convoy on that eventful night.

My compatriot Mr Gawthorne the First Radio Officer was a survivor and was rescued. He managed to cling onto the upturned boat. I know because we came together later on in the war and worked on the same ship together.

On 28 June 1941 SS *Oberon*, (1996 grt), the Dutch ship that had so gallantly come to our rescue was sunk by U-boat *U-123* off Freetown, Sierra Leone, West Africa. Six lives were lost. The remainder were picked up by a Corvette and taken to Freetown. They were later repatriated on *Empress of Australia*, a big old three funneller used for trooping.

Noel's account was fascinating and gave me a real insight into how the ship had sunk. It has been a privilege dealing with him – we had a shared affinity for the sea. We had also both spent time in the same stretch of water and touched the same ship – but in very different circumstances. I had been cocooned inside a modern 21st century dry suit and he had nothing but the clothes he had been standing in. Again I thought that was the end of the story but there was more to come. Another comment was posted by a Betty Treacy on my Random House Author's Place website on 26 March 2010:

> My late father Pakie (Patrick) Bowe from Waterford, Ireland was also on the SS *Creemuir* during the Second World War and I would be most interested to hear how the ship was sunk. My father was born in 1902 and died at 60 years of age on 1 January 1963. I was the eldest of his three children and was only just gone 16 years when he died, so would love to hear any news about the torpedoing of the ship. I was always told he was torpedoed and while in the water was fired at by Germans, against all the rules of war. Needless to say, this is only hearsay.

I was able to put Noel and Betty in touch with each other and Noel was able to fill in all the gaps that Betty had about the sinking. On 22 May 2010, Noel posted the following comment:

> Betty Treacy and I wish to thank you most sincerely for bringing us together after all these years: 70 to be exact. It does not seem possible. We now know that her father and I shared the only raft that survived after the sinking of the SS *Creemuir* off Aberdeen in 1940. To be truthful I cannot remember him, but I know there were four of us on this raft: her father (who was a stoker); a cabin boy; a sailor; and me – 2nd Radio Officer. It really is wonderful to be reunited and we are most grateful. The other Radio Officer – Mr Gawthorne – also survived by clinging to an upturned lifeboat. I sailed with him later in the war on another ship. I think he came from Northampton. Again, many thanks Rod.

After that Helen King – whose uncle had been lost on *Creemuir* – contacted me. He had been a young deck-hand, sadly only on his first trip to sea. And then there was a further posting by an Austin James whose great grandfather – a master mariner – had been lost on *Creemuir* as well.

It has been amazing and very rewarding to see what has transpired from a simple one-line posting about a single wreck we had dived. It demonstrates the power of the Internet. Noel has been in touch with each of the relatives and has given them what information he can. He has been very willing to assist with this Chapter – his selfless purpose being to help other relatives and to highlight the role of the Merchant Navy during World War II. I cannot imagine what it must be like from Noel's perspective after 70 years to meet the daughter of a man he shared a raft from a sinking ship with. Likewise, Betty tells me that as a child she didn't pay too much attention to her father's stories about the sinking and as he died in 1963 when she was 16, she had never heard the full story. Imagine what it must be like from her perspective to meet a man with whom her father shared a raft, and to hear first-hand what took place that cold November night in 1940.

POSTSCRIPT

This book is very much a chronicle of our work in progress as technical divers interested in Scottish shipwrecks. My last book *Into the Abyss* started out at the very beginning of my diving career in the early 1980s and went through all the adventures I had along the way, as my diving skills developed. It encompassed our conversion from standard air diving to the use of commercial mixed gases in the mid 1990s.

The Darkness Below is essentially a continuation from where *Into the Abyss* left off. It would be rash to assume that everyone who reads this book has read *Into the Abyss* – so to give context to this book, I have devoted the first few chapters to a condensed summary of how our band of technical divers formed and developed.

But the main thrust of the book is deep Trimix diving and my conversion from open-circuit diving to closed-circuit rebreather diving with the changes and benefits that brought. Along the way I have been privileged to be able to find, research and dive many, many virgin wrecks – some lost for aeons. From this I have learned and gained so much.

Each shipwreck has a traumatic story attached to it. For those of us who have not experienced shipwreck, it is hard to imagine what it must be like to have your seemingly secure floating home disappear beneath your feet and to be cast into freezing cold water. The water is so cold in the North Sea that survivors say it is like a thousand knives being stuck into you. How many poor seamen have ended up in the water turning their eyes forlornly to the distant land, praying for rescue and salvation before grimly accepting there would be no rescue? In the North Sea a man would survive 30–50 minutes before being overcome by the cold and slipping away. When do you give up and accept your fate? There have been a few times in the water when I have felt up against it, ready to be overwhelmed by the immensity and power of the sea. As a crewman on the Stonehaven lifeboat, we have pulled people out of the water who have been immersed unprotected for 40 minutes, with just 10 minutes of life left, well past the shivering stage, incoherent, unable to function and so, so physically cold.

When I started out diving shipwrecks I just saw the rusted metal before me – the actual event of the wrecking seemed remote and almost inconsequential, having happened a long,

long time ago. It never occurred to me that I would come in contact with people with a direct connection to some of the vessels I have researched.

Over the years I have been contacted by survivors of wrecks such as HMS *Repulse* and *Prince of Wales*, and by relatives of crew who lost their lives in many of the shipwrecks. Each one has brought a sense of realism to what I am doing and I have often been helped enormously by their comments, photos and recollections. I had wondered whether as divers, relatives would regard us suspiciously. Without exception however, the relatives who have been in touch with me have been interested, cooperative and genuinely grateful for whatever information we have been able to give.

My diving has brought me many like-minded soul mates and good friends. I now seem to live in a bubble where just about all my closest friends are tech divers. We speak in an unusual language unintelligible to the non-diver: of 'PPO2'; 'hypoxia'; 'hypercapnia'; 'oxygen toxicity' and the like. We have a shared bond, an affinity and a comfortable understanding of what the other has seen and done. It is only now as the years have gone by that I can look back and see how lucky I have been to have done the things I have done and gone to the places I have been to. But my diving has also brought me in contact with many other people interested in the sea that I wouldn't ordinarily have met, from local fishermen to historians.

Whilst writing the book I was always unsure how it should end. There is no climactic chapter. No one dies (although we have had a few scares along the way). But the story of the *Creemuir* and the bringing together of such lovely people – all touched in different ways by an almost-forgotten event 70 years ago – seemed a fitting ending to a book about diving and shipwrecks. A positive story showing that although divers sometimes get a bad press, we do help in other ways.

But this book is also a story of work in progress. There is still a lot to do and I accept that I am now getting older and won't be able to continue at this pace indefinitely. We have done so much over the last 20 years, yet there is still so much left for the next generation of technical divers to discover – even in just our small section of coast along the north east of Scotland. I will welcome, and look forward to, the mysteries we have left behind being solved by other divers.

At some stage there will be another quantum leap in diving technology, as we had when the Trimix revolution descended on us in the 1990s. Suddenly wrecks that are at the very limit of our diving ability in depths of 100–150 metres or more, will become easily achievable. The next generation of divers should have as much fun and adventure as we have had.

For the meantime my group still has a long list of jobs to be done, such as: finding and diving the bow section of the *Queensbury*; positively identifying the two remaining steam trawlers that are not the *Lowdock*; locating the German destroyer *T6*; roping off the *Gowrie* and *Fernside*; locating and diving HMS *Tithonus*, SS *Desabla* and many others; as well as visiting all our old favourites.

To be continued...

Take care down there.

Rod Macdonald